APPLIED RESEARCH IN LIBRARY and INFORMATION SCIENCE

Edited by

Prof. G. Devarajan Ph.D

Head, Deptt. of Library & Information Science

University of Kerala

Thiruvananthapuram

Ess Ess Publications

4837/24, Ansari Road, Darya Ganj,

New Delhi-110002

✆ : 23260807, 51563444

Fax : 011-51563334

E-mail: info@essessreference.com

url:http://www.essessreference.com

First Published 2005

ISBN : 81-7000-462-4

Price : Rs. 725/-

Published by :
Ess Ess Publications
4837/24, Ansari Road, Darya Ganj,
New Delhi - 110 002
✆ : 23260807, 51563444
Fax : 011-51563334
E-mail: info@essessreference.com
url:http://www.essessreference.com

Laser Typesetting:
Mukesh Graphics
T-1264, Mangolpuri, New Delhi
Ph. : 27922304
E-mail:mukeshgraphics29@hotmail.com

Printed at :
Print Line

1
Agricultural and farm information services in Kerala

Dr. R. Raman Nair

1. INTRODUCTION

Agricultural development rests heavily on information available to managers, scientists and farmers. However, this aspect gets least consideration and inefficiencies have become obvious in managing information resources. Vitalization of agricultural information systems is a matter of urgent concern and priority to protect the interest of agricultural sector in the context of increasing requirement for food grains as well as globalization. The cost of establishing information infrastructures for agriculture may be expensive, but the costs of not doing so are likely to be much higher in terms of productivity, quality and value addition.

A clear policy framework coupled with sound planning and implementation backed by generous research and development investments and efficient information support is essential to ensure sustained production of food grains and other agricultural commodities. Meeting the domestic food requirements has been the foremost social priority before India since independence. Hence, thrust was given to food production beginning with First Five-Year Plan, particularly during mid-sixties[1] . India has put in unstinted and aggressive efforts towards agricultural development. This has increased 51 million tones of food grain production in 1950- 51, to 195.92 million tones during 2001-2002. According to the estimate of

Indian Council for Agricultural Research (ICAR) India now need about 230 million tones of food grains i.e. an increase of 30-35 million tones[2] . Further, large increase is essential in coarse cereals, pulses, oilseeds, fodder, fuel wood, fruits, vegetables, milk, meat, eggs, fish, a wide range of industrial, and plantation crops.

The situation becomes further complicated when we view a rising population graph against decreasing productivity graph of major agricultural commodities. The yield per hector of most crops is still quite low as compared to other countries. Land available for cultivation is limited, and it goes on decreasing due to the ever growing demands of industries, roads, houses, etc. Experts are of the opinion that problems will become acute unless a second revolution takes place in agriculture.

We need to take measures based on research to stabilize the annual agricultural production, which fluctuate due to weather, pests and plant diseases. Many problems are there to be solved also in, animal husbandry, veterinary science and fisheries. Sustainable agricultural production on long-term basis has also become a cause of concern. Unless we strive continuously to improve present level of crop production, we may again face severe food shortage.

It has been widely held that future growth in production has to come exclusively from growth in productivity. As the area under cultivation cannot be increased and the growth of population cannot be controlled, the alternative is the qualitative improvement in farming, which requires improved agricultural production technology. For this an efficient research and development programme is needed. Quality and quantum of research by our agricultural scientists, in turn depends on efficient information support systems[3] . Sustainable agriculture in the 21st century will be based on the appropriate use of biotechnology, information technology and eco technology[4] .

As India is getting integrated with world economy, it is

imperative to develop techniques, technologies, processes and products, which are competitive in terms of cost and quality at local, regional and global levels. All these suggest for a strong, vibrant, effective and dedicated agricultural research supported by efficient information systems at regional and national levels.

Hitherto, agricultural libraries have played a vital role in knowledge communication and in keeping the scientists, administrators, planners and farmers posted with latest knowledge and advancement in their area of work and respective fields of specialization. However, extension and intension of the field of agriculture and emerging specializations under it has made management of information resource very complicated. The present trends of development in agricultural research and the nature and quantum of information generated by it have brought in various challenges to traditional systems.

Definition of the Main Concepts

The main concepts in the title of the study are *'agriculture and farming'*, *'information services'*, '*resource sharing'* and '*networking'*. Webster's Dictionary defines agriculture as the science or art of cultivating the soil, harvesting crops and raising livestock and in varying degrees the preparation of these products for man's use and their distribution.[5] Farm or farming is growing crops and rearing animals. In the context of this study, 'information' is considered synonymous with the scientific knowledge irrespective of its manifestation. In terms of manifestations, information includes oral and written, documentary and non-documentary, audio and video, in their traditional or digital forms from formal or informal sources. 'Information services' here means acquiring, organizing and managing relevant information, processing and repackaging it if essential and delivering or making available the same to the user community in agricultural sector as per their requirement at the right time.

'Resource sharing' may appear to be a new term for the traditional concepts of 'interlibrary loan' or 'library

cooperation'. However, even though resource sharing includes the activities meant by these earlier terms there is significant difference in the approach. The terms interlibrary loan and library cooperation take the existence of libraries for granted and describe how they can achieve their objectives better by working together. But the new term 'resource sharing' appears rather to assume a range of physical, intellectual and conceptual resources on the one hand and covers the activities involved in organizing the one into a set of optimum relationships to meet the needs of the other.[6] So resource sharing may be seen here as a term for working out inter institutional relationships for the benefit of users of agricultural information systems which has to change from material orientation to client orientation.

'*Networking*' is the most important means to give practical shape to this philosophy of resource sharing. When two or more libraries formally engage in a resource sharing programme that is in a common pattern of information exchange through communication for some functionally independent purpose it becomes a network meant for sharing information resource.

Definitions and Scope of Agricultural Science

In applied sciences, agriculture is one of the youngest professions. Like medicine, scientific agriculture rests on the principles of basic sciences. However, agriculture must draw not only from botany, zoology, chemistry, physics and mathematics but also from geology, ecology, meteorology, engineering, economics, sociology and statistics. The profession of agriculture includes a wide diversity of practices and specializations because it is closely knitted with the production of the fundamental elements of man's food, shelter and clothing, which are derived from plants and animals. Most broadly, agriculture must also be concerned with the production, conservation and improvement of the plants and animals and the natural environment in which they grow as well as with their marketing and distribution[7].

The subject covered by the term agricultural sciences

can be listed as follows based on the sub disciplines of agriculture specified by Encyclopedia of Agricultural Science[8] and Agripedia[9] .

Crop Sciences: Plant Breeding, crop production and horticulture, crop protection etc are the major subdivisions of crop sciences. However, as no discipline under agriculture can stand in a watertight compartment there will be overlapping and many other subjects may seem to have a place under this heading in various contexts.

Forestry and Related Areas: Forestry comes under agricultural sciences from the point of planting and propagation through management and harvesting, to the processing of timber and the various wood and non-wood forest products. The management of forestland, in the widest sense, and agro forestry, an area of increasing importance also comes under this discipline[10] .

Animal Sciences: This discipline covers veterinary and animal sciences, their medical aspects, dairying, poultry, and fisheries and all areas related to them.

Food Science and Human Nutrition: This field deals with food and nutrition for both man and animals. In addition, policy on malnutrition, food aid and food supply are covered. Aspects of human nutrition covered by the field are; analysis and techniques for the determination of nutritive value of foods, nutrients, anti-nutritional factors, toxic substances and toxins in foods, whole range of foodstuffs, physiology and biochemistry related to food intake, and nutritional disorders.

Biotechnology, Engineering, Economics and Other Areas: As agricultural sciences covers work on all animals and plants of economic or domestic importance and related wild species as well as their management, production and protection issues no area that can be considered, as coming under biosciences is alien to agriculture. In addition the sub fields of economics, engineering, Information Technology, medicine, newly emerging areas like biotechnology and a host of such subjects are highly relevant to agriculture and have sub disciplines specializing in agriculture.

2. NATURE AND USE OF AGRICULTURAL INFORMATION

The above discussion on nature and scope of agricultural sciences reveals that information services to agricultural sector have to deal with published literature on research and development related to the fields of agriculture, animal rearing, fisheries, forestry, human health, human nutrition, animal health and the management and conservation of natural resources as well as various disciplines and sub disciplines coming under the broad area known as biosciences.

The rate of accumulation of knowledge in the above areas is a hundred times more than it was at the beginning of the last century. We have progressed from a low productive agricultural society to an information society of high productivity. At a moderate estimate, we have over forty million documents for use annually in the world in different languages and are doubling every six to eight years[11]. No other single discipline has shown so much growth of published material as in agriculture today. In agriculture, we have 2 to 2.5 lakh primary documents annually. Of the world's approximately 85000 journals and bulletins the biggest contribution is from agriculture i.e. a thousand research papers per day[12]. About 9000 periodicals and more than a lakh books are published annually related to agriculture along with innumerable number of other documents in different languages of the world.

The published documents in agriculture mentioned above consist of research reports, books, journal articles, CDROMs, magnetic tapes, videotapes, etc. From the documents resulting from agricultural research worldwide since 1973, items that have relevance to all countries and agro climatic systems selected by Centre for Agriculture and Biosciences Information (CABI) for its database, comes to over four million documents. Approximately 180,000 documents of high relevance are added to that at CABI each year. These documents related to agriculture selected by CABI are published in more than 50 languages. They include research papers published in over 9,000 learned, professional and trade journals specializing in agriculture and related areas from all over the world. They also consist of serials including irregularly issued reports, bulletins and monographs, proceedings of conferences, symposia, workshops, etc. books, doctoral dissertations, annual reports, project reports and other papers, patents and standards related to agriculture and allied fields.

Approximately thirty percent of the specialized publications that cover latest developments are presently available in digital form only. Various lectures and awareness and training programs meant for extension workers as well as farmers were available now as video films and interactive multimedia programmes. Accessibility to all these are important for our agricultural sector for supporting the scientists to update their knowledge as well as to help the farmers for applying what has been invented by the scientists.

Information output is measurable in agriculture also as in many branches of knowledge. For instance the estimates have been that if a scientist researches and studies 60 minutes an hour, 24 hours a day throughout his life, he would have by end of his life, just read only $1/10^{th}$ of the total literature output on his specialized area of research[13] . Due to information explosion, retrieval of required information has also become a serious problem. A scientist will need a long time to find out and read all the literature relevant to his work from three lakhs and more articles on agriculture published annually which will steal away his time for applying what he has learned. Repackaging and transferring research information to the farm also has become a specialized function.

Information Flow and Users in Agriculture

The flow of information in an agricultural sector is grouped into four levels according to their place in the continuum from knowledge policy making to knowledge generation, knowledge exchange and finally to knowledge utilization[14] . The users of information in agricultural sector can be generally classified into three the managers, scientists and farmers.

a) Managers: This category of users in Kerala include

Vice Chancellor, Directors, Secretaries and other decision making authorities of Kerala Agricultural University (KAU), ICAR Institutes, Government Departments of Agriculture, Animal Husbandry, Poultry, Fisheries, Dairy Science, Food and Rural Development of the State as well as those from NGO's and private groups. They will require the following information for effective decision-making:

* human and physical resources
* research, extension and development projects
* budgeting
* physical targets

b) Scientists: This category of users will include personnel working in research systems of the State coming under KAU, ICAR etc as well as various research and extension units of the Departments of the Government of Kerala related to agriculture. Their information requirement can be listed as follows:

* research and extension trends in agriculture and related disciplines
* plant animal and fisheries genetic resources, soil profiles, and natural resources
* agro climatic factors
* economic and social indicators
* feedback from fields
* results of previous research at both national and international levels

c) Farmers: The farmers and the public form the most important category of users. They may require information on aspects like the following:

* input/output prices
* market information
* location specific improved varieties, farm machinery, cattle breed, fish etc.
* improved techniques and methods
* complete package of practices

* post harvest value additions

* information about input supply system

Agricultural Information Related to the Region

The agricultural information generated in Kerala, the areas where research is going on in the region, and the requirement of managers, extension activists and farmers discussed above are related to the crops and animals reared in the region. The agricultural institutions in Kerala where research extension and development are going on generate information on the crops cultivated in the region. They also acquire and store information generated elsewhere on these crops. In addition, they require information on those crops generated and stored in other institutions in Kerala.

The representation of information on agricultural research conducted in India in international information systems and databases is good. But even than we cannot fully rely on such systems for our activities at grass roots level. When agricultural development at the regional level like within Kerala is considered unrecorded indigenous knowledge held by the farmers, literature generated in the region, in the regional language and specific to the region and our farmers; like extension literature, farmers' literature, product literature, newspaper, radio and television reports, audio-visual materials etc are also important. We cannot expect such resources to be covered by international or even national information systems.

The details of information generated and required in the sector identified by the study points out that the State can not refrain from modernizing the information support systems which is very important for achieving quality and efficiency in managing the crops and animals. This necessitates improving the existing information management facilities on a priority basis to offer appropriately tailored and well defined services required for different crops and categories of users.

Information for Agricultural Research

Agriculture being the major determinant of livelihood destiny of the majority of people of India, development of this sector will determine the country's economic and political future. Synthesis of technology, public policy and farmers cooperative action is essential to shape this future in a desirable direction[15] . If we can achieve that our country will be one of the major nations of the world with farm power. If we fail due to in appropriate public policies and research priorities that result from lack of right information at right time the country will collapse. This stresses the importance of information services for agricultural research.

The main function of agricultural research is to seek information and knowledge. If the information does not exist or is not available in the researcher's institutions, it can be generated by experiment. If experimentation is ruled out due to resource limitations or other factors, researchers will scan knowledge sources outside the institution, hoping to identify information, ideas, and technologies that can be borrowed and adopted for local use[16] .

No research system however large it may not generate all the technologies it requires. Therefore, an effective national or State agricultural research system must have the capacity to borrow both knowledge and materials from the entire world[17] . In advanced countries this capacity to borrow from outside is desirable and complements the capacity of the country to generate technology. In countries like India and its constituent States, where sources for technology generation are scarce, it is essential to be able to borrow. Borrowing technology is mainly acquiring knowledge or information for application as it is or adoption for further development. Getting knowledge and information generated elsewhere or in-house for the use of researchers is a critical management function. This only can ensure that past investments in research and information are adequately assessed, evaluated, and utilized before experiments begin. This can also limit duplication of previous efforts and ensure that current activities use, and benefit from, existing knowledge.

Information and Agricultural Education

With the impact of Information and Communication Technologies (ICT) perceptions of the scope of education also is changing as societies come to recognize that time to learn now is the whole lifetime and not just during the period of childhood and youth.[18] With the power given by ICT, synergic effect also occurs when important information is coupled with a second modern advance – the new capacity to communicate among the people of the world. The opportunity exists to harness this force and use it positively, consciously and with design, in order to contribute to meeting defined learning needs. The agricultural educationists and extension activists of advanced countries are long since using computers having multimedia capacity with links to digital libraries which store text, animations, audio and video files, to create interactive learning environment as well as effective extension activities. Their librarians and extension activists work in close cooperation. Any one from any remote location with a computer, a modem and a telephone can access virtual libraries with such training materials mixing, text, animation and video. Digital library technology combined with communication systems of State Information Infrastructure can materialize high-tech teaching learning environment for agriculture as well as training and extension facilities at Krishi Bhavans, veterinary hospitals, or village libraries at low cost.

Information and Agricultural Extension

Effective transfer of technology is very important for accelerating production. This is a complex task – interdisciplinary, multi-institutional in approach, and content. Integrated functioning of research, education, information and extension has been the cardinal principles of agricultural development in advanced countries. The extension system in the country and State involves research institutions, educational institutions, training centers, marketing system, extension organizations, input agencies, village institutions and farming communities. But the involvement of institutions or units, which have to undertake the most important function -

information dissemination is lacking at national and State level. Information in various media, repacked for various categories is the main tool and resource for extension activity. The major institutions dealing with this resource is libraries and information units. Hence as a strategy of development an integrated systems view of information and extension agencies is needed. Functional linkages of library, information and extension are to be created. Our State's extension system has to deal with millions of farmers including farmwomen, and agricultural laborers. An extension system however vast cannot reach them quickly or acquire organize and manage the information and documents meant for them. What is required is developing and maintaining strong functional relationship with library and information service units at higher levels in production of information materials and programmes for extension as well as use of existing village library networks and facilities near the farm to transfer the technology. Utilizing the resources at the command of specialist's areas of information science together with village library services is essential for success of transfer of technology programmes covering the whole State.

Information and Agricultural Marketing

Economic and financial policies of the country have recently undergone dramatic transformation and many structural changes have been brought into the traditional system, so that the country can integrate itself into the new and reemerging world economic order. Liberalization and globalization have become the keywords in the present policies. With the signing of the Marrakech Accord (WTO) in 1994 largest increase in global trade is expected in clothing, agriculture, forestry and fishery products and processed food and beverages – areas where India has a competitive advantage.[19] The new Export and Import Policy (EXIM) announced by government seeks to complete the process of India's integration with global economy by removal of various restrictions. It seeks to provide fresh directions to setting up Agricultural Export Zones and providing them special benefits. Agro exports would be reorganized based on specific products and specific geographic areas. Focusing specially on areas where there is a convergence of these two factors would make a beginning. Such zones will be made as Regional Rural Motors of Indian Export Economy. The more will be the end-to-end development of export specific products.

Kerala will have constraints in fully participating in International Trade. It will be because of various critical gaps including availability of information on prices, demands, quality, standards etc. Efficient information systems will be essential to fill these gaps by transmitting international signals to the farmers. They need to be encouraged and enabled to respond to these signals through the State. Internationalization of our agriculture will have several implications. It can give great opportunities to our farmers. The terms of trade, which have, for long been in favour of industry is expected to shift in favor of agriculture. Huge investments will be diverted to agriculture. If our farmers are equipped to rise to the occasion, we will be able to make a mark in the international trade in agriculture with this farm to port approach. Information systems have a crucial role to play in equipping the farmers.

Kerala's agricultural sector is heavily dependent on foreign trade and approximately 80% of agricultural produce in the State is in one way or other affected by foreign trade. This necessitates an efficient information system to enable the stakeholders to evolve appropriate strategies and plans for minimization of negative impacts of the new multilateral trade regimes on specific crops, products and sub sectors. Good understanding about the different aspects of the WTO Regime by all stakeholders in the field of agriculture including cultivators, traders, exporters, scientists, breeders, plant protection personnel, staff of the development departments, and media persons is very important.

To fulfill the above needs an information system, which can enable the farmers to achieve higher income and prosperity through productivity improvement, quality enhancement, value addition, and farmer friendly marketing of agricultural products is important. Such an information system should generate and disseminate technical and marketing information to farmers and other stakeholders to take maximum advantage of the emerging worlds trade regime in agriculture. It should also act as a decision support system to the government for planning appropriate strategies to take advantage of the dynamic market situation and minimize adverse impact of market fluctuations on the one side and competition from other countries on the other.

3. AGRICULTURAL LIBRARIES

Because of the multidisciplinary nature of the subject of agriculture, in an organization concerned with it the role of library becomes very important. The discipline of agriculture unlike most other disciplines as we have discussed earlier is very vast and complex. Diverse subjects are studied and researched under Agriculture in one context or other. Such a phenomena has a direct bearing on the agricultural library, its users and managers.[20] It is almost impossible to quantify the information output in the field of agriculture and related sciences. Hence, the role of the libraries in acquiring, organizing and disseminating required information to their patrons could not be over estimated.

Agricultural library and information systems have to discharge a multiplicity of functions, catering to a wide clientele having divergent interests, and representing varying states of intellectual development. There modernization is very important for agricultural development. They can no longer exist as those old institutions charged with preservation and conservation of books. They are now saddled with the task of collecting, organizing, managing, repacking and communicating information and knowledge of a colossal magnitude and variety with speed and efficiency[21] .

The current developments in agricultural sector necessitate creation of library and information service units in all agricultural institutions, which are not presently having them. Information service outlets are to be established at different levels up to villages. It is also important that information systems existing in the institutions in the sector be vitalized to meet the challenges in terms of quality, efficiency and cost effectiveness. The method of working of most of the libraries coming under various organizations in agricultural sector in the State needs thorough restructuring and overhauling, keeping in mind requirements of the agricultural sector. The libraries of the organizations around which agricultural, education, research, extension and development activities are centered should be capable to provide effectively the knowledge and information support required for those activities. All these indicate the important role that the library and information systems have to play in agricultural development.

The systems, which bridge the gap of information downpour on the one hand, and the information needs of the users on the other are libraries. In Kerala the libraries attached to KAU and its constituent colleges and Research centers as well as ICAR institutes, and Agricultural Department of State Government are responsible to fulfill the information needs of the agricultural sector in the State. They offer various traditional and modern library and information services to the users. But their efforts are presently individual and isolated[22] . So the scope, comprehensiveness, coverage and cost effectiveness of their services is limited. In addition to them there are also many other libraries of organizations coming under government, private organizations, and NGOs which are struggling hard to cope up with the problems of expanding agricultural research information, increasing information needs of their clientele, complexity of the ways of acquiring information and ever declining financial resources. Facing all these problems they have to provide the information support required for education, research, extension and development programmes of their parent organizations.

Estimates about the amount spent on agricultural research and also the annual production of publications in agriculture reveal that we have sufficient recorded knowledge in agriculture, which can be used as input for improving production. But the existing knowledge is not reaching the users. This gap is to be reduced. Sharing the resources can narrow this gap. Generation of technology and its application are two different issues. A country may not generate technology but can use it skillfully if it has good information network. It has been said that there are advanced countries because they take advantage of the work of other countries. Therefore creation of basic information infrastructure, support and services is crucial in agricultural development.

Harnessing Possibilities of ICT

Harnessing the possibilities, ICT can help us to improve in the right direction with speed and efficiency. Capability in areas of science and technology, like biotechnology, information and communication, give hitherto unavailable opportunities. They can help the country for achieving sustainable agricultural development based on knowledge and biological inputs in the place of chemical and capital-intensive production methods that can harm. Integrated attention to regulation, education and social mobilization has become very important for sustainable development. Research strategies need to be restructured to make possible strategic, anticipatory and participatory research. Extension services are to be decentralized and should be capable of converting generic into location specific knowledge essential for taking to precision farming methods. The farmers themselves should maintain the rural knowledge centers. They should act as service outlets of, and form part of national and State level agricultural information systems. They should be able to use State level information infrastructures, public library networks and village library facilities for information access, management and dissemination. They should provide computer aided and Internet connected information access and processing facilities so that farmers have timely and relevant technical as well as methodological management and marketing information. Hence national and state level information infrastructures extending to the villages catering to the needs of agricultural sector has become the need of the time.

In the above contexts, a study of the resources, facilities and services of library and information units of agricultural organizations in the State as well as an attempt to check the feasibility for establishing resource-sharing programme among them becomes very important. The present study is initiated by an awareness of this fact.

4. OBJECTIVES , METHODOLOGY AND HYPOTHESES

This study consists of a systematic investigation and evaluation of the resources, facilities and services of the library and information units of the organizations engaged in agricultural education, research, extension and development in the State of Kerala with specific primary and secondary objectives.

Objectives of the Study

The primary objectives of the study are:

a. to examine the existing facilities for resource sharing among the information systems in agricultural sector in Kerala;

b. to examine how far access to international and national databases in agricultural sciences is available to the research institutes in the State;

c. to assess the effectiveness of the existing systems and methods; and

d. to determine the factors that affect efficiency and extension of information services.

The secondary objectives of the study are:

a. to ascertain the feasibility of resource sharing and networking as also to determine areas where resource sharing can be resorted to with advantage;

b. to propose a plan for establishing an agricultural and farm information system – computer communication network interlinking the agricultural research institutions in Kerala that can allow agricultural scientists in the State, access to up-to-date information; and

c. to suggest the measures that can enable flow of results of research down to the grass root level to improve productivity in agriculture.

Methodology

The sources from where the investigator initially covered the major organizations in the agricultural sector like Kerala Agricultural University, Farm Information Bureau and State Departments of Agriculture, Animal Husbandry, and Fisheries and from there identified and covered institutions under them and also various other government and non governmental organization for further study.

The sample institutions identified are divided into three categories for the convenience of the study; major, minor and out steam institutions based on their resources, infrastructures and funding agencies. The study was conducted with mixed methodologies and instruments consisting of different sets of questionnaires for farmers, scientists, librarians etc in English and Malayalam, visits to these institutions, interview with librarians and or staff in charge of institutions and services, interview with members of the staff who were connected with the collection development, automation and services and interview with farmers and other information users.

The samples used for the study, constitute 77 librarians and officers in charge of information systems, 437 users that include scientists, students, and extension workers, 220 farmers and the public, and 300 scientists and staff in charge of organizations at grass roots level interviewed for the purpose.

Constraints

The information required for the evaluation was not available in any organized way at most of the institutes. The information, provided by many libraries were incomplete and had to be supplemented as well as updated from the Annual Reports of their parent institutions as well as from handbooks, brochures etc related to those institutions. A good deal of data had to be collected from the librarians and the staff of the libraries concerned through formal and informal communications and personal interviews. The study being a qualitative evaluation of the systems the librarians or officers in charge of information services were normally found disinclined to provide details thinking about the observations and comments the study may make about the systems managed by them.

Hypotheses

The following hypotheses are formulated for the study.

a) the agricultural information and extension services in Kerala fail to utilize the available resources for providing need based services to various categories of users in the agricultural sector;

b) there is lack of efficient infrastructures for information management, access and dissemination as well as effective programmes for coordination of the information services in the agricultural sector of Kerala.

5. REGION AND SCOPE

Kerala is taken as the geographical area within which the study is limited. It stretches from Manjeswaram in the north to Parassala in the south. It is 576 Kms in length and 32 to 125 km in width.[23] The region is bounded by Western Ghats in the east, the Arabian Sea in the west, Tamil Nadu in the south and Karnataka in the north. Physiographically Kerala can be divided into three natural regions – highland, mid-land, and coastal low – land. These divisions form parallel belts running across the length of the State. The high land consists of the Western Ghats and high mountain peaks, long spurs, extensive ravines and dense and evergreen forests. The mid land consists of undulating terrain, rivers, valleys and plains and lies between high land and low land. The low land runs along the 576 Kms coastal belt of the Arabian Sea, charactering beach ridges, beaches, lagoons and sandy coastal belt[24]. For agricultural purposes these regions are technically divided into five agro climatic zones. They are Northern, High range, Central, Special and Southern Zones. There are some problem related zones also. Research institutions and stations dealing with a specific agro climatic region are normally established in the concerned region. The State measuring 38, 863 Sq.Kms comprises only 1.8 percent of the total geographical area of the country and is one of the smallest of the Indian States. The state sustains 2.9 crore population

The State gets rain from the southwest and northeast monsoons. So the rainfall is almost spread throughout the year. This continuous rainfall and the undulating nature of the land bless the State with about 44 rivers[25] . The State has also ample ground water potential. It also has many backwaters, which includes lakes and ocean inlets. All these aspects are favorable to agriculture. The forest area account for 28.63 percent of the total geographical area. The records of land use reveal that the net sown area is around 59 percent[26] .

5.1 Present Agricultural Scenario of the Region

Kerala cultivates a large variety of vegetations of food crops and non-food crops. The food crops include cereals, pulses and tuber crops. The non-food crops are diversified in nature namely, oilseeds, cash crops, perennial cash crops, spices and plantations, rice, jowar, ragi and other millets. The rice is the predominant food crop. Tuber crops; tapioca a near substitute for rice and sweet potato are extensively cultivated. Coconut and arecanut constitute the perennial tree crops. Kerala's spices are pepper, chilies, ginger, turmeric, cardamom and cocoa. The plantation crops are tea, coffee, rubber and cashew nuts. Coconut is the major oilseed of the State. Besides coconut, other oilseeds are groundnut and sesamum. The State has widespread tobacco cultivation. In addition to these, horticultural crops like banana, mango, jackfruit, and pineapple are grown in different parts of the State. Vegetable cultivation is also on the rise.

The State has a high intensity of cropping and has already utilized about 58.31 per cent of its total geographical area for cultivation and an increase in this will be at the cost of other development purposes[27]. For the last few decades, the net area sown has shown steady but marginal increase.

Since the British Raj Kerala has inherited a unique crop pattern that lays stress on cash crops. The agro-climatic condition of the State is biased in favor of cash crops. In the colonial period, the Europeans initiated plantations in the highland to exploit the agro-climatic condition of the State. The Kings of Travancore also promoted the cultivation of cash crops to tap the benefits of European capital, technology and expertise.

Predominantly, a cash crop economy, Kerala grows a large variety of high value cash crops to earn valuable foreign exchange. Of these, the cultivation of some crops like coconut, pepper, rubber, cardamom, ginger, etc. enjoy a higher concentration. In pepper, Kerala's contribution is 97 per cent of India's production, rubber claims 85 per cent, and cardamom enjoys 70 per cent, ginger 60 per cent, and coconut 43 per cent. There was a rapid improvement in the area under different cash crops since 1972. During the period area under coconut cultivation increased from 7.45 lakh Ha to 9.14 lakh ha and rubber from 0.62 1akh ha to 4.431akh ha, pepper from 1.161akh ha to 1.881akh and coffee from 0.34lakh ha to 0.821akh ha.[28] In addition to the extension of the area, the production and productivity of majority of the cash crops have went up sufficiently to attract more attention over the years. But productivity of important food crops has declined.

Since the 1970's the area under food crops in general and rice in particular has been declining at an alarming proportion due to a host of reasons. The cultivation of rice is not a relatively profitable affair due to its high cost of cultivation, including the wage cost. The occupational mobility has taken place in favor of the tertiary sector among the second generation of farmer tenant families. This has restricted the mobility of family labor for the continuation of cultivation. The implementation of land reforms since the 1970s by covering paddy field under the provisions of ceilings on land holdings has adversely affected the food crop cultivation in the state. Sub-division and fragmentation of paddy lands through generations have discouraged the intensification of food crop cultivation and encouraged the pattern of fallowing of the paddy lands.

Given lucrative profits, paddy growers are turning to cultivation of cash crops like rubber, coconut, areca nut and other garden crops. The wages of laborers have risen due to the intervention of militant trade unionism. In addition, the cost of other inputs has also increased. The shortage of labor is another important reason for this change in crop pattern. Non-availability of information and inputs, including high yielding varieties of seeds, are other factors that force paddy growers turn to cash crops.

Since the 1980s, Kerala has witnessed another trend, the conversion of paddy farms for non-agricultural purposes due to the high value offered for paddy land. The processes of cash crop orientation and conversion of paddy land for coconut gardening have undergone a serious set back since 1996-97 due to a sharp decline in the prices of coconut. The area under coconut cultivation has shown a downward trend which has adversely affected our agricultural sector.[29]

The homestead cultivation is the unique feature of Kerala crop pattern, which is the result of the settlement pattern of the people that exists in the State. Due to successful implementation of land reforms and subdivision and fragmentation of holdings, majorities of the land holdings are small, being less than one hectare.

With such small holdings, the growers prefer cultivation of a number of horticultural and perennial tree crops like coconut, arecanut, mango, jack tree, banana tree, etc. to a single crop. The agro-climatic and social conditions of the State are highly suitable for the cultivation of horticultural crops and have led to the shift away from food crops.

Organizations in the Region Covered

Kerala has one State Agricultural University (SAU) with ten constituent colleges and about 40 research stations spread over the length and breadth of the State. Then there are also many agricultural research/development organizations under State Government, Central Government, ICAR and other agencies. State Government also has its Farm Information Bureau (FIB) and Departments of Agriculture, Animal Husbandry, Poultry, Fisheries, Food, Diary etc looking after concerned areas of agricultural sector. The present study confined its scope to all resource rich institutions in the agricultural sector and selected few samples of various types of minor libraries inside and outside the sector in the State. The library and information systems of institutions covered in detail are the following:

a) Kerala Agricultural University (KAU) and its eight constituent colleges,

b) Five ICAR Institutes existing in Kerala

c) Selected institutions having good information collections on Biotechnology, forestry and other natural resources and agriculture related aspects.

Considering the horizontal and vertical levels of activities and programmes in agricultural sector representative sets of libraries belonging to various organizations at different levels with activities relevant to agricultural sector is also studied. They include the following libraries.

a) Departmental libraries of biotechnology, biochemistry, zoology, botany etc of University of Kerala, Mahatma Gandhi, Cochin, Calicut and Kannur.

b) Research Station libraries under KAU and ICAR.

c) Rural Libraries with Agricultural Information Service Corners, Krishi Bhavans and Veterinary Hospitals..

d) Libraries or Information Services units under agriculture related departments of the State.

e) Krishi Vijnana Kendras run by KAU, ICAR and NGOs.

f) Libraries of NGOs dealing with agriculture, animal husbandry, fisheries, rural development and cooperation.

The libraries of constituent colleges of KAU came into existence in seventies, and those of other organizations during the next three decades. The high tech central library of KAU came into existence in second half of nineties. Of the other libraries, some have limited resource-sharing facilities. Some are supported only by Central Government, some partially by ICAR and some partially by State and Centre.

Aspects Covered

Details about the strength of scientists, collection of books, journals and electronic publications, ICT equipments, budget, etc of the institutions covered by the study. All these institutions covered came into existence during the period from 1970 to 1995. The strength of users varies from 20 to 1000.

The aspects of the libraries in agricultural organizations, which are relevant to resource sharing and networking only are covered in detail. Detailed evaluation of the selected libraries of Kerala under KAU, ICAR and State and Central Government has been done in regard to the following aspects.

a) Mandate: Objectives, Functions
b) Organizational Setup and Budget
c) Staff: Professionals, Non Professionals
d) Collection: Books, Journals, Documents in Digital Media, and other Non-Print items
e) Infrastructure: Equipments, Building
f) Automation and Networks.

Significance of the Study

Agriculture is the lifeblood of our economy. It contributes to nearly 25% of Gross Domestic Product and about 70% of the population is dependent on agriculture for their livelihood[30]. So growth in the productive capacity of the agricultural sector is crucial to the survival and development of the country. Technological transformation that can boost agricultural production consists of improvements in material inputs, farming techniques, storage technology marketing and research. Effective integration of these factors is tied closely to adequate information flow, which can be ensured only by an efficient agricultural information system. So evaluation and improvement of existing information system is very crucial for agricultural growth.

There are a number of studies on development of information systems, resource sharing and networking in the context of special libraries serving engineering, health science, management, and other areas. There are also many studies related to agricultural information systems in foreign countries especially USA, UK, Russia and China. But there are only very few studies on agricultural library and information systems of India and their networking at the national or State level.

In evaluating the information services for agricultural sector in a region the effect of various factors, which interact to help or retard the operation, is to be noted in order to arrive at some sound judgement. An assessment of the achievements and failures of such information systems are essential to formulate realistic norms for their healthy growth. This needs a systematic study of the resources, organisation, and services of various representative libraries serving different functions related to agriculture at its various sub sectors in the region. The present research work has been undertaken with this motive.

No earlier studies have dealt comprehensively with an integrated view of the library and information system supporting agricultural sector as a whole in the country or a State. Available studies limit their scope within a specific research institution, selected universities, and some sub sector or on building theoretical frameworks. The present study is the first attempt towards an in-depth investigation and evaluation of the resources, facilities and services of the libraries serving the different aspects like education, research, extension and development of the agricultural sector of a State. It covers sample libraries of different levels and categories, from different sub sectors and functional areas.

The study advocates resource sharing in the areas of

journal subscription, specialized databases and HRD for ICT, which can contribute to maximizing the utility of resources at our disposal. The suggested model for resource sharing and networking at state level is a very important outcome of the study. The study proposes the establishment of Agricultural and Farm Information Network for Kerala AGFISNET-K. The network configuration standards for software and hardware as well as the HRD programmes required for the AGFISNET-K are recommended based on tested functional models from those covered by the study with technology options if any, that has become essential.

AGFISNET-K can serve as a model for other State agricultural information systems also. The following of such a model and standards recommended by the present study can enable the development of State level agricultural information system in India on a uniform pattern and their successful coordination at national level for effective integration under national AGFISNET.

6. THE PHASES OF THE STUDY

The present study was done in seven phases. At the initial, phase the scope of agricultural science, nature of agricultural information as well as importance of information as an input for agricultural education, research, extension and development was studied. Attempts were made to define the key terms, form the objectives of the study, methodology, and the hypothesis, mark the region and scope, identify the samples to be used and also to prepare the scheme of work. The relevance and importance of the topic are also ascertained in the initial phase.

In the second phase literature generated in India and abroad on various aspects of agricultural library and information systems is surveyed. It includes books, reports, dissertations, seminar presentations and journal articles. Most studies have occurred in foreign countries and they deal with settings of concerned countries. The survey revealed that literature dating before 1950 on agricultural libraries is very uncommon. In India, the first initiative to study agricultural library and information system was in 1957 by the Shaw and Rao Committee constituted by ICAR[31] . A search for literature on the topic conducted at libraries of major agricultural institutions in India like IARI at **Pusa**, ICAR at New Delhi, National Library at Calcutta, NAARM and MANAGE at Hyderabad and Agricultural University Libraries of West Bengal, Maharashtra, Andhra Pradesh and Karnaṭaka along with searches in CABI Abstracts, LISA, AGRIS and Internet unearthed only less than 60 papers, reports, dissertations and books pertaining to India. Total items about all countries of the world are also found to be less than 350 on aspects related to agricultural information services. Out of the 300 PhD and MLISC dissertations in Library and Information Science done in India up to the year 2000 only 3 PhD Dissertations and 20 MLISc dissertations were related to library and information services in agriculture related areas. The major research done earlier on related topics are found to be by Subbaiah[32] , Pracher[33] , Deshmukh[34] , Singh[35] , Gokul[36] Rathore[37] and Raman Nair[38] . Pracher has studied the management aspect of agricultural university libraries based on four of the largest State Agricultural Universities of India. Subbaiah has built up a conceptual framework for implementing a national level agricultural information system. Deshmukh has worked on the standardization aspect of agricultural library and information services. Arjun Singh has evaluated the information resources and services for forestry. Rathore has studied marketing of information services and products in agricultural sector in the ICAR libraries. Gokul has studied information requirements of veterinarians and the resources and facilities of veterinary libraries in India. Raman Nair has studied the aspect of staffing of agricultural information systems in the Indian context. These studies are on specific groups of libraries in agricultural sector or on specific aspects. The survey revealed that a study evaluating all aspects of the agricultural library and information services in total of a region, a State, or country in regard to India is not done earlier.

In the third phase the study concentrated on the development of infrastructures in agriculture sector in the country and in Kerala in a historical perspective. It makes a detailed assessment of institutions and organizations of Kerala engaged in agricultural education, research, extension and development and their library and information service units. The mandates of the institutes, the areas where research is going on under them and other aspects that may reveal their information requirements are studied. This is essential for effective planning of information systems and resource sharing and networking programmes.

The survey of institutions in agricultural sector of the State of Kerala showed that they together undertake the functions of education, research, extension and development in the fields of agriculture, animal husbandry, home science, fisheries, forestry and allied sciences. The subject fields these institutions cover include agricultural botany, agricultural economics, agricultural engineering, agricultural entomology, agricultural extension, agricultural meteorology, agricultural statistics, agronomy, animal husbandry, home science, horticulture, olericulture, processing technology, plant breeding & genetics, plant pathology, plant physiology, plantation crops and spices, pomology and floriculture, soil science & agricultural chemistry, biotechnology, computer science, forestry, wood science, environmental sciences, wild life, ecology, aquaculture, fishery biology, and processing technology, irrigation and drainage engineering, machinery and energy, post harvest technology and processing, anatomy, animal reproduction, animal breeding & genetics, bio-chemistry, clinical medicine, diary science, livestock product technology, microbiology, nutrition, parasitology, pathology, pharmacology and toxicology, physiology, poultry science, preventive medicine, surgery, statistics, veterinary public health and also many others coming under the broad group of agriculture and biosciences. Research or development in none of these areas can be conducted as in watertight compartments. So cooperation between these institutions is important. The success of our agricultural sector in a free and competitive national or international market would depend on inter-institutional participation in development. Efficient information systems, the complex gamut of interacting activities that can enable continuous identification of problems under changing environment and development and utilization/ transfer of appropriate technology will be essential for sustainable agricultural development.

In the fourth phase a comparative evaluation of the selected libraries and information systems in agricultural sector of Kerala. The mandate, budget, collection, infrastructure, networks and services, quality and quantum of staff, physical facilities, and computer and communication systems were evaluated. Qualitative evaluation of the system and services based on results of survey conducted among system managers and users is also attempted in this phase.

The evaluation of infrastructure and facilities revealed that the resources at the disposal of the libraries taken together are sufficient for reliable services. However, when individual libraries are taken resources at their disposal are not adequate, full or reliable even for major libraries. For the institutions coming under minor group surveyed the resources are far from satisfactory. It is also found that the libraries in the agricultural sector of Kerala as independent units face various constraints in providing efficient information services. The libraries, which have to serve the majority of user community that is farmers and the public that is Krishi Bhavans, village libraries, etc in total possess only less than 1% of the information resources available in the State. There is no provision for this majority groups or their libraries to access the information stored in resource rich institutions for the sake of the farming community.

In the fifth phase a detailed investigation and evaluation of information resources available under six different sub sectors of agriculture; Crop Sciences, Veterinary Sciences, Fisheries, Forestry, Agricultural Economics, Agricultural Engineering etc. Institutions that are to take leadership in resource sharing in each of these areas are identified. Important aspects in which resource sharing is essential and cost effective; are traced out. How institutions in the sector can fill the gap between what is published in agriculture and what is made available to their users is the aim of the investigation.

The available information resources when considered with the publisher's statistics and annual additions at ICAR library[39] it is found that the book collection strength in agricultural libraries is not strong. Most of the new publications as well as information on current research in agriculture are escaping the attention of those in our agricultural sector, which will surely affect the quality, and speed of development. However, if it is considered in the light of the financial resources that will be available to these libraries we cannot expect drastic changes or improvement in our resource allocations for collection development. The options available to these libraries will be subject specialization in collection development by each institute. All institutions can lessen cost of collection development by limiting their acquisition to allotted specialization. By a resource sharing programme, access for all institutions to the total information resources available in the State at different specialized institutions will become possible. The data analysis revealed that an effective resource-sharing programme requires planned development of the institutions as well as competent and tough managers at the institutions. Well-defined areas for sharing resources, and assignment of specialization at the institutional level are also found essential by this study. There should be a detailed agreement on terms and conditions. A resource sharing programme even in selected areas like foreign journals, databases etc can effect considerable savings of recurring expenses for agricultural sector. It can also increase the quantum and quality of information resources available in the sector.

Based on the analysis in the fifth phase of the information resources available in Kerala under different sub sectors of agriculture and their usage and possibilities for extending services in the sixth phase proposal for establishing an Agricultural and Farm Information System (AGFIS) for Kerala was put forward. The functions of AGFIS, the categories of information to be included, the user categories and their training needs, levels of implementation etc are outlined. Phasing and timeframe for implementation are suggested. Standards required, network options, architecture etc is suggested. Organizational and management aspects related to implementation, functioning and sustainable development of AGFIS is also presented.

In the final phase recommendations evolved by the study for improving information services in the agricultural sector of Kerala are provided in detail.

7. MAJOR FINDINGS

The study revealed that institutions and individuals in the agricultural sector of Kerala are in constant need of information. They require information on diverse aspects like plant, animal, fisheries and other natural resources, agro climatic data, projects, budget, improved varieties, techniques and methods, packages of practices and also on the trends and developments in agricultural sciences and technology. They also need current information about agricultural prices, market trends, loans, supports, subsidies and other aspects. So agricultural sector may require various types of information services. The sector has already developed various information systems and service facilities at huge cost. To justify the expenditure on information systems in terms of their use it is essential to extract their maximum utility. This needs an integrated approach to information infrastructures their subsystems, libraries and content, which form the heart and lifeblood of the system.

Lack of Resource Sharing Programmes

Presently most libraries in agricultural sector serve users from their parent institutions only. The data collected for the study revealed that no resource sharing programme exist in the sector. There is no cooperation and coordination between institutions in managing information resources. This causes duplication of costly resources. The sector fails to extract optimum utility of the information resources built up at considerable cost. The information infrastructures should enable to extend the services offered by libraries of the agricultural institutions. The libraries in addition to catering the requirements of parent organizations should be responsive to the needs of the agricultural scientists, students, officers, extension workers, administrators, farmers and other users from outside also. An extension of information service along with cooperation between libraries for that purpose will fulfill the long felt needs of the agricultural sector of the State. It will also ensure optimum returns by maximizing the utilization of the knowledge collections held by the institutes in agricultural sector.

Challenges and Solutions

There is information explosion in every sphere of human activity including agriculture. The agricultural libraries with their limited resources face great difficulties in developing the collections and managing reliable services in the midst of the flooding of documents in various media, their cost escalation and cut in budget allotments. This also necessitates them to modernize their systems, share their resources and organize services on a cooperative basis to satisfy collectively the information needs of the users. Current developments in ICT enable the networking; cooperation and resource sharing among geographically dispersed and remotely located agricultural institutions. Now information available everywhere can be integrated, disseminated and shared easily. Agricultural sector should harness the possibilities offered by ICT and use the available information infrastructures to link farm to the lab.

Library in the Institutional Setup

The mandate of institutions coming under the ICAR, Government of India and State Government, functioning in the agricultural sector of Kerala are found to be in total to plan, undertake, and promote education, research, extension and development in agriculture, forestry, veterinary and animal sciences, diary sciences, fisheries, food, nutritional sciences, agricultural engineering and allied areas. The mandate of the libraries under them expressed by the mission statement of their parent institutions and library guides available are to provide information support for the above-mentioned activities. This is of equal importance to the activity of any other division of those institutes.

For the development of an efficient library and information system with need based, resources, facilities and services a legal basis for the system is essential. Successful participation in resource sharing and networking programs also necessitates such an authority. But this is found to be absent in most of the institutions.

The instruments of governance of the agricultural institutes and university does not define the organization, and status of their respective library systems as clearly as they have done for their other divisions or units. They also do not provide for the appointment, responsibilities, functions, powers, status, qualifications and service conditions of the library staff in the same fashion in which they have done such things for their other academic/scientific staff.

The librarian should be directly responsible to the Head of the Institution to facilitate quick and professionally sound decisions. This is essential for the successful implementation of library policies and programmes. But in ICAR Institutes library is put at third level and the head of another scientific division comes between librarian and the Director. In departments of GOK and institutions under them, also library and its officer in charge come in third or fourth level. In KAU libraries, the position is better. An earlier study in this aspect has recommended the reorganization of institutions in agricultural sector by bringing Library to the second level unit.

Library Advisory Committee (LAC)

The LAC has to serve as a link between the library and its users. LAC exists in almost all the institutions surveyed. But their constitution differs. In KAU Libraries; library management councils in which staff from lowest level to the manager participated in decision-making have been constituted. The revision of constitution of LAC's is essential to make it an effective mechanism. Participatory Management Councils have also become the need of the time.

Internal Organization of Libraries

The internal organizational set up of libraries surveyed also differs. In view of the objectives of the agricultural libraries; range of activities and services to be performed and staff available, the internal organizational structure should follow the model of KAU library combining different functions in accordance with size of the library's requirements and needs at the stages of development if essential.

Qualification and Status of Staff

Most of the institutions are having only one staff for looking after the library. They are mostly unqualified and usually library management is an additional duty allotted to them. Such staff cannot effectively handle information services. Presently no standards or norms for provision of library staff exist in most of the organizations except KAU and ICAR institutes. But in KAU also majority of the libraries are lacking professional staff. The managerial post, University Librarian is also vacant for a long time. In ICAR Institutes the library professionals do not enjoy parity of status and pay scales with scientific/academic staff. There are wide variations in the designations, salary scales and the qualification of the professional staff in agricultural libraries.

The library staff has to support and guide the scientists in their information search for research, extension and development work. For fulfilling this responsibility they require minimum qualifications prescribed by the UGC/ICAR. The professional staff of the library needs to be accorded the status and pay scales at par with other academic and scientific staff of the corresponding levels. The designations, which at present vary also, needs to be standardized and made uniform. Two detailed studies have already come out with necessary recommendations on this aspect. In institutions under State staff formula, qualifications and service conditions recommended by the KAU Expert Committee on Staff Pattern can be adopted. ICAR can consider the recommendations put forward by the detailed studies on staffing agricultural information systems already undertaken, with necessary modifications if any required.

Managerial Positions

The post of University Librarian incepted by KAU Act 1971 who is to give leadership for the system providing services at more than 48 stations spread over the State consisting of resources worth approximately 20 crore and an annual expenditure running above one crore was vacant from 1971 to 1995 and is again vacant since 2000. The annual reports of the university clearly presents the wide difference in quality of development and functioning of the information system and the returns received for the expenditure met for library resources at KAU for the periods with and without the manager in position. This can serve as a revelation to the fact that only with a competent manager in position an institute will be able to develop its library in a planned and need based way as strong sustainable system.

Financial Allocation

The library budget of the institutions covered by the study except a few varies between 2 to 5% of the parent institution's budget. Even at KAU the library budget is less than 3% of the university budget. The agricultural sector spends only less than 2.69% of total budget for library and information facilities. Agricultural University Library Commission has recommended, a minimum 6% of the institution's budget for the library. A study on resource allocation for university libraries has also supported the 6.5 to10% of the institutional budget recommended by Kothari Commission. Agricultural institutes should have a separate and regular budget for library and information services. At present there is no norm for that. The budget allocation to the libraries of agricultural institutes is not only inadequate but is also fluctuating from year to year. This should be avoided. It is very critical for resource sharing and networking programmes because there will be commitments of various kinds with other participating libraries.

Expenditure on Collection Development

It is seen that the expenditure on collection development accounts for 71% of the total library budget. From that 87% is used for printed materials, which includes books and journals. Only 13% is used for electronic documents. Among books and journals, the trend is towards spending more on duplicate copies of the latter. Very important source materials are available in other physical forms more cost effectively. The practice of considering only print media needs to be stopped. A rational policy should be framed by each institute for proportion of expenditure to be met for the resources in various media.

Information Resources

The information resources available in agricultural sector of Kerala can be grouped under different subject specializations. They also belong to different media and type. The evaluation of information resources available covered different areas of specialization mentioned below to consider possible resource sharing and networking.

a) Crop Sciences and Horticulture
b) Veterinary and Animal Sciences
c) Fisheries and Marine Sciences
d) Forestry, Soil Sciences and Water
e) Agricultural Economics, Statistics and Marketing
f) Agricultural Engineering and Technology

The survey revealed that information resources are available for use in the above areas of agriculture sector in Kerala at different institutes covered by the study. It is held by various organizations in Kerala with mandate on the above subject areas. They are engaged in education, research, extension and development activities. These institutions have also at their disposal, various physical and technology related facilities to provide information services. Their resources mainly document and journal collections in print and digital form as well as other facilities were comparatively evaluated for this study. Based on that possibilities for resources sharing and networking are identified.

Eight institutions ranking one to eight in size of the collections on each of the six sectors of agriculture are taken for evaluating their possibilities for subject specialization and leadership for resource sharing. Based on that data KAUC was found apt for specialization in crop science and horticulture, College of Veterinary and Animal Sciences, Mannuthy in veterinary and animal Sciences, KFRI in forestry and related subjects, CIFT in fisheries related area, CCBM for agricultural economics, marketing etc, CAE for agricultural engineering and technology.

Types of Information Resource

Information resources on agriculture, biosciences and related areas held in the agricultural sector are found to be of various types. They consist of books, journals, reports, thesis and working papers, video films, interactive multimedia programmes, CDROM databases and web pages. Of these books, reports, thesis and bound journals constitute 97.5% of the resources. The libraries in major institutions together spend approximately Rs. 135 lakhs for the purchase of books and Rs.208 lakhs for journals every year. The subscription of current journals consumes 53 % of the total budget for collection development.

Book Collections

When quantity of collection is considered libraries under KAU and ICAR are found to top the list. The collections in most of the institutions under KAU and ICAR are found to be adequate to serve the user community of those organizations. But the collections in other institutions especially under government departments are found to be highly inadequate.

Even though books are not very costly items there is considerable duplication on them between institutions and between different stations of the same institution. Presently there is no union catalogue in agricultural sector of the State.

Preparing a union catalogue of books available in the sector can help to avoid unnecessary duplication in regard to book purchases. This can publicize the availability of agriculture related books in different collections. The resources will then become useful beyond the walls of an institution to the whole agricultural sector.

Journal Subscriptions

Journals subscribed by major agricultural institutions in Kerala causes a recurring expenditure of Rs 208 lakhs, which come to 52.58% of the allotment for collection development. Even with that expenditure the sector fails to provide accessibility to most of the important journals at many institutions.

The study found that the number of periodicals subscribed is declining every year. But the expense towards subscription for the decreased number of journals is increasing. During the five year period examined by the study the journals subscribed in agricultural sector in Kerala has gone down by 11.7 %. But at total expenditure on journals has gone up by 94%. The new journals on newly emerging subjects related to agriculture also remain out of reach.

Cost of Duplication of Foreign Journals

Being primary sources of information and being the group of documents causing huge expenditure journals subscription aspect was examined in detail by the study. It is found to be an important area for specialization and resource sharing in agricultural sector.

The major institutions in agricultural sector taken for detailed evaluation, together subscribed 1545 journals. But this constituted only 891 different titles. Of this 659 foreign journal subscriptions constituted only 360 titles. Out of this 299 numbers were duplicate titles. Of the foreign journals 158 titles have 360 subscriptions. Duplication goes up to 8 copies for many titles.

Detailed analysis of two sample groups of journals duplicated revealed important facts. Details of the first group show that 1 journal costing more than Rs 2 lakhs is duplicated at 5 institutions, 5 journals each costing more than Rs 2 lakhs per year are subscribed at 3 institutions, another 2 journals each costing more than Rs two lakhs per year are duplicated in 2 institutions. 4 journals each costing between Rs one lakh to two lakh each per year is duplicated in 2 to 5 institutions. Of the 158 foreign journals duplicated 12 titles costing Rs.1 lakh to Rs 2 lakh are subscribed in 2 or more copies. The total cost of single subscription for them was only Rs.23, 17, 400. But the total expense including their duplication was found to be Rs.68, 44,650. The expenditure due to duplication comes to Rs.45, 27,250. Cost of one copy each of another 14 foreign journals come to Rs.9, 05,735. But the total subscription cost met by the sector for these journals including their duplicate copies is Rs.27, 56,499. The expenditure for duplication is Rs.18, 50,764. The actual total cost of single subscriptions for 158 foreign journals duplicated in the sector is Rs.51, 59,103. But total amount spent by the agricultural sector of the State for this 158 journals is Rs.154, 51,613. Hence it was found that Rs.102, 92,510 per year go for duplicate copies of the 158 foreign journals in the State.

Duplication of journals consumes a considerable amount of library budget. Their price is also increasing every year and they cost our foreign exchange. Library budget also shrinks causing discontinuation of many journals every year. In such circumstances, it is very important to avoid duplication of costly foreign journals and to make subscribed titles accessible to all. This will enable the institutions to divert the amount for duplication to the tune of Rs.103 lakhs for meeting the escalating journal cost, avoiding discontinuation of existing journals and addition of new journals in emerging fields of agriculture. So instead of foreign journal titles worth Rs. 52 lakhs available presently, the institutions will be able to have titles worth Rs.103 lakhs at their disposal if they establish a resource-sharing programme. All the institutions will also get full benefit.

Databases in CD ROM

A significant portion of allotment for collection development in institutions like KAUC (35%) and CPCRI (22%) is utilized for electronic publications from foreign countries. Even though these are essential to most of the institutions in the sector, cost makes them unaffordable. Only 11 institutions are subscribing to any of these titles. But these titles are normally not accessible to those from outside the institution. The present study revealed that against a total of 52 subscriptions of databases costing Rs.99 lakhs the libraries received only 30 titles costing Rs.40 lakhs. Duplicate copies of 11 titles related to agriculture are subscribed in 2 to 4 copies in Kerala. There is a net expenditure of Rs.67 lakhs for this duplication.

Back files of most of these titles from 1971 are available from publishers but not subscribed. About 50 titles of relevance to agricultural sector are published. Their total cost comes to approximately Rs.55 lakhs only, which includes back files also. By avoiding duplication and through a resource-sharing programme the libraries can subscribe to all the 50 titles with full back files at a cost less than that which is met presently to subscribe 30 titles. Their use can also be extended to all institutions in Kerala.

Reference Sources in Digital and Other Forms

Various reference sources in digital form are available at KAUC, CPCRI, IISR, and CAGI. They include, reference books, specialized libraries in digital form, current back files of abstracting journals, and complete collections of back volumes as well as current issues of a few primary journals. The cost of these materials ranges from Rs.1000 to R.15 lakhs per title as subscription or annual license fee. The major collection of audiovisual materials on agriculture useful for teaching, extension and awareness programmes among farmers and tribal groups and the general public is available at KAUC library.

These documents can form important tools for extension activity at KVKs and Krishi Bhavans, which interact with the farmers. But they are rare and not available through normal trade channels.

The libraries surveyed also hold significant collections of theses, reports, maps, posters etc mostly generated in-house. These documents are prepared at huge expense. They being unpublished are not available for other institutions. The theses collection at KAU includes 3870 PhD and MSc dissertations in different branches of agriculture. Traditional universities also have PhD thesis very relevant to agricultural sector. There is also a good collection of research reports and maps generated in-house spread through different libraries. All the above items can be made accessible to their expected users in agricultural sector only through a resource-sharing programme. A resource-sharing programme has to publicize the availability of these materials among all institutions. Sharing these resources with other institutions can effect savings of space and cost of binding, purchase, indexing etc of their printed equivalents at many institutes.

Collection Development Policy

Each library should evaluate the strength of the existing collection against the current and future teaching, research, extension and development programmes. The libraries should frame policies that can ensure consistent and comprehensive collection development in the areas mandatory to the institution. Quality of collection and services depends on such policies and planned development. To fulfill commitments related to resource sharing programmes all the participating libraries should have appropriate collection development policy.

The Library Building and Access

Presently the technological devices like computers, communication stacks and other such gadgets are becoming normal tools in libraries. Hence in building design, along with electrical wirings and fittings, UPS and network cabling and other such requirements should be appropriately considered. Along with space planning for readers, staff and reading materials, new servers, work stations, digitization equipments, electronic document storage systems, CD servers, juke boxes, digital presentation systems etc are becoming critical and are to be considered. The involving of the librarian in the planning and design of the library building as well as librarian's ICT literacy has become very important in the present day context. The projections regarding the space requirements for various items including stacking of books, periodicals, other materials, reading areas, staff areas, as well as ICT related aspects like IT Labs, network control rooms, record storage rooms of the digital library, conference/seminar facilities etc should be made with a vision for next 20 years according to the norms and standards specified for the purpose by concerned agencies. KAUC is found to be an excellent model for physical facilities on this line. CTCRI, CPCRI, CIFT, etc also have excellent physical facilities.

Access and Opening Hours

Of the Libraries, which responded to the survey, 40 libraries were following open access. In 21 libraries closed access system is followed. The libraries surveyed function from 10 AM to 5 PM only. The institutes being in remote locations and staff mostly residing inside the campus itself it is advisable that opening hours should be adjusted as per the demand of users and should be at least from 12 to 15 hours a day. KAUC is a library in main campus which has invested about 9 crore for its development. More than 1000 students, scientists, teachers and other staff are residing in the same campus where the library is situated. It is accessible to those from nearby campuses also. Hence it should be kept open day and night to extract optimum returns for the investments made.

Areas for Resource Sharing

The study has analyzed in detail the possibilities for resource sharing in regard to book, journal and electronic publications and databases. The findings suggest that resource sharing will bring in cost effectiveness and efficiency not only in collection development but also in many other processes and services of library and information systems. Important areas identified are technical processing, storage of less used materials, HRD in ICT, reprographic services, documentation services including abstracting and union catalogues, conservation activities etc.

Technical Processing

In most of the libraries in agricultural sector in Kerala the collection is not classified, catalogued and arranged accordingly. Only major institutions have technically processed their collections at least partially. There is large extant of duplication of titles in different collections. Libraries presently do the technical processing independently. Technical processing works like classification, cataloguing data entry in computers, preparation of union catalogues, OPACs, production of bibliographies and abstracts, HRD etc can be done cost effectively under a resource sharing programme. It can by pooling together the catalogues of participating libraries make available an online public access union catalogue. The libraries can download the records related to their newly acquired titles and can save the effort for cataloguing, classification and data entry work. This will avoid huge waste of human and financial resources caused by the duplication of technical processing work.

OPACS and Bibliographies

A resource-sharing programme can also circulate a union Monthly New Addition List for Books pertaining to the libraries participating in the programme. It should be based on the records received from participating libraries. Nodal Centers can prepare and periodically publish in digital or printed form bibliographies on the area of their specialization.

Documentation Services

Most of the agricultural libraries surveyed provide various documentation services. These are not automated and are presently done individually by the libraries. Documentation services are costly when done by individual institutions. If the services are provided jointly it becomes less expensive. Resource sharing also improves their scope, comprehensiveness, coverage, speed, quality and reliability.

Current Awareness Service

Agricultural libraries have to expand existing document identification capabilities by establishing Contents, Abstracts and Photocopies Service (CAPS) as run by INSDOC. The institutions suggested by this study for acting, as nodal centers in the six sub-fields of agriculture are capable to provide CAPS service on their subject area. These nodal centers should be supported by government or other agency to run CAPS in their particular area of specialization as well as maintain common facilities. In return for such increased financial support, libraries at these institutes are to be authorized by their parent organizations to build up collection in well-planned way to provide services including CAPS to other institutes also. In a resource-sharing programme for journals each library can prepare and transmit content pages of the journals received in those institutions every month to a leading institution which is to publish a monthly bulletin or volume of the content pages and circulate it to all libraries participating in the programme.

Abstracting and Indexing

A resource-sharing programme can create instruments for conduct of bibliographic searches in articles contained in the journals subscribed by participants. Libraries at the nodal centers should plan their journal subscriptions jointly without over lapping of titles between them. They should prepare a computerized database of articles pertaining to Kerala in their mandatory subject available in the journals and other documents subscribed at the nodal center as well as other institutes cooperating with it. For this all article titles and accompanying abstracts, should be computerized. This database should form the key to document provision through CAP services also. Based on this database Monthly Abstracts on Agriculture limiting to the agro climatic regions of Kerala can be published under a resource-sharing programme. Major agricultural databases like CABI, ASFA, AGRIS, AGRICOLA and MEDLINE are subscribed in Kerala. Records related to agro climatic regions relevant to Kerala could be downloaded at the institutions subscribing them. These records can be organized for reference under a resource-sharing programme.

Full-Text Retrieval

As most of the important reports, thesis etc on agriculture is not published; developing full text digital libraries of such materials are very important for agricultural research. Many big collections from groups of agricultural libraries of foreign countries are available in digital version. Already attempts on development of full text thesis library have been successfully conducted in one of the libraries surveyed. A resource-sharing programme should develop full text digital archives of the documents generated in-house by all participating institutes as well as documents relevant to the agro climatic regions of Kerala produced elsewhere.

Other Services

Inter library loan between participating institutions, establishing common storage facility for less used materials, common preservation labs and, common printing facilities etc are found to be other areas which can be considered under a resource sharing programme.

Human Resource Development

Success of resource sharing and networking will depend on continuous training of the librarians in the knowledge, skills and techniques in information work. Training facilities are costly and each and every institution cannot establish their own training facilities. AGFIS should take leadership in providing such training. In the institutions covered by this study KAUC was found to have excellent training facilities for librarians. Use of this facility for HRD will extract the optimum utility of public money invested there.

Resource Sharing Network

Based on the facts and needs discussed above this study

proposes the establishment of an Agricultural and Farm Information System (AGFIS) and Network for Kerala covering agricultural institutions in the State under KAU, ICAR, GOK and other agencies. It will be a State level network intended to strengthen Information Management (IM) within the agricultural sector of the State of Kerala. AGFIS proposed by this study will have an integrated view of information system and content. The system will be a common one to support, managing and making available for use information and documents meant for different activities in the sector like planning, administration, research, education, extension and development. Considering the needs of the agricultural sector of the State the AGFIS network is proposed to be implemented with five levels.

Status of ICT Facilities at Institutes

Minimum ICT facilities in the concerned institutes are one of the essential prerequisites for the successful implementation of resource sharing network. The survey conducted for this study revealed that most of the major institutions in agricultural sector have already acquired computers. But for AGFIS some costly common facilities will become essential and are to be created by the DAGI the agency managing AGFIS. The participants normally will have to make their own arrangements for required hardware, software and other peripherals to become a nodal center or to participate in the programme. Government has to provide minimum computers and connectivity at lower level institutions like research stations, KVKs, Krishi Bhavans, veterinary hospitals, village libraries etc. This can enable such institutions to develop local capabilities and give farmers and the public the poser to use the information system.

Phasing and Time Frame

Considering structure of the agricultural sector of Kerala and also factors such as information resources, infrastructure facilities, manpower and level of computerization at present in various agricultural institutions this study proposes launching of the AGFISNET in three phases running over three financial years.

The first phase has to cover the library and information systems of six nodal centers, other ICAR Institutes, major institutes under KAU, FIB etc. The second phase will cover remaining KAU colleges, concerned Departments of GOK and other institutions. In the third and final phase all the research stations, Krishi Vigyan Kendras Agricultural Offices, veterinary, hospitals, Krishi Bhavans, village libraries, NGOs and all concerned institutions under government and private agencies in agricultural sector of the State will be brought into the network programme.

By the end of third year AGFISNET implementation is to be completed and services should be extended to the farmers and extension workers in villages through their nearest accessible service outlets. Scientists from any remote location of the State will then get linked to State, national and international information systems in agriculture.

Common Standards, Formats and Procedures

Successful participation in AGFIS system will require uniformity in various aspects. Hence common standards for hardware, software, MIS work, library processes etc will be essential. Standard formats are to be used for different processes. For MIS most of the required formats are already specified in commonly used, hardcopy. All that has to be done in this regard will be to recreate these forms in a spreadsheet program for the computer. Cooperation for technical processing works, documentation services etc will require the use of common standards and codes for cataloguing classification, computerized databases etc by libraries participating in the programme. A prior agreement on standards for bibliographical and DBMS format is essential. Presently among 30 major libraries; for Classification 7 institutions uses DC, 6 institutions UDC and 8 institutions CC. For cataloguing 7 uses AACR, 10 CCC and 1 their own scheme. Others have no specific standards or schemes. For database development 14 uses CDS/ISIS 6 uses other software.

INFLIBNET, which supports most of the academic and research libraries in India, has recommended the use of DDC for classification, AACR for cataloguing and CCF format for database development. In CCF records can be generated much faster and they can be interchanged with any ISO-2709 based format in the world. Presently DDC has an electronic version also. INFLIBNET has also developed library automation software ILMS, which can be also be considered by AGFISNET for use in participating libraries.

Hardware

Presently there is no prescribed standard for computer hardware in institutions surveyed. It is recommended that AGFISNET participants should go in for computer systems, which have components of current technology, scope for up gradation and compatibility to packages used for highly specialized functions in the system. A minimum configuration is to be recommended by AGFIS for workstations/PCs at the institutions like Krishi Bhavans, village Libraries etc for enabling their access to the network. Based on current technology and affordability a Pentium IV 2.5.GHz, 256 MB RAM, 40GB HDD, CDD 54x, CDRW 48x, 17 Inch Color Monitor, Speakers, Scanner, Keyboard and Scroll Mouse, Web Camera and Internal Modem and an Ink jet Printer and scanner is proposed by this study for service outlets at Krishi Bhavans, village libraries etc and for use as workstations. This costs less than Rs. 20000 and can fulfill the requirements at these service points.

People and Technology

The study considers that awareness about AGFIS is to be created among the people for the success of the system. Training is also to be provided to scientists, teachers, extension workers, farmers and the public to make the system useful for agricultural developments.

Organizations And Management

The overall policy and management of the AGFIS is to be coordinated by the Department of Agriculture, GOK. But a special department of required status with delegation of concerned powers needs to be constituted.

For the implementation and future management of the AGFIS this study considers it essential to form a Directorate for Agricultural Informatics (DAGI). It should have mandate for agriculture and biosciences information that runs beyond management information, extension activities, libraries, publications and computers. Constituting Management Council for DAGI by GOK with Agricultural Production Commissioner as Chairman is also found to be a requirement. An Information Management (IM) Unit in the DAGI with ICT experts and subject experts from each sub sector of agriculture also is proposed. The discussion in Chapter 6 suggests that organizations of repute in ICT ventures outsourcing business are to be contracted for network design, hardware procurement, installation, and commissioning in DAGI and institutes participating in AGFIS as nodal centers.

Demonstration Sites

Mass Media will be very important for dissemination of agricultural information. DAGI will in future require independent studio and radio facilities. It will be a blessing if DAGI could work near and in close association with regional Doordarshan Kendra and All India Radio. Presently GOK has that facility. It has an adjacent campus to Doordarshan under it where presently a few extension and training activities are going on. DAGI can establish a campus in State capital near Doordarshan where sufficient space for that is available to it. AGFIS central hub at the campus should start research and development as well as education and training for participating institutions.

Network Options and Architecture

There is good telecommunication infrastructure in the State. NIC is likely to participate in various projects of Department of Agriculture, (GOI). Its expertise in the management of district-level telecommunications will be of importance for strengthening the IM capabilities of farmers and extension services and also the research/extension linkages. Network designs based on available functional models can be adhered to in AGFISNET. Such Networks to be initially established in DAGI and nodal centers under AGFIS programme have to grow rapidly through topology assimilation, aggregation and absorption into Enterprise Networks at later stages. All network development has to be done with this in mind.

DAGI under GOK should establish a well-planned Campus, campus wide network as well as required premises networks at headquarters where the central hub of AGFIS will be established. Six nodal centers also should establish similar networks. The institutes should acquire required LAN/ communication stacks and solutions as per standards prescribed by DAGI in consultation with it.

Technology Choices

The technology choices available and their positive and negative aspects are discussed in detail by the study. AGFIS should consider only the technology that has proven to work, that will still be appropriate for at least another ten years, which can be afforded as well as simple. Based on current trends it is found advisable to use a combination of landlines both leased and dial-up, satellites, and radio in AGFISNET.

Quality and Utility of the Systems and Services

The assessment of the utility of libraries in agricultural sector for their qualitative evaluation was done through users responses to the questionnaire. In the survey of the 427 users from manager, scientist and student categories who responded to the questionnaire 15% of the users rated the book collection as excellent, 19% as very good, 23% as good and 11% as poor. Journal collection was rated as excellent by 4 % of users, as very good by 19%, as good by 40 %, as average by 15 % and as poor by another 15 %. Data on users ratings of the library staff shows that 26% of users rated staff in agricultural libraries as excellent, 24 % as good, 26 % percent as average and 18 % as poor. Users awareness and use of the information resources was also assessed by the study. Of the users 24% reported that they were fully aware of the resources of the library and 9 % stated that they were making full utilization of the resources. Another 4 % was utilizing the resources at least up to 75%. Only 3.56 % reported that they were not at all aware of the resources of the library. Rating of the users on the organizational set up, presentation of the library system and quality of services from the experience of users was obtained through the questionnaire. The overall system of the library was rated as excellent by 13% of users, 19% as very good, 29% as good, 18% as average and 7% as poor. Of the 77 librarians that responded to the survey from inside the system 3.5 % rated the library as excellent, 2 % as very good, 26 % as good, 25 % as average and 23 % as poor.

Lack of Farmer Orientation

A few of the major libraries surveyed are having excellent collections specially meant for the farmers. But farmers are not using such libraries. Krishi Bhavans are not having any such document resources, but village libraries are rich in this aspect. Of the expected users of agricultural information systems less than 1 % are scientists and administrators (who exist to serve the farmers) and 99 % are farmers. But presently the information systems under agricultural sector are not accessible or inviting to the farmers whom they have to serve directly and indirectly.

A survey using a questionnaire in regional language was conducted among randomly selected farmers and public living near the regions of the major agricultural institutions. The intention was to check the sources they use for agricultural information, its accessibility and use. Of the 220 responses only 17 % stated that they were aware of the agricultural institution existing near them and 8 % stated that they approach those institutions for information. From this less than 1 % only stated that they are satisfied and another 5 % opined that the service is not satisfactory or relevant. For 32 % the procedural difficulties and the psychological barriers prevented them from using the services of those institutions.

Among the farmers and public who responded 77 % stated that they were aware of the Krishi Bhavans existing nearby and of this 14 % stated that they approach Krishi Bhavans for information. From this 7% stated their service as satisfactory and 20 % as unsatisfactory. Among the responses 93 % stated that they were aware of the village library and 32 % of the total responses stated that they approach them for agricultural information. The survey revealed that village library was the most sought after institution by farmers, and that procedures and psychological barriers in using those collections were less there.

But 65 % of the respondents were of the opinion that Krishi Bhavans are the apt place for providing agricultural information services to the farmers. But 59 % preferred village libraries and 12 % research institutes for providing agricultural information services to farmers.

Possible Hindrances to Resource Sharing

The present study obtained the views of the librarians/ officers in charge of libraries from institutions covered by the study in regard to the hindrances for resource sharing programmes. Of the librarians who responded 60% have stated that absence of planning is an important factor hindering resource sharing programmes. Then 76 % stated absence of institutional leadership as an important factor. Of the other factors hindering resource sharing programmes absence of spirit of cooperation (64 %), inadequate resources (66 %), inadequate finance (68 %), lack of communication (69 %) etc, were rated as high by the librarians.

From the analysis of the responses of librarians collected for this study it is to be concluded that an effective resource sharing programmes requires planned development of the institutions, and competent and tough managers at the institutions. Well-defined areas for sharing resources, and assignment of specialization at the institutional level are also essential. There should be a detailed agreement on terms and conditions.

8. THE OUTCOME OF THE STUDY

Agriculture is the lifeblood of our economy. It contributes

25 percent of Gross Domestic Product. In agricultural sector of Kerala there are approximately ten thousand professionals, which include scientists, extension officers and other staff working. Agriculture continues to be the occupation and way of life of more than half of our population even today. Sustainable prosperity of this class; the farmers and the landless agricultural laborers holds the key for improving the overall human resource development scenario in the country. The efficiency and effectiveness of education, research, extensions and development at the farm depend upon several factors amongst which information is one of the important.

The study revealed that we have rich and relevant knowledge/information resources in our agricultural sector. But it is not getting connected to the scientist and managers and extension activists who require it. The information to reach over the farmers spread over the blocks and villages mostly in remote areas is an up hill task. The diversity of Kerala's agro ecological situation adds to this challenge further. In today's world farmers needs are much more diversified and the knowledge required to address them is beyond the capacity of the present extension functionaries.

But today, its is possible to find a solution to this situation by using the potential of Information and Communication Technology. This can enable pooling and sharing of the available resources. It can also enable information systems access to resources available world wide to cater to the requirements of the scientists and extension workers as well as the location specific needs of the farmers.

The present study could identify the institutions and groups that require information services and the facilities available to them. The study also assessed the agricultural information resources available in the State, their location, accessibility, usage, hindrances for access/usage, the extent of loss of public money due to unnecessary duplication, provision for coordination and resource sharing available etc. Based on the above the study could formulate various recommendations for extracting the maximum utility of the available information resources by extending their accessibility to the whole agricultural sector to all levels. A model plan for resource sharing and networking in the agricultural sector also could be put forward by the study.

Recommendations

Based on the findings of the study and the discussions in the above paragraphs the suggestions and recommendations on important aspects of agricultural library and information system of Kerala are given below. Implementation of these recommendations can improve the quality, efficiency and cost effectiveness of agricultural information services in the State and contribute to increased production.

a) the agricultural institutes should clearly define the organizational set up of their library divisions along with that of other divisions. They should clearly define the terms of appointment, responsibilities, duties, powers, status, qualifications and service conditions of the library staff

b) Library should be brought into second level unit in the organizational set up of institutions in agricultural sector.

c) Library Advisory Committees (LAC) in all institutes should incorporate representatives from every unit/ department that library has to serve. The head of the institution should chair LAC and Librarian should act as the Secretary. Library Management Councils with intra departmental representation should also be constituted in all libraries with Librarian as Chairman.

d) Staff formula, qualifications and service conditions recommended by the KAU Expert Committee on Staff Pattern for University College/Research Station and other institute libraries may be adopted for libraries under KAU and State government. ICAR should also consider revising qualifications and service conditions of library and information service professionals for its institutes in the changed context of ICT inroad to libraries.

e) Qualifications prescribed by UGC/ICAR and additional qualifications on specialization in agricultural information handling prescribed by concerned expert committees should be strictly adhered to for filling up the posts of librarians at managerial level in all institutes.

f) It is very important that the chief librarian of all institutions small or big should be appointed right from the inception of the institution. He/she should be a professional. The foundations for library development should be laid under his/her supervision. Such library posts at the managerial level should never be kept vacant considering the importance of information systems for development.

g) A minimum 6% of the institution's budget should be earmarked for the library. Agricultural institutes should have a separate and regular budget for library and information services.

h) The nodal centers specializing on different sub sectors should lead in providing services in concerned areas to agricultural sector. Based on present study KAUC is recommended for specialization on crop science and horticulture, CVA for veterinary and animal sciences, KFRI for forestry and related subjects, CIFT for fisheries related area, CCBM for agricultural economics, marketing etc, and CAE for agricultural engineering and technology.

i) Web based union catalogue of books, reference sources in electronic media, audio and video documents, dissertations, reports, maps etc available in the agricultural sector of the State should be published. This can help to avoid unnecessary duplication in purchase as well as technical processing works. This can publicize the availability and maximize the use of resources.

j) Development of digital full text library of theses and dissertations of doctoral studies in agriculture and biosciences conducted in Kerala in KAU and other traditional universities as well as other documents generated in-house at the institutions in agricultural sector of Kerala like project reports, journals, annual reports, experimental data, resource data etc should form priority item under AGFIS. Technology developed in the region itself for full text library like Nitya Archive by CAGI should be given preference if parameters related to cost, efficiency and possibilities for future scaling stands equal with others considered.

k) The scientists, extension activists, librarians managers and the farmers should be trained under AFGIS in various aspects of ICT relevant to each group in institutions at various levels under AGFIS.

l) Duplication of foreign journals should be stopped. Journals should be subscribed under a resource-sharing programme, and made accessible to all institutions. The funds presently put on duplicate titles should be utilized to subscribe new titles.

m) Duplication of subscription to CDROM databases between institutions should be stopped. They should be subscribed under a resource-sharing programme. The savings should be diverted to purchase new titles and full back files.

n) The projections regarding the space requirements for various aspects in libraries should envisage IT Labs, network control rooms, record storage rooms of the digital library, conference/seminar facilities etc also and should be made with a vision for next 20 years.

o) To extract returns for the amount spent at the costliest information service infrastructure of KAUC, that facility should function 24 hours a day, 365 days a year with maximum publicity on that aspect.

p) It is recommended that technical processing in libraries should be done on cooperative basis.

q) An Agricultural and Farm Information System (AGFIS) and Network covering agricultural institutions in the

State under KAU, ICAR, Departments of GOK and other agencies should be established. It should be a State level network intended to strengthen information management within the agricultural sector of the State of Kerala. AGFIS should have an integrated view of information system and content. The system should be a common one to support, managing and making available for use information and documents meant for different activities like planning, administration, research, education, extension and development.

r) For the management of the AGFIS creation of a Directorate for Agricultural Informatics (DAGI) under Department of Agriculture, GOK with mandate for agriculture and biosciences information that runs beyond management information, research information, extension activities, libraries, publications and computers is recommended. The Director of DAGI should be a senior information scientist with proved record of achievements, innovation and commitment to information management issues in agriculture. Management Council for DAGI also should be constituted by GOK with Agricultural Production Commissioner as Chairman. An Information Management (IM) Unit with ICT experts and subject experts from each sub sector of agriculture should also be created.

s) It is recommended that DAGI should establish a campus in State capital near Doordarshan where sufficient space is available to the Department. AGFIS central hub at the campus should start research and development as well as education and training; for participating institutions.

t) Networking facilities offered by NIC should be utilized for extending the service of AGFIS to the farm for cost effectiveness and also to get the management and technical experience that NIC possess.

u) DAGI should chart and craft a technology, product and

capacity plan that will emerge through modest beginnings and evolve in a non-disruptive migration continuum into an elastic and scaleable network that can easily imbibe any future local and cross-campus requirements of the Institutes as well as AGFIS.

v) At DAGI main Campus and at all nodal centers the central hubs of the concerned campus networks, their administration, and digital information storage and processing systems should be located in the buildings of the information handling divisions of the institutes, which will normally be the library.

w) AGFIS should use the technology that has been proven to work, that will still be appropriate for at least another ten years that can be afforded as well as simple.

x) Every agricultural institute's library should build up an important unit for providing information service to farmers. Their collections should consist of information materials repacked for them. Preferably they should be in regional language. Interactive multimedia programmes, videos and poster as well as facilities for using and presenting them should be available in this unit. At least one access terminal to AGFISNET should be provided at this unit. Continuous training on use of ICT facilities as well as extension programmes related to sustainable methods of farming, animal rearing, fisheries etc should be conducted in association with this unit. There should be facilities for farmers to present their innovations as well as for recording and preserving traditional knowledge obtained from them at this unit. There should be a well-qualified professional librarian with ICT literacy and aptitude to manage this unit. If the institute and its library are located in an urban area this unit should be located at a nearest village relevant to the mandate of the institute concerned. The expenditure incurred for an agricultural institute can in no way be justified unless such a service is provided by it.

9. FULFILLMENT OF THE OBJECTIVES OF THE STUDY

The study was conducted with the objectives to evaluate the resources, facilities and services of the information support systems in agricultural sector of the State of Kerala. Investigation on the factors hindering their efficiency, finding out solutions to overcome them, as well as evolving proposals for resource sharing and networking also formed the objectives. The study has made a general assessment of information resources and facilities of 105 institutions in agriculture sector which consisted of 30 resource rich institutions, 75 minor institutions consisting of samples of all categories of institutions from among approximately 200 existing in the State. Appraisal from inside the system was done by a survey and interview schedule conducted among librarians and officers in charge of information services. The quality and relevance of the collections and efficiency and accessibility of the systems were evaluated through surveys among managers, scientists and farmers.

The study observed the richness of the existing collections, lack of provision for extending their use outside the institutions, recurring loss of crores of rupees occurring due to present need for duplication of resources, and lack of coordination and cooperation in managing and disseminating information in the sector. Based on these findings the study succeeded in framing various recommendations for improving the situation as well as preparing a plan for establishing a resource sharing network for agricultural sector of Kerala. The recommendations and proposals if implemented can enable the optimum utility of agricultural information resources available in the State; can ensure accessibility to the managers, scientists, and farmers from any part of the State to the complete agricultural knowledge available. An effective communication link will come into existence between the laboratory and the farm, enabling quick transfer of technology; which will lead to improved quality and production in the sector.

The Tenability of the Hypothesis

The hypothesis formulated at the beginning of the study are that; agricultural information and extension systems in Kerala fail to utilize the available resources for providing need based services to various categories of users in the agricultural sector and that there is lack of efficient information infrastructure and coordination form information management, access and dissemination in the sector. The hypothesis was proved to the extent that the sector is holding valuable information resource but the resources and facilities are not spread according to the requirement. It was also found that available resource is not accessible to most of the expected users, there is no resource sharing programme as well as provision for coordination of the information services to extract the maximum utility of the resources developed at huge cost.

Areas for Further Study

As agriculture is concerned with the production, conservation and improvement of the plants and animals and the natural environment in which they grow it is a vast subject with various sub disciplines. Agricultural science may require research information from various branches of biosciences. This necessitates the agricultural information systems to specialize on different disciplines under it and share that knowledge with scientists working in other disciplines under agriculture as well as facilitate access to information from a wide variety of topics coming under agriculture and biosciences. Then agricultural sector is also an area in which two types of information dissemination systems exist - extension activities provided by scientists themselves and information services by librarians. They exist independently, duplicate resources, and fail to achieve efficiency and effectiveness. One system holds information and the other system hold facilities for disseminating it.

Also library and information service scenario where most aspects of ICT were initially tested and perfected is witnessing revolutionary changes in the mediums and methods for accessing, storing, organizing, processing and disseminating information. In live agricultural libraries traditional hard copy materials, online databases and familiar CDROM products have been joined by the World Wide Web, electronic journals and Intranets. Continuous professional improvement to cope up with these developments has become very essential for agricultural librarians. Resource sharing, cooperative technical processing and access to centrally located collections have become the standard of the time. In Library and Information Science field agricultural information systems is a neglected area of research and hence all the above aspects of agricultural information systems needs to be studied and can be listed as follows.

* National and State level agricultural information systems resource sharing networks.
* Information systems on specific disciplines of agriculture like crop sciences, veterinary and animal sciences, forestry, fisheries, agricultural engineering, agricultural economics etc.
* Agricultural university libraries: general and specific
* ICAR institute libraries: general and specific
* Information services for extension activities in agriculture
* Agricultural information services at local community, Krishi Bhavans, village libraries etc.
* Agricultural libraries and their organization, management, staffing, standards etc.
* Information sources in agriculture relevant to India.
* User studies in agricultural libraries.

Of the above areas studies has already been made on conceptual framework for establishing a National Agricultural Information System by Subbaiah, SAUs by Prasher, user studies on veterinarians by Gokul and forestry libraries at national level by Singh. The present study has covered establishment of an agricultural information system at State level including possible resource sharing and networking mechanisms. Studies on the other aspects at national and State level are also open to researchers in library science. At State level the following aspects are virgin fields for research.

* Specialized information systems at State level on the six sub sectors of agriculture; like general agriculture, veterinary and animal science, forestry, fisheries, agricultural engineering and agricultural economics.
* Information systems at agricultural colleges in the State
* Information systems for the organizations under Departments of Agriculture, Animal Husbandry, Poultry, Fisheries, Diary Sciences etc.
* Organization, management, staffing etc of agricultural libraries at different levels in the State
* Information services for the farmers and village level systems for managing local information.

10. CONCLUSION

The study has brought to light the richness of information resource available in Kerala on various aspects of agriculture. It has also revealed the factors that hinder the State from extracting optimum utility of the resources. The observations have helped in framing necessary recommendations to improve the situation as well as for planning an integrated information system and resource-sharing network for agricultural sector.

A resource-sharing network programme like AGFISNET proposed by this study will lessen the duplication of costly journals, books and databases. Even in selected areas like foreign journals, electronic databases etc it can effect considerable savings of recurring expenses to the tune of approximately one crore per year. This amount can be diverted to increase the quantum and quality of information resources available. AGFISNET will also ensure availability of all the materials held by the institutions in agricultural sector in Kerala to each and every institution and user in the State. This will ensure access to all the scientists of Kerala, teachers, researchers, extension workers, development activists, and administrators, farmers and public, the whole wealth of knowledge/information resources on agriculture available in the State. Availability and accessibility to more resources at less cost by all institutions and to all concerned will become possible.

While developing Infrastructures for AGFISNET, the managers should see extension activities, publication, library and information services, management information, research information, and computer and communication networks with an integrated view. This will help to harness the maximum utility of the information infrastructures developed as well as contribute to the quality and efficiency of all the activities in agricultural sector. Such an integrated view will avoid duplication of computer and communication infrastructures between management, library and extension information systems. It will also keep the information component connected to Information Infrastructures. The failure of most of the information infrastructures is due to the lack of such an integrated approach.

REFERENCES

1 Randwa, N.S. History of agriculture in India, V3. New Delhi, ICAR, 1980: 273

2 India, Agriculture, Ministry of, DARE/ICAR. Annual Report 2000-2001. New Delhi, the author, 2002: 14.

3 Devarajan, G. Information Technology for agricultural development. In *Agricultural Information Systems: Vision 2020.* Thrissur, IASLIC Study Circle, 2000: 6.

4 Swaminathan, M.S. Century of Hope: Towards an era of harmony with nature and freedom from hunger. Chennai, East West Press, 1999: 51.

5 Babcock, Philip, Ed. Webster's third new International dictionary, V1. Chicago, Merriam Webster, 1993: 44.

6 Sewel, Philip. Resource sharing: Co-operation and

coordination in library and information services. London, Andre Deutsch, 1981.

7 Subbaiah, R. Conceptual framework for an Indian National Agricultural Information System (INAGRIS). (Unpublished PhD Thesis). Trivandrum, University of Kerala, 1985: 41

8 Ritter, Allen, M. Encyclopedia of Agricultural Science, V1. New York, Academic Press, 1994: 173.

9 University of Kentucky. Agripedia. http:www.ca.uky.edu/agripedia.

10 Lipton, Kathrylyn L and Reine, Luzne. Dictionary of agriculture. New York, Holt, 1995: 16

11 Prasad, C. Information Science and Technology. In *Information Technology* Ed by Swaminathan. Madras, Macmillan, 1991: 10.

12 Ibid.

13 Raman Nair, R and Francis, AT. Information needs of agricultural scientists in India: Problems and prospects. Co-authored with Sri. A.T. Francis. *Proceedings of the IASLIC National Seminar- 1996*, University of Calcutta, 1996: 121-126

14 Blum, Abraham. Mapping and comparing agricultural knowledge system as evaluation and improvement instruments. Keynote Address delivered at the *National Conference on Frontiers of Extension Education in 21st Century.* Lucknow, November 8, 1997: 14.

15 Deshmukh, P.P. Role of libraries in agricultural education, research and extension. In *Information systems for agricultural sciences and technology Ed by P.P. Deshmukh.* New Delhi, Metropolitan, 1987: 137-149.

16 Ballantyne, Peter. Managing the flow of scientific information for agricultural research in small countries: An Issue paper. Hague. ISNAR, 1991: 11.

17 Ruttan, V.W. Towards a global agricultural research system. In *Policy for Agricultural Research,* edited by V.W.

Ruttan and C.E. Pray. New York, Boulder, 1987: 84.

18 UNESCO. International Commission on Education for the Twenty-First Century, Report. Paris, the author, 1996: 14.

19 Ashok, A. Liberalization and globalization: Issues in agricultural marketing. In *Southern Economist. 14 (19), 2002*: 5-6

20 Raman Nair, R. Content management for agricultural, research and development in India. In *Proceedings of the IASLIC Conference – 2001*, Calcutta, IASLIC, 2001: 35-36.

21 Op cit.3.

22 Raman Nair, R. Agricultural and Farm Information System for Kerala. In *Proceedings of the ILA National Seminar - 1996*. Directorate of Public Libraries, Andhra Pradesh, Vijayawada, 1996: 298-312.

23 Ramachandran Nair, Adoor K.K. Kerala State Gazetteer. Vol.2, Part 1. Trivandrum: State Gazetteers, 1986: 21-32.

24 Ibid.

25 Ibid.

26 Surendran, P. Kerala economy: Growth and survival. New Delhi, Vrinda, 2002: 19.

27 Op.cit.35: 20.

28 Ibid.

29 Op cit. 35: 21.

30 India, Information and Broadcasting, Min of. India 2003: A Reference Annual. New Delhi, the author, 2003: 395.

31 Shaw, Ralph R. and Krishna Rao, D.B. Report on Library and bibliographical services for Agricultural teaching and research in India. New Delhi, ICAR, 1957.

32 Subbaiah, R. Conceptual framework for an Indian National Agricultural Information System (INAGRIS). (Unpublished PhD Thesis). Thiruvananthapuram, University of Kerala, 1985

33 Prasher, R G. Managing university libraries. New Delhi, Today and Tomorrow, 1991.

34 Deshmukh, P P. Standardisation of library and information services with special reference to scientific and agricultural libraries, New Delhi, ABC, 1990

35 Singh, Arjun. Assessment of resources, facilities and services in libraries of forestry institutions in India: A proposal for resource sharing and networking. (Unpublished PhD Thesis). Jaipur, University of Rajasthan, 2002.

36 Gokul, Adarsh N. Information needs and use pattern of veterinarians in the IT environment. (Unpublished PhD Thesis). Thiruvananthapuram, University of Kerala, 2002.

37 Rathore, Jag Mohan. Marketting of information products and services in agricultural sector: A study of marketing management of the libraries of agricultural research institutes of ICAR. (Unpublished Phd Thesis). Jaipur, University of Rajasthan, 2004.

38 Raman Nair, R. Staffing agricultural information systems. New Delhi, Ess Ess, 2000.

39 India. Agriculture, Min of. Annual Report 2002-03. New Delhi, the author, 2003:121.

2

Application of Information Technology in Tribal Medicine

— *Dr. S. Asha*

1. INTRODUCTION

The world today is in transition from industrial age to information age. The Information Technology (IT) revolution is making a tremendous impact on the society by relentless technology innovation, massive growth in computer power, world wide net works and ever growing electronic factories (Pathak and Tripathi, 1998). It has taken a new turn in order to make the human life not only informative, but also easier and comfortable. Owing to the untired efforts of the scientists and technologists, several new technologies have been introduced, creating havoc in information acquisition, processing, and retrieval through a combination of computer and satellite based technologies in particular. Such technologies interestingly seem to have not fixed any parameter in respect to their level of operation (Panda and Gautham, 1999).

Information technology represents an assemblage of technologies. These technologies are the computer ability to store and process information, the communication technology, which represents transmitting information to location where it may be needed (Gopinath, 1985).

Right from ordering a pizza with a restaurant far from the home, till the saving of a precious human life from possible cardiologic arrest in an operation theatre, such technologies seem to have proved their capabilities beyond human imagination. Today computers are no more restricted to the corporate or elite class. It is not very costly and everybody can access it. Now the word computer is on everybody's lips, computers are now in the hands of layman.

Importance of IT

Information Technology has penetrated so much into every discipline that the management of information and knowledge has been more efficient, cost effective and almost at real time. The phenomenal expansion of the world wide web and the internet in every nook and corner of the world has made access to the internet from anywhere in the world smooth, fast and efficient. Websites have been created by several millions of specialized institutions on the world wide web thereby making searching and browsing the net an integral part of the new professionals daily routine (Menon, 2000).

All countries in the world are attempting to formulate their own strategies to make use of IT as a tool for progress and overall development of the country and thereby providing better quality of life to their citizens. There is a great potentiality for the third world countries to take advantage of the information technology as a whole for their overall development. Application of IT is not just confined to the hardware, software, importing or exporting software packages. It can be effectively applied as a tool for the development of the society as a whole

IT and Development

Even though the developed countries have already tapped the potentialities of IT for the development of the whole society, in developing countries like India some multinational companies and computer professionals enjoy the benefits of IT only. The application of IT is just confined to hardware, software, importing, exporting of software packages. But it can be effectively used as a tool for the development of the society as a whole.

Information Technology includes hardware and software,

telecommunication devices and networks besides brainware and orgware. Brainware means theories, strategies and policies in the development and social application of IT and orgware concerned with the organizational and management aspect of IT (Mathew, 1985). The above aspect of Information Technology requires the social application of IT, which has more relevance in the modern context.

IT can be used as an effective tool to meet the developmental needs of the society. But till now, there is a tendency among the IT experts to delimit IT application in the traditional areas like office automation, industrial design, information communication sectors, etc. There is an urgent need to re-design the traditional concepts of Information Technology for achieving social development. For this purpose IT application has to be extended to the non-conventional areas like agriculture, traditional health care, education, etc. IT application on a social aspect will have much relevance in the present context. But however no major works have been conducted in these fields. The present study is an attempt to explore the potentialities of IT application in developing and modernizing the tribal medicine practices in Kerala based on the forest medicinal plants with an aim of wider application of this system of medicine to the mankind as a whole.

IT and Medicine

Computers are now widely used in modern medicine and medical research in improving the overall health care system. Consequent on the wide application of the IT in the entire aspects of modern medicine a new branch of study namely Medical Informatics has emerged (Collen, 1995). Experts in different parts of the world are fastly developing the theoretical, methodological, operational and applicational aspects of the IT in health care and in modern medical services.

Traditional Medicine

Traditional medicine or ethno medicine is a heterogeneous term referring to a broad range of ancient and natural health care practices, which was dominant until the applications of modern scientific methods in the beginning of the nineteenth century, (Pushpangadan, 1999). Traditional medicine might also be considered as a social amalgamation of dynamic medical know how and ancestral experience (WHO, 1978). Indian traditional systems of medicine include Ayurvedic, Unani, Sidha, Naturopathy.

There are many reasons for the promotion of traditional medicine. Firstly, traditional medicines have intrinsic qualities. So it need to be evaluated, given due recognition and developed so as to improve its efficiency, safety and availability and wider application at low cost. They are particularly effective in solving certain cultural health problems. Secondly, traditional medicine has a holistic approach. It views the man in his totality within a wide ecological spectrum, and of emphasizing the view point that ill health or disease is brought about by an imbalance or disequilibrium, of man in his total ecological system and only by the causative agent and pathogenic evolution. Thirdly traditional medicine is one of the surest means to achieve total health care coverage of the whole population using acceptable safe, economically feasible method (WHO, 1978).

Tribal Medicine

Tribal medicine can be considered as a part of the traditional medicine, which is mainly practiced by the tribals settled in the forest area. This system is mainly confined to the medicinal plants available from the forest. The practitioners possess rich and valuable knowledge about the medicinal properties of these plants. The drug 'Jeevani' is developed from the plant 'Arogyapacha' (Trichopus zeylanicus) on the basis of the medicinal knowledge possessed by the 'Kani' tribes in Thiruvananthapuram district of Kerala. Many such medicinal knowledge of the tribals are getting scientifically validated in this manner.

Medicinal plants

India is rich in medicinal plant diversity and has a special position in the world today. Because it is one of the few countries that is capable of producing most of the important plants used both in modern as well as traditional system of medicine - a result of its vast area with wide variation in climate, soil, altitude and latitude (Lambert, 1997). Majority of India's medicinal plants are found in the tropical zone, mostly in the forests of the Western and Eastern Ghats.

The tropical evergreen forest of Kerala is noted for its rich presence of valuable medicinal plants and herbs. The tribals in these forest areas are able to tackle their health problems mainly with the help of these forest medicinal plants and herbs available in abundance from their surroundings. This medicinal knowledge of the tribals has served as the basis for the preparation of many new drugs in the modern medicine.

2. NEED AND SIGNIFICANCE OF THE STUDY

Kerala has a rich and valuable collection of forest medicinal plants and a number of tribal practitioners possessing a lot of knowledge about the curative aspects of these medicinal plants. This potential natural resource of Kerala has not been properly utilized so far. If this natural resource is properly utilized, it can solve many of the social development problems of Kerala. But such studies in this direction have not been made so far.

Today one can see that many of the tribal knowledges of medicine are getting scientifically validated through research and development. As in the case of 'Arogyapacha', the traditional knowledge of 'Chackarakolly' - a plant effective to control blood sugar was scientifically proved after successful tests of trials at Council of Scientific and Industrial Research (CSIR) and Sri Chitra Thirunal Institute of Medical Science and Technology [SCTIMST], (Mukundan, 1999). Tests conducted at Regional Research Laboratories had shown that 'Neeruvatti/ Chembravalli' (a plant used by the Kani tribals) was capable of reducing blood sugar level.

There is a global clamour for herbalism today. People are fed up with the ever-increasing price and dangerous side effects of the modern allopathic medicines. This factor together with the scientific validations of many tribal knowledge of medicine has created a greater awareness in Kerala towards tribal medicines. The people have realized the intrinsic value, safer and economically feasible aspects and curative efficacies of tribal medicine. So the study about the tribal medicine assumes much relevance in the context of the 'health for all' concept of the WHO.

The tribal medicine system in Kerala is still in its primitive form and follows the ancient system and practices. At the same time other traditional systems in India like Ayurveda, Sidha, Unani, etc., slowly but steadily adopted modern scientific and technological methods of treatment and earned much acceptance. But the tribal medicine showed reluctance to accept any modern scientific methods of treatment and kept in traditional forms.

The gems of knowledge of tribal medicine are not recorded anywhere. They are handed down the generation by word of mouth. Even these words are accessible only to a selected few, very often to a chosen, most loved and dedicated descendent. Usually practitioner is reluctant to transfer his knowledge of medicine because he knows that the social recognition and influence that he enjoys from the society is because of his knowledge in medicine. So he keeps the knowledge as a private treasure. Such secret knowledge has inbuilt dangers of extinction. The tribal medical practitioner could die incommunicado without being able to transfer his knowledge to the younger generation. This leads to the decrease in the number of knowledgeable tribal medical practitioners and finally to the extinction of the light of knowledge.

Today a cursory glance at the tribal medicine reveals the signs of their erosion. The younger generation shows disinclination to initiate the profession. But loss of this indigenous system will be a loss to civilization and heritage. "Medicinal practices among the tribesmen are not just limited to the curative aspects but are integrated with many facets of their life" (Burman Roy, 2000).

The tribal medical system, which has evolved through centuries of observation, has time-tested remedies for many diseases. Now the tribal medicine or ethno medicine has become a treasure hunting ground for other medical systems and multinational drug firms. Professionals of modern medicine approach the tribal healers to collect the secret of their curing recipes. The tribal traditional knowledge is usurped and the intellectual property of the tribes is alienated. The tribal's right over their knowledge on the medicinal plants and herbs should be safe guarded. Preserving and protecting the intellectual property right from the piracy would provide economic and social benefits to the tribals as well as the state of Kerala. Further research and analysis of such knowledge of medicine is imperative for the wider application of the efficacious valuable medicine.

The immobility of the Tribal medical system to adapt to the changing societal needs and the technological advancement is a major handicap and this system challenges even the very existence of the system. This light of knowledge which has survived through long years of experience and possessing valuable knowledge about the treatments of many diseases of the present world will become extinct unless efforts has been made to preserve it. Modern scientific and technological advancement has to be applied in tribal medicine for making it beneficial to the whole mankind. The present study is a pioneering attempt towards this end.

3. STATEMENT OF THE PROBLEM

The present study is stated as "A Study of the Application of Information Technology in Tribal Medicine in Kerala with regard to Forest Medicinal Plants".

* Definition of key terms
* Study

The word "Study" means the activity of gaining knowledge of a particular subject. (Oxford advanced learner's dictionary of current English, 5th ed., 1996).

Application

The word 'Application' means the action or an instance of putting a theory, discovery, etc., to practical use (Oxford advanced learner's dictionary of current English, 5th ed., 1996).

Information Technology (IT)

Several definitions of information technology covering its various aspects are available.

UNESCO defines Information technology as scientific, technological and engineering disciplines and the management techniques used in information handling and processing, their applications; computers and their interaction with men and machines and associated social, economic and cultural matters (Varalekshmi, 1992).

According to the Webster's new world encyclopedia (1992), Information Technology is the collective term for the various technologies involved in the processing and transmission of information. They include computing, tele communication and microelectronics.

According to the US report, IT means the collection, storage, processing, dissemination and use of information. It is not confined to hardware and software, but acknowledges the importance of man and the goals he sets for this technology, the values employed in making these choices, the assessment criteria used to decide whether he is controlling the technology and is being enriched by it (Chartrant and Morentz, 1979).

Teague (1994) defined IT as the conversion of technologies that are useful and profitable to their own right to form together a powerful new approach to information storage, transfer and retrieval. These are the technologies of computers, telecommunications and micro graphics with microelectronics as the facilitators (Patel and Kooganuramath, 1994). Even though several definitions of IT are available, the present study is mainly based on the definition given by UNESCO.

Tribal Medicine

Majumdar (1961) considered a tribe as "a group speaking

a common language and inhabiting a common territory". He further describes them as a "collection of families or groups of families bearing a common name, members of which occupy the same territory, speak the same language and observe certain taboos.... and have developed a well-assessed system of reciprocity and mutuality of obligations".

According to Dube, (1977) most popular definitions... tended to see in the tribes some, if not all, of the following characteristics: **(1)** their roots in the soil date back to a very early period; if they are not the original inhabitants, they are at least some of the earliest inhabitants of the land; **(2)** they live in the relative isolation of the hills and the forests; **(3)** their sense of history is shallow for, among them the remembered history of five to six generations tends to get merged in mythology; **(4)** they have a low level of techno-economic development; **(5)** in terms of their cultural ethos, language, institutions, beliefs and customs, they stand out from other sections of society and **(6)** If they are not egalitarian, they are at least non- hierarchic and undifferentiated.

In 1982, the World Bank in its operational manual statement defined 'tribal people' as "those ethnic groups typically with stable low energy sustained-yield economic systems, as exemplified by hunter-gatherers, shifting or semi-permanent farmers, or fishermen", and exhibiting varying degrees of characteristics such as geographical isolation, un acculturated or only partially acculturated into the social norms of the dominant society, non-monetised or only partially monetised, producing largely for subsistence and independent of the national system-ethnically different from the national society-non literate and without a written language, linguistically different from the wider society, identifying closely with one particular territory, having an economic life style largely dependent on the public natural environment, possessing indigenous leadership but little or no national representation etc. They generally have loose tenure over their traditional lands, which may not be accepted as legally binding by the dominant society. Thus they have weak enforcement capabilities against encroachers even when tribal areas have been delineated. (Encyclopaedia of Dravidian Tribes. V. I, 1996)

According to the McGraw Hill Encyclopedia of Science and Technology, (1997) the term 'Medicine' has two general meanings. The first indicates any material, notably in the drug category, which is given to prevent, alleviate beneficially alter, or stop a disease process. On the second and broader sense, medicine denotes the field of science devoted to healing.

A tribal medicine or folk system of medicine is a set of dynamic medicinal practices, based on the principles of trial and error, and on empirical evidence, which has evolved over a period of time- given a set of supports necessary for its growth and development within a unique socio-cultural and physical-environment (Johari and Karki, 1999).

Kerala

Geographically Kerala is located in a narrow strip of land in the southwest corner of India. It stretches from Kasaragod in the North into Thiruvananthapuram in the South (about 600km) and from the Western Ghats in the East to the Arabian Sea in the West (about 120 km at the widest point). Kerala is a small state comprising of only 1.03 percent of the total area of India. (The Encyclopedia District Gazetteers of India, 1997).

Forest

A Plant community consisting predominantly of trees and other woody vegetation, growing closely together is a forest. (Mc Graw Hill Encyclopaedia of Science and Technology, 1997).

Medicinal Plants

According to Oxford advanced learner's dictionary of current English, medicinal denotes "having healing properties". Plant is an organism that belongs to the Kingdom Plantae (Plant Kingdom) in biological classification. The term is also loosely used to indicate any organism that is not an animal. (Mc Graw Hill Encyclopaedia of Science and Technology, 1997).

So medicinal plants denotes those plants having healing properties.

4. OBJECTIVES

1. To study the present status of the tribal medicine practices in Kerala.
2. To study the nature of collection of forest medicinal plants and the methods of preparation of medicines.
3. To examine the potentiality of information technology applications in tribal medicine for modernizing the tribal medical system for a wider applicability.

5. HYPOTHESES

1. Tribal medicine practices in Kerala is getting general acceptance and is maintaining a steady growth.
2. Tribal medicines have a greater relevance in the modern context.
3. Information Technology can be applied in tribal medicine for its modernization with a view of achieving wider recognition even at the global level.

6. METHODOLOGY

The general nature of the present study was empirical. Data has been generated from the field study. Since the population of the study was large, sample study was conducted. Earnest effort has been made to take a representative sample from the population.

After considering the relevant characteristics of the population, the geographical area consisting of the three revenue districts of Kerala viz., Wayanad, Idukki and Thiruvanathapuram were selected for the study purpose. After a complete enumeration of this study area, 30 tribal medical practitioners were identified. 100 clients (users) of these practitioners were selected in two different ways. Half of them (50 users) were selected by circular systematic sampling from the address record of the users maintained by some practitioners (10 in number) and the other half (50 users) from the clients of the remaining practitioners (20 in number) on spot selection by a Simple Random Sample With Replacement (SRSWR) technique by interviewing the users immediately after their visit to the TMPs. The researcher itself has conducted interview. Data collected from the practitioners and users were separately analysed with appropriate statistical techniques. Observations made during the field study were also interpreted with the help of relevant studies.

7. LIMITATIONS OF THE STUDY

The present study was conducted from the point of view of an information scientist rather than that of a pharmacologist or biochemist. After considering the relevant characteristics of the population, the three districts of Kerala namely Wayanad, Idukki and Thiruvananthapuram were selected for this study. The curative efficacy of the tribal medicine has been assessed on the basis of user survey.

8. ORGANISATION OF THE STUDY

The thesis is organized into 6 chapters as detailed below.

Chapter I — Introduction

This chapter contains the need and significance of the study, statement of the problem, definition of key terms, objectives and hypotheses of the study. A brief methodology is also provided.

Chapter II — Tribal medicine - an overview

This includes a bird's eye view of traditional medicine and tribal medicine.

Chapter III — Review of related literature

Some relevant studies in tribal medicine are given in this chapter.

Chapter IV — Methodology

This chapter consists of the detailed description about the characteristics of the population of the study, the criteria adopted for selection of the

	study area and description about the procedures followed for selection of true representative sample.
Chapter V	Analysis and interpretations This chapter contains mainly the analysis of the data collected from the field. The observation made from the field were also analysed with the help of relevant secondary data and other relevant studies.
Chapter VI	Summary, conclusions and policy implications This chapter consist summary and conclusions made from the analysis of the data and some policy implications.

9. SUMMARY, CONCLUSIONS AND POLICY IMPLICATIONS MAJOR FINDINGS

Socio-economic Background of Tribal medical practitioners

From the study it was found that the tribal medical profession in Kerala is dominated by males. Female presence is only 7 percent. The mean age of practitioner is 64 years. 90 percent of the practitioners were literate and 46 percent of the practitioners have monthly income below Rs. 2000. Wide variation in income earned from the profession was noted.

Old population

The tribal medical practitioner's population is relatively an old population with nearly 43 percent of the practitioners are above 70 years. Significantly it was noted that these practitioners have already crossed 69.5 years, the average expected life in Kerala.

Loss of knowledge

As already mentioned, the knowledge in tribal medicine is not recorded anywhere and is transferred from generation to generation by word of mouth. During this transferring process, there is an inevitable loss of considerable amount of knowledge. The same has been clearly revealed from this study. Table 5A.4.1 shows that 17 practitioners have so far transferred only a part of their knowledge and 2 practitioners have no sishyas or disciples to transfer their knowledge.

So 19 practitioners (63.33%) has not so far fully transferred their knowledge, when this is compared with the fact that 43 percent have already crossed their expected life (in other words, only 57 percent are below their expected life span), which indicates that at least in some practitioner's case (6.36%), there is a greater probability of losing knowledge without being able to transfer it to their next generation. Another chance of the knowledge loss was also noted from the study. A practitioner usually transfers the valuable and secret knowledge at relatively old ages, by that time many will lose their vitality and memory power. This will also increase the rate of knowledge loss.

Virtual extinction of the profession

Lack of motivation in the younger generation to initiate to this profession was noted in the study. All practitioners of this study were initiated to this profession before 28 years. But all tribal practitioners of the present study were above 30 years and no tribal practitioners of ages between 28 to 30 years were found. This shows a clear declining trend with regard to the transfer of knowledge to the younger generation. If this trend persists for a longer time, a virtual extinction of the group of practitioners is certain.

Monopoly loses in the tribal society

Social recognition and prestige were the major rewards to the tribal practitioners in the past. They enjoyed the monopoly in handling the health problems of the tribal society. But with the introduction of modern medicine in the tribal belts, the tribal practitioners lost their monopoly and influence in the society. This is one of the reason for the lack of motivation in younger generation to initiate to this profession.

Remuneration

The tribal practitioners are not particular about the

remuneration for their rendered service and are satisfied with whatever the patient gives. For many of them, the income earned from this profession is hardly sufficient to meet their family expenses. They generally believe that demanding remuneration for the service will destroy their medicinal knowledge. They find some other job for earning money, and treat this as a part-time profession. But this cannot be generalised. 10-20 percent of them are potential and influential practitioners who were able to attract large number of patients, income and social status. On an average there are seven patients per day per practitioner.

Pedagogy

The tribal practitioners start on their profession at relatively younger ages as if they know the modern pedagogical principles. In modern pedagogy, it is a widely accepted fact that in order to maintain quality and skill in a profession, one should get trained at a young age.

The disciples acquire the knowledge and practices of medicine as an apprentice to the tribal practitioner by living and working with him. In many cases, the disciples will be a close blood relative of the practitioner. They identify the most potential disciple after continuous evaluation and assessment of all relevant aspects such as attitude and interest towards the profession, dedication, service mindedness, etc.

Primitive methods

The diagnosing methods used in tribal medicine are primitive. If they have some experience in use of some modern methods, they can work wonders. For example, some tribal practitioners are excellent bone-setters, but in rare cases, the patient may get permanent disability after treatment. This can be avoided if they have some experience to utilise the X-ray methods. The tribal practitioners have no method to assess the severity of the disease. They always use freshly prepared medicine, which avoid the deterioration of their medicine from physical, chemical or biological effects.

There is no quality control and standardisation in the

preparation of tribal medicine and no hard and fast rule to determine the dosage of medicine according to the severity of disease, age or body weight. In tribal medicine, the emphasis is on curative aspect rather than preventive aspect of disease.

Tribal medicine users

Socio-economic background

The study revealed that 74 percent of the users were males. Moreover 71 percent of the users were in the age group of 30-59 years. The mean age of the user was 45 years. Wage earners, agriculturists, traders or businessmen, constituted 38 percent, 19 percent, and 22 percent, respectively. 46 percent of the users have monthly income less than Rs. 1000. 13 percent of the users were illiterate and 4 percent are post-graduates. 31 percent has got only primary education.

More non-tribal users

The tribal, non-tribal distribution showed that nearly two-third of the users are non-tribal, which clearly indicates the acceptance of tribal medicine in non-tribal areas. Today there is awareness in the modern society about the positive aspects of tribal medicine. This is mainly due to the proper coverage given by media about the scientific validation of many tribal medicine knowledge and also due to the efforts of KIRTADS and other such agencies.

Curative aspect

The study revealed that diseases of the 63 percent of the users were completely cured and 34 percent partly cured while 3 percent not cured. The disease wise study showed that 84 percent not cured of the Headache/Migraine complaints and 58 percent of back-pain/body-pain/neck-pain complaints are completely cured while 16 percent and 29 percent are partly cured. All jaundice cases are completely cured. All piles complaints are only partly cured. 33 percent of the arthritis cases are completely cured, 67 percent are partly cured.

Attitudes

Four factors, which were likely to affect or reflect the

attitude of the users towards tribal medicine were identified as:

1. Opinion about curative aspect of the medicine.
2. Expense incurred.
3. Convenience and difficulties to access the system of medicine.
4. Side effects, if any.

The users were asked to consider all the above four factors and judge the system of medicine and to mark their preference on a three-point scale as fully satisfied, partly satisfied and not satisfied. 65 percent were fully satisfied, 30 percent partly satisfied and 5 percent were not satisfied.

Further statistical analysis with the help of chi-square test were made to know the income, occupation, age and education-wise attitude of the users towards tribal medicine.

The income and occupation-wise studies revealed that these characteristics were not associated with the attitude of the user.

The education and age-wise studies showed some association with the attitude of the user. Even though the users with high educational level such as graduation and post graduation are approaching tribal practitioners, people with lower education level showed a small dominance in the set of users. The age-wise study showed a slight positive skew ness or more precisely people having more than 39 years old (mode value) has shown more affinity towards tribal medicine. However, both these associations were found to be weak, since the Karl Pearson's coefficients of mean-square contingency was small.

Disease-wise approach

One-fourth of the users of the tribal medicine have headache or migraine complaint, 24 percent have back-pain/ body-pain/neck-pain complaints, 6 percent are jaundice patients. Piles, asthma and chest pain patients were 4 percent each, while diabetic, skin-disease and kidney-stone patients were 3 percent each.

Source of information about tribal medicine

91 percent of the non-tribal users become aware about the curative efficacy from the opinion of the satisfied user. 9 percent, from other sources like newspaper reports, camps, seminars, etc.

Medicinal plants collection

All the practitioners preferred early morning time for collection of medicinal plants. They face some inconvenience from forest officers during collection of medicinal plants from the forest area.

Tenability of the hypotheses

In the light of the analysis of the data, the tenability of the hypotheses were examined.

Tenability of the first hypotheses

Now tribal medicine is not confined to the tribal people alone. In fact, it has more non-tribal users than tribal users. The study revealed that there is no occupation-wise or income-wise preference of users towards tribal medicine, which shows general acceptance of tribal medicine as far as these two characteristics are concerned. Even though the age-wise and education-wise analysis of the users showed some association, it was weak. Hence the tribal medicine practices in Kerala is getting general acceptance.

The lack of enthusiasm of the younger generation of the tribals to initiate to the profession of a tribal medical practitioner was revealed from the study. The study identified the possibility of the loss of tribal medicinal knowledge without being able to transfer to the next generation. Presently, tribal medicine is not maintaining a growth but shows signs of extinction or erosion at the knowledge level.

Tenability of the second hypothesis

User study revealed that tribal medicine has effective treatment for some of the chronic diseases like migraine, back-pain, arthritis, etc. Generally, chronic diseases can only be controlled and cannot be cured completely with modern allopathic drug therapies.

Patients who were not satisfied with the treatment of other systems of medicine are also found satisfied with tribal system of medicine. 'Less expensive' and 'no side-effect' were other attractions of tribal medicine besides its curative value. Tribal medicine has a greater relevance in the modern context for achieving the 'health for all' concept especially when the allopathic medicines are costly and having poisonous side effects.

Tenability of the third hypothesis

The study found that most of the existing methods of treatment in tribal medicine are primitive and crude ones especially in diagnosis, preparation of medicine and dosages.

Tribal medicine can achieve wider recognition by adopting modern methods in treatment and scientific validation of the tribal medicinal knowledge. Modern methods include, scientific diagnosis, standardisation and quality control of drugs, scientific determination of dosages, etc. The infinite capabilities of information technology can be effectively used in modernising almost all the areas of tribal medicine.

Scientific validation of tribal medicinal knowledge is possible only through research and development. Here also, Information Technology can be applied for creating database of the scientifically validated knowledge, which will definitely invite inter and multi-disciplinary research.

Policy implication of the study

Kerala is blessed with rare species of medicinal plants possessing effective curative value and a number of tribal practitioners having valuable medicinal knowledge about these plants. If these natural resources are properly utilised and projected at global level with adequate legal framework to protect Intellectual Property Right (IPR) issues, Kerala can make tremendous development. It will create a number of job opportunities and can earn a lot of foreign exchange.

While making tribal medicine a tool for development, the Government must recognise the cultural, intellectual and commercial importance of tribal medicine. Government should safeguard the cultural heritage and background of the tribal and tribal medicine. Government should also enact proper legislation to protect the intellectual property right of the tribal. Thirdly, Government should tap the commercial potentiality of the trading of medicinal plants and the tourism aspects of the tribal surroundings. *Tribal Tourism Centres* - a centre where the natural beauty is blended with tribal rejuvenation therapies like steam-bath (medicated bath), wild food, etc., is a new concept.

Appropriate health policy has to be formulated to integrate tribal medicine with modern medicine. On a broader plane, it could be said that the government has given all its patronage to the spread of Allopathic system of medicine. This approach has to be changed.

Strategies

Raising the social status and prestige

For attracting the younger generation of tribals towards the tribal medical practitioner's profession, steps should be taken to raise the social status and prestige of the profession. This can be achieved by:

a. Introducing tribal medicine as a part of the curricula in the tribal schools. It can be made as an optional subject for all other schools also.

b. Starting of tribal medical colleges (like that of siddha medical colleges) and appointing the potential tribal practitioners as tutors or professors.

c. Government should start some tribal medicine centers and dispensaries and appoint tribal practitioners as doctors and should take initiatives to produce potential tribal medicine drugs in a scientific way.

d. Proper identity certificates to all eligible practitioners should be given for enjoying some benefits and collection of medicinal plants from forest.

Integration and co-ordination of research

Government must link all research and development institutions like, Regional Research Laboratories (RRL), Tropical Botanical Garden and Research Institutes (TBGRI), etc., which are doing phytochemical studies. All research work in the areas of phytochemical studies should be integrated and coordinated for a speedy result.

Strategies for Information Technology application

Documentation of Knowledge

As mentioned earlier, the tribal knowledge of medicine is not recorded anywhere and it is scattered. A comprehensive collection, classification and documentation of all these knowledge is the first step to be taken to avoid further loss of knowledge and also to equip tribal medicine to make it convenient for application of Information Technology.

A special team of experts in Botany, Pharmacology, Phytochemistry and Anthropology, as well as legal experts with sufficient experience and knowledge in patent rights, trademarks and related issues has to be constituted for a comprehensive collection of the tribal medicinal knowledge through field-study, interview and other relevant methods.

On the basis of the ownership or possession of knowledge, tribal medicinal knowledge can be classified it into three categories as given below:

1. Individual knowledge kept as family secret from generation to generation.
2. Therapeutic recipes known to more than one healer of a tribe of a region.
3. Traditional knowledge known to the community members and tribal healers, which can be treated as community property.

While documenting the knowledge, the ownership of

each knowledge has to be recorded to avoid future dispute about patent rights and sharing of monitory benefits if any generated from commercial exploitation of this knowledge.

There should be a separate authority to register this knowledge and he should act with the same powers and duties of a registrar of revenue documents/copyright controller as provided by the general law of intellectual property rights prevailing in the country. He should settle all future disputes about ownership and other matters.

After proper documentation and registration of tribal medicinal knowledge, information Technology can be effectively applied in tribal medicine in the following areas:

a. For encouraging research and development in this area

Create a database containing all the known details of a plant, such as its family name, botanical name, parts used for medicine, therapeutic action, indication, specific indication, contra indication, if any, dosage, botanical description, active constituents, phytochemical constants such as total ash, foreign organic matter, acid insoluble ash, alcohol or water soluble extractives, etc. These details will encourage more researches towards the topic.

b. Encouraging plant trade

The potential world market of phyto-medicines or herbal medicines is very large. Supply is not sufficient to meet the demand. Tribal co-operative societies should be formed and some forest land has to be distributed to these societies for cultivation of medicinal plants. Large scale production of medicinal plants in these forest areas under the control of these tribal co-operative societies and marketing of these plants through Internet or web portals aimed singularly at international trade will definitely earn a lot of foreign exchange and generate employment opportunities.

c. Concept of tribal tourism centres

Tourism is the fastest growing and second largest industry in the world. It has tremendous potentials for earning foreign exchange, providing employment and development of backward regions.

Much of Kerala's exotic appeal is centered in the Western Ghats. The forest of Western Ghats are punctuated with small water-falls. Some of the scintillating cascades in the forest can be developed into tribal tourism centres. In these centres, tribal rejuvenation therapies like steam-bath (medicated bath) and wild food, tribal arts, crafts, music, etc., can attract tourists.

The potentiality of information technology can be used for marketing these tribal tourism centres through the creation of sites in the World Wide Web and other multimedia integration, which will generate income and employment opportunities for the tribal.

10. SUGGESTION FOR FURTHER RESEARCH

Every country or state should utilize the natural resources for its overall development. Kerala has abundant natural resources in tribal medicine, which has unlimited potentialities. But unfortunately, no attempt has so far been made to explore these possibilities. It is hoped that this pioneer study will shed some light about this untapped natural resource of Kerala.

There is ample scope for a series of further research projects in this field by a team of experts in Information Technology professionals, Tribal medical practitioners and Information scientists.

REFERENCES

1. Burman, B.K.R. Protecting folk and tribal herbal medical knowledge. University Today. March 2000.
2. WHO. The promotion and development of traditional medicine. Technical Report Series 622. Geneva, WHO, 2001.

3

Design and Development of User Education Programme in Agricultural Universities

— Dr. K.S. Ambili

1. INTRODUCTION

The process of globalization, liberalization and modernization are forcing institutions for extensive use of Information technology in information handling. Rapid growth of the Internet and the web, has led us to a new communication paradigm; a shift from face to face human contact to human machine interaction; from paper based information transfer to electronic delivery; from text centered mode to multimedia; and from physical presence to telepresence or virtual presence. Since Gutenberg invented the printing press in 1452 AD, the publishing industry, which has been flourishing for more than 550 years, is now being shaken up with the advent of e-media. Jurisdictions are widening and become meaningless. The origin of user education can be traced back to 1883, to a statement by Columbia's president in his annual report when he suggested that a little systematic instruction would so start our students in the right methods that for the rest of their lives all the work in the libraries would be more expeditiously accomplished.[1] Users of published literature should understand the patterns of information generation, communication and the ways to retrieve information economically, effectively, efficiently and expeditiously.

Technological advancement coupled with information

revolution has given rise to tremendous capacity to man to record, encode, reproduce, disseminate and repackage information and has brought out significant changes in learning and teaching strategies and in educational system as a whole all over the world. It is high time for us to adopt these changes into our stream of education by providing necessary user education to facilitate efficient and optimum use of digital information, computers and Internet and thereby enrich the life long learning, teaching and research.

A Librarian's duty does not end with the collection of fairly good books, CD-ROMs, capture and subscription of journals but only starts with its procurement. Librarian must understand the varied information needs of the faculty and students in order to integrate user education into the curricula and create intimate group of readers who infuse life into a library by intelligent training, information organization and providing personalized reliable content delivery tailored to individual needs within reasonable times.

2. RELEVANCE OF THE STUDY

UNESCO Guide has stated the importance of user education in the preface as users of information are an integral part of and the final link in the information transfer chain, they are the raison d'etra' of every instrument made for bettering the storage, processing and retrieval of information. In every country from the least developed to the most advanced certain amount of scientific and technological information - locally produced or of international origin is stored in some fashion for the benefit of users. Unless these users know how to find relevant information available to them, the information 'Machinery' falls short of its main goal.[2] A library is rather like a laboratory where books are the apparatus. Just as in a laboratory, it is difficult to use the apparatus without instruction.[3] According to Harper the equipment of the library will not be finished until it shall have upon its staff, men and women whose entire work shall not be the care of books, not the cataloguing of books, but giving instruction concerning their use.[4]

The socio-economic developments of a country mainly depend upon the development and transfer of information on science and technology from the scientist to farmers and industrialists. In an agricultural library, users at two extremes i.e., highly scientific and technical users working with diversified subject specialties at one end and tradition bound farmers at the other extreme are to be fed with information. The user is an important component in an information system. Though the fact that the user study is a precondition for efficient library service was realized in western countries half a century ago, it is a recent phenomenon in India. For an efficient and effective information service Librarian should ascertain the information requirements - user needs, use pattern and use behavior of his library users from time to time.

To obtain relevant information economically and pin pointedly the researcher, the teacher and the extension officer have to be acquainted with different components and services of library. Developments in the information and communication technology have improved the access to information from a wide variety of information centres in agriculture. But the users of Kerala Agricultural University (KAU) libraries are observed to be not fully aware of these modern developments and the key role of the library in providing the required information to the user. It is felt that users at present are not able to utilize all sorts of information sources, retrieval devices and services. The advancement in information technology, the information explosion, the complexities of publications, emergence and growth of bibliographic tools, automation of library operations and introduction of sophisticated information services necessitates orientation programmes geared to the requirements of different groups of users for the maximum utilization of its resources and also from relevant centres outside.

Uncoordinated information networks, poor telecommunication facilities and shortage of well qualified trained professionals in handling digital information and IT gadgets and user education programmes are crucial problems facing agriculture information services in the third world countries. Information explosion, increased rate of publications in electronic form and the multidisciplinary nature of agriculture, further complicates the effective coordination and integration of agricultural information. Specialized information requirements of users of agriculture makes libraries not only to switch over to the modern techniques of information storage and retrieval but also to devise modern methods and programmes of user education.

Over the past few years, computer networks have increased dramatically and have spectacular increase in respect of speed and data capacity. The Internet imagined as the electronic mobile library in the cyberspace providing infomap of global resource centre has accelerated the process of data communication. The Internet offers seamless access to variety of information sources of valuable resource centres scattered in different parts of the world as well as expose their resources for the users dispersed world wide. Librarians need to be proactive and must train users to exploit the full potential of modern gadgets and Internet sources.

Diversified users of agricultural information such as planners who need packages of information with facts and figures, scientists and students who need recent scientific and technological information, extension officers who need processed information in the palatable form for farmers at grass root level are to be fed with recent right information at the right time. User education is indispensable to get information at the fingertips of students, scientists, research scholars and teachers in spite of geographical location.

Mews argues that training in the use of information should be part of all students' education. She stresses the need for instruction in the use of libraries and information services as a continuous process, which should cover use of the catalogue, abstracts, bibliographies and reference books and detailed instruction in methods of searching and formulation of clear requests at the post-graduate level.[5] Ministry of Education, China recommended three levels of user education based on the users educational background. The first level is library orientation for freshmen; the second courses of bibliographic instruction for juniors and seniors; and the third is more sophisticated user education involving the sorting and summarizing of documentation and the studying and analysing of information for all graduate students.[6]

Tiefel opines that 'broadly defined, library user education (also called library instruction) teaches users how to make the most effective use of the library system'. At Ohio State University, user education encompasses all activities undertaken to help students become efficient users of information - i.e., how to identify the information needs and then how to find, evaluate, and select the best information to meet that need. Activities to achieve that goal include orientation sessions, workshops, handouts and course-related and course integrated instruction. According to him the term 'library user education' has more recently been broadened to include the concept of information literacy.[7] Green, and Gilbert argues that "Information literacy will be essential for the growing cadre of knowledge workers in the 21st century".[8]

The Think Tank II report on bibliographic instruction defined information literacy as encompassing the entire world of information and seeking to prepare people to pursue the concept of lifelong learning. Information literacy extends its objectives to teaching information-seeking skills to all ages and at all times. It prepares people to use information effectively in a situation. There are no boundaries for information any where in any format. Information literacy may be defined as the ability to access and evaluate information effectively for problem solving and decision-making. Information literate people know how to be life long learners in an information society.[9]

The above views indicate that user education is a continuous process, which has to be performed for all user groups. To ensure that users are equipped with efficient methods of accessing, evaluating information from a variety of sources and tailored to their needs, training can be organized based on level of difficulty to find information and or users educational background.

User education strategies are the subject of much lively discussion and development in foreign countries. User education stands as a link between the user, information and the librarian. Librarian introduces his library and the library without walls, the cyberspace and its resources and services especially WWW the lifeblood of Internet, tips on searching for information and on scientific writing through user education. The key factors in user education configuration are the users, information sources and tools and the librarian. Hence while designing the user education programme one has to study the users their approaches to information, their information needs and their use pattern, the librarians ways and means and methods to link the user with appropriate information expeditiously and his methods in educating and orienting the users to access the right information.

It is high time to review the user education programmes that exist in various Agricultural Universities, as there are a variety of services and procedures, which could be considered as part of library's user education programme, in the background of drastic development in IT and the information explosion. Recent changes in the University teaching methods, composition and size of the student community, recognition of the importance of study skills, efficiency and quality monitoring and pressure on staff time demand this change in delivering user education. The quality of user education provision by libraries is crucial and hence several national initiatives such as EDUCATE (End user Courses in Information Access through Technology) have been established to enhance user education provision and to share scarce resources.

User education should be directed towards designing programmes for all categories of users depending upon their information requirements while it has to be integrated into the course curricula of undergraduate and postgraduate students. New methods and skills with media mix have to be developed to make it more appealing effective and meaningful. Considering all these factors in mind the investigator has undertaken a study entitled "Design and Development of User Education Programme based on Information Needs of Users in the Kerala Agricultural University Library and Information System ".

3. TITLE OF THE STUDY

The study is entitled: "Design and Development of User Education Programme based on Information Needs of Users in the Kerala Agricultural University Library Information System".

DEFINITION OF KEY TERMS

The terms, which are not self-explanatory in the title, is defined below.

USER EDUCATION

Freeman and Maltby state that "User Education can be seen as a major strand within a "Study Skills" Programme equipping the trainees with the knowledge and abilities to use libraries and information effectively and confidently; a skill of inestimable and enduring value to any manager or administrator who has to handle and evaluate the flow of information emanating from official or non official sources."[10]

Wajid Ahmad Alivi defines user education as that facet of library service, which is concerned with educating the library users in efficient use of library resources so that they are able to exploit them to the best of their advantage.[11]

UNESCO defines[12] user education as any effort or programme, which will guide and instruct existing and potential users, individually or collectively with objective of facilitating:

a. the recognition of their own information needs;
b. the formalization of their needs;
c. the effective and efficient use of information service; as well as
d. the assessment of these services.

User education in the present IT environment of 'Library without Walls' needs a wide connotation. Hence User education in the present scenario can be defined as a fostering programme whereby the users of information are equipped with awareness of formalization of their needs, knowledge and experience of general as well as specific information sources, basic research and study, library and information skills to identify, find, evaluate and select the best information for life long perpetual education.

INFORMATION NEEDS

The Librarian's Thesaurus defines information need as "that need which library services or materials are intended to satisfy".[13] According to Brenda Dervin "an information need is an impediment preventing an individual from moving forward in cognitive time and space. The person is faced with a gap that must be bridged by 'asking questions, creating ideas and / or obtaining resources'. Such gaps do not occur in the abstract but arise out of particular critical events and situations".[14] Maurice B. Line has defined information need as "what an individual ought to have for his work, his research, his edification, his recreation etc".[15] Hence information needs may be described as the actual and potential needs of users for documents/information /any other services.

KERALA AGRICULTURAL UNIVERSITY LIBRARY AND INFORMATION SYSTEM (KAULIS)

Kerala Agricultural University Library and Information System (KAULIS) consists of the central library, the constituent college libraries and various station libraries, the user communities, computer networks and other gadgets, resources, and staff and other services of Kerala Agricultural University Library.

OBJECTIVES

The main objective of the study is to design and develop user education programme suitable for various categories of users in the Kerala Agricultural University Library and

Information System. In order to attain this goal the following specific objectives are formulated

i. to assess the extend of use of library tools available in the Kerala Agricultural University Library and Information System by the user community;

ii. to assess the present use of information sources and services available in the Kerala Agricultural University Library and Information System;

iii. to examine the information needs, use pattern and use behaviour of the various categories of users in the system;

iv. to examine user education programmes and facilities in Agricultural Universities in India;

v. to assess the existing user education programmes in Kerala Agricultural University Library and Information System; and

vi. to design and develop user based user education programme.

4. HYPOTHESES

The following hypotheses are formulated

i. The varied information needs of the students, research scholars and teachers are not adequately met by the KAU library and information system.

ii. The existing library tools especially IT tools and sophisticated information services available in the system are not fully utilized by the user community.

iii. The existing user education programmes in Kerala Agricultural University Library and Information System is not user based in the present IT environment.

5 SAMPLE AND METHODOLOGY

The major methodology adopted for the investigation is questionnaire method. The observation and interview methods are also used to corroborate the findings arrived at questionnaire method.

QUESTIONNAIRE METHOD

Under this study a self completed, well structured, pretested questionnaires (Appendix I) were distributed to the under - graduate and post - graduate students, research scholars and teachers of various faculties of Kerala Agricultural University. The questionnaire was so framed as to gather information on the following points.

1. Personal data such as qualification, age, nature of job and experience in the case of teachers etc.
2. Information needs, approaches and preference to various types of information sources and information services.
3. Awareness about the information sources and services.
4. Use of computer, software, Internet, CDs and other IT gadgets.
5. Details of user instruction / education received and opinion about its effectiveness, type of instruction they prefer etc.
6. Details of information technology courses undergone and the topics covered.
7. Suggestions for facilitating better services including user education by maximum exploitation of the resources of KAU.

The number of large user categories varies widely making a fixed percentage of samples impossible for statistical analysis. Hence sample was collected on three different proportions of the corresponding population. Sample Questionnaires were collected from 311 (50 per cent) teachers, 100 Post Graduate / Ph. D Students (40 per cent) and 514 (30 per cent) Under Graduates which comes to a total of 925. Among the respondents 24 (33.80 per cent) teachers, 10 (37.04 per cent) Post Graduate / Ph. D Students, and 168 (41.90 per cent) Under Graduates of various faculties were interviewed and observed to corroborate information revealed through questionnaire.

Status-wise and Faculty-wise analysis of questionnaires were made as and where necessary to infer into the users faculty-wise actual information needs and to find out the facets at which user education has to be given for various categories of users such as Teachers, Post Graduate / Ph. D Students, and Under Graduates and to design an effective package for the Kerala Agricultural University Library and Information System (KAULIS) to satisfy the information needs. Kerala Agricultural University Library and Information System will be here in after referred to as KAULIS through out this study.

Status-wise Distribution of Respondents

The respondents were grouped into three categories such as Teachers, Post Graduate / PhD Students, and Under Graduates Students for status wise analysis. Post Graduate / PhD Students, and Under Graduates Students will be here in after referred to as P G Students and U G Students respectively through out this study.

The teacher group consists of 311 (33.62 per cent) teachers including those who are engaged in part - time research and extension work in ten Colleges, six Regional Agricultural Research Stations (RARS), twenty six Research Stations, and five Krishi Vigyan Kendras, Instructional Farms, Dairy Plant, Meat Plant, etc. The U.G students group consists of 514 (55.7 per cent of the total respondents) undergraduate students of ten constituent colleges of Kerala Agricultural University. The P.G students group consists of 100 (10.81 per cent of the total respondents) postgraduate students and full time research scholars of ten constituent colleges of Kerala Agricultural University. There is only three and one P.G students each in College of Fisheries and Kelappaji College of Agricultural Engineering and Technology during this study.

Faculty-wise distribution of respondents

All the faculty staff and students of ten colleges and faculty staff of various research stations are working under four faculties such as Agriculture, Veterinary and Animal Sciences, Fisheries and Agricultural Engineering. The faculty of Basic science and Humanities has not been started and teachers are deployed in the other four faculties. Hence the four faculty groups taken for faculty-wise study are Faculty of Agriculture (58.16 per cent), Faculty of Veterinary and Animal Sciences (28.76 per cent), Faculty of Fisheries (7.68 per cent) and Faculty of Agricultural Engineering (5.40 per cent). Here after they will be referred as Agriculture, Vety, Fisheries and Agrl. Engg., respectively in this study. Another questionnaire (Appendix II)was distributed to the librarians of forty-one agricultural universities in India(Appendix III).

The first part of the questionnaire was intended to collect the general information about the university such as exact address, e-mail address, year of establishment and facility of the main centralized library etc.

The second part of the questionnaire was intended to elicit information about modern IT applications / facilities such as library automation, Internet and CD-ROM database facility to get an idea about the level of sophistication of the libraries for the preparation of uniform course content for user education.

The third part of the questionnaire was dealt with the level, structure and content of user education. Much care was taken to collect exact data on various levels of user education such as orientation lectures, credit course on technical writing/ user education at UG and PG courses, number of credits, information about course teacher, facilities for conducting the course, prescribed text books for the course if any etc. Finally sets of questions were directed to elicit comments on uniform course contents for user education and suggestions/ modifications for user education programme if any and details about various surveys conducted if any. The total response to the questionnaire was 82.93 percent.

Observation

Observation of use of libraries by students and teachers was also conducted to avoid any possible distortion of information that might otherwise creep into the questionnaires furnished by the respondents and to obtain a first hand idea about the information seeking behaviour of the clientele.

Interview

Unstructured interview was conducted. The selected under graduate and post graduate students, teachers and research scholars of various faculties were interviewed to ascertain their approach to information, information needs and the effectiveness of present user education programme.

6. SIGNIFICANCE OF THE STUDY

Technology is creating the basis for new paradigm shifts in the scholarly information storage, retrieval, and transfer though the information needs of an individual will not vary considerably. The acceptance of any new method mainly depends on the convenience in terms of effort and knowledge required by the individual in using the facility, the comprehensiveness and the cost involved in it. The graduates coming out of our universities are expected to possess necessary qualifications / knowledge and skills in popular software packages, programming and Internet in this IT era of globalization to compete in the international market of knowledge and better placement. Traditional services cannot provide all the required knowledge and skills to the students

Declining library budgets and growing user expectations force the librarians to move to fee based value added information services and to access free online information. For equitable access to this digital information the general IT information literacy of the reader for management of IT gadgets and for quick reliable retrieval has to be improved through user education and continuing education.

7. LIMITATIONS OF THE STUDY

The study is confined in respect of data collected from students, researchers, scientists and teachers of Kerala Agricultural University, its users of Central library and constituent college libraries while data has been collected from all Agricultural Universities in India to study the IT facilities and user education pattern followed and to incorporate the comments and suggestions of various Universities in India to design and develop user education programme to implement in all Agricultural Universities.

8. ORGANISATION OF THE STUDY

The study is organized under the following chapters.

1. Introduction

This chapter deals with relevance and title of the study, definition of key terms such as User Education, Information needs, Kerala Agricultural University Library and Information System etc., the objectives, hypotheses, sample and methodologies such as questionnaire, observation and interview, significance and organization of study.

2. Review of Related Studies

Review of Literature gives a background as well as a broad overview of research methods and procedures used by earlier investigators in the field of study and points out briefly the findings of related studies.

3. Agricultural Universities and Information Infrastructure in India.

This chapter gives an account of Information Infrastructure of forty-one Agricultural Universities in India including four specialized universities.

4. Kerala Agricultural University and Library and Information System

Chapter four gives a summary of historical background Kerala Agricultural University, its five faculties consisting of ten constituent colleges, academic programmes and a detailed account of Kerala Agricultural University Library and Information System (KAULIS).

5. Information Needs, Use Pattern and User Education of Users of Kerala Agricultural University Library and Information System : Analytical Study

In chapter five an in-depth analysis of information needs, use pattern and user awareness of user community of Kerala Agricultural University Library and Information System is provided.

6. User Education Programmes in Agricultural Universities in India : Analytical Study

This chapter provides a detailed analysis of modern IT application and facilities and user education programmes conducted in various Agricultural Universities in India.

7. Findings, Design of User Education Programme and Recommendations

This chapter provides the summary of major findings evolved out of the study. It also contains design of user education programmes suitable to Agricultural University.

Appendices

Appendix-I.	Questionnaire for the Survey of Users Awareness about Information Sources and Services in Kerala Agricultural University Library and Information System.
Appendix-II.	Questionnaire for the Survey of IT application and User Education Facilities in Agricultural Universities in India.
Appendix-III.	State-wise List of Agriculture Universities in India

9. FINDINGS, DESIGN OF USER EDUCATION PROGRAMMES AND RECCOMENDATIONS

The analysis and discussion in the foregoing chapters have revealed a number of significant findings. The major findings that have evolved from the discussion in the previous chapters are summed up here under various heads. The findings and inferences evolved out of the study are used for the Design of User Education Programme.

Findings

1. Status wise analysis reveals that 61.41 per cent teachers have Ph.D. degree and 45.98 per cent have guided thesis at P.G. level and 11.89 per cent teachers have guided for Ph.D. programmes and 67.52 per cent of them have

undertaken research project. The information need of teachers and application of IT tools are greater than Post Graduate and Under Graduates Students.

2. Kerala Agricultural University library and information system (KAULIS) users as a whole while ranking preferred information sources in terms of usefulness to meet their information requirements have given the top priority to Internet (95.24 per cent) followed by learned periodicals (92.32 per cent). On Faculty - wise analysis the three faculties Agriculture, Veterinary Science, and Agricultural Engineering and technology ranked Internet and periodical as their first and second preference respectively while the first and second preference of Faculty of Fisheries go to periodical and books respectively. While general ranking third, fourth and fifth preference go to Books (91.35 per cent), Abstracting Periodicals (88.22 per cent), Conference/Seminar Proceedings (78.05 per cent) respectively. The Status-wise analysis reveals that there is a lot of similarity in preference of information sources by teachers and PG students as their first three ranks are the same. The percentage of top priority of usefulness given to periodical by teachers and PG students was 100 per cent as it includes original contribution or information or formulation of new ideas, observation, development and experience of various scientists and teachers. Teachers preferred Internet and books with 91.64 per cent and 91.32 per cent respectively whereas PG students preferred Internet and books with 98 and 96 per cent respectively. The last two ranks were given to Reviewing periodicals (20.97) and Bibliographies (19.68).

3. In general 91.57 percent out of 925 respondents utilize the library facilities. While 99 per cent P.G students utilize the library facilities it is 91 and 90.47 per cent each in the case of teacher and U.G students respectively. Among various status groups 38.59 per cent teachers, 40.08 per cent UG students and 63 per cent PG students utilize the

resources of KAU Central library. But 57.95 percent respondents have never utilized Central Library and 11.46 utilize it only once in a while. On faculty-wise analysis it can be seen that Vety faculty library come to the top in total as well as daily use of library with 92.86 and 19.17 per cent respectively. Daily use of Faculty/College/ Station Library is 8.55, 4.23, and 10 per cent in the case of Faculties of Agriculture, Fisheries, Agrl. Engg. respectively The percentage of use of other libraries by 39.23 teachers, 35.80 U.G students and 45.00 P.G students indicate the need for additional information and services for day-to-day updation of their knowledge. Among the respondents 2.46 per cent teachers and 35.57 per cent P.G students use two libraries other than Central / college / Station library. As the colleges of KAU are geographically distributed central library is not easily approachable to about 58 percent teachers and students.

4. About 37 per cent respondents are not satisfied with present bay guide and shelf guides which has to be immediately rectified as this will be a hindrance to easy access of readily available information.

5. Among the population 25.08 per cent 27.24 per cent and 35 per cent teachers U.G and P.G students respectively are not familiar with the classification scheme followed in the library. It is a clear indication that the general orientation provided to users and existing user education for P.G students is not so effective.

6. In general, only about 33.19 per cent respondents make frequent use of catalogue. It is never being used by 16 per cent of Agrl. Engg. faculty, 15.24 per cent of Agriculture Faculty and 5.64 per cent of Vety faculty members. User education for all categories of users are essential for improving the use of catalogue and there by the optimum utilization of materials.

7. Only about 59 per cent of population under study use the right method for ascertaining the availability of

reading materials in the library i.e. consulting the Library Catalogue. The order of preference of various status groups of users is astonishingly the same. Faculty- wise analysis reveals that consulting the Library Catalogue is the first preference of professionals of all the three faculties other than Agrl. Engg. which gives its top preference to examining of the books on the shelf.

8. Of the respondents about 76 per cent of teachers 50 per cent U.G students, and 78 per cent P.G students use computers in library/ research station. 38.16 per cent are not at all getting opportunity to use computers in library/ research station, which necessitate immediate refinement.

9. In general 90.38 per cent and 81.08 per cent KAULIS users are familiar with Microsoft Windows and MS-Office respectively. In the present information era cent percent professionals should acquire knowledge in these Operating Systems and Software Packages. Cent percent teachers and students of Agrl. Engg faculty is familiar with Microsoft Windows and MS-Office. P.G students (cent percent) occupy the top most position in the familiarity of Microsoft Windows as well as in the case of UNIX/LINUX (27.00 per cent). Necessary provisions have to be given to include recent and important software packages in the integrated curriculum of User Education of students and of teachers.

10. Internet is used by 67.46 per cent of KAULIS users. P.G students top with about 81 per cent use followed by U.G students (67 per cent) and teachers (65 per cent). Use of Internet is above 60 per cent in all the three faculties except Fisheries where only 57.75 per cent use it. While correlating the use and need of Internet on faculty basis, it is seen that in the same way top preference was given to Internet by three faculties (Agriculture, Vety and Agrl. Engg.) except Fisheries to meet their information requirements. The use is as high as 78.95 per cent in Vety. Internet use through the institutions is as high as 76.12

per cent among teachers, 81.48 per cent among PG students and 40.94 among U.G students as this facility is provided in all the departments of the colleges. Internet access facility of U.G students at colleges has to be increased by providing sufficient facilities. A list of 119 favourite websites given by the respondents was brought into light though it is hard to find any unanimity on this topic.

11. Only 37.41 per cent respondents use Internet for e-mail correspondence with professionals of their subject field for exchange of scientific information while 67.46 per cent use Internet. About 61 per cent of teachers, 78 per cent of P.G. students and 15 per cent U.G. students use it for this purpose. Of the 37.41 per cent users, 9.84, 12.76, 7.35 and 3.46 per cent use this facility only once in a week, once in a fort-night, once in a month, and once in a while respectively. Faculty - wise analysis reveals that Agrl. Engg. tops in e-mail correspondence (52 per cent) followed by Agriculture, Fisheries, and Vety. Better awareness in IT may be the reason for better utilization of this facility by Agrl. Engg. faculty. This directs towards the need of more training in IT and encouragement to form user groups in various fields or to become members of already existing user groups for better and speedy use of scientific information.

12. CD-ROM database, the cheapest storage device, which permits digital copying is used by cent percent P.G. students while 5.79 per cent teachers and 18.09 per cent U.G. students have never utilized this facility. Agrl. Engg. faculty tops in its use (92 per cent) followed by Vety (91.35 per cent) though none of the respondents from these faculties use it daily and on considering the frequency of use agriculture faculty tops. The frequency of use of CD-ROM is not up to the mark in the case of U G students as the use is only 7.20, 10.31, 15.37 during once in a week, once in a fortnight and once in a month respectively and about half of the U G students use it once in a while,

which has to be improved by providing more facilities including training in its use.

13. In general Encyclopaedias (88.76 per cent), Yearbooks & directories (76.97 per cent) and Abstracting journals (67.89 per cent) are most utilized publications in the order of priority in CD format and same is the order in print media (93.95, 85.95 and 66.16 per cent respectively). Subject dictionaries and indexing journals in CDs are utilized by 38.49 per cent and 39.14 per cent respectively by the users. In the case of Abstracting journals Vety tops (86.47 per cent) followed by Agriculture while Agriculture faculty tops in the use of encyclopaedia in CD (92.01 per cent) followed by Fisheries (88.73 per cent) and Agrl. Engg. (88 per cent). Users in general prefer print media to CD except in the case of Abstracting journals and Union catalogue of serials. Less utilization of publications in CD than print are due to their non-availability / lack of sufficient gadgets and / or low level of awareness in IT.

14. CAB CD is very often used by about 7 per cent respondents and occasionally used by about50, 34 and 61 per cent teachers, U.G. students, and P.G. students respectively. Faculty wise analysis shows that Agriculture faculty tops in the use of CAB CD followed by Vety and Agrl. Engg. while in the case of use of MEDLINE, Vety tops followed by Fisheries. Vet CD is used by about 15 per cent as this CD was not procured by Vety at the time of collecting data.. In general P.G. students use CD ROMs more frequently than teachers. CAB CD (49.08 per cent) occupies top position in use followed by AGRISEARCH (32.76 per cent) AGRIS (29.30 per cent) and AGRICOLA (20.86 per cent) in the use. Vet CD and FSTA are more used by Vety and Fishery faculty respectively being specialized subject CDs. Derwent Biotechnology abstracts and current contents have to be procured for KAULIS and provided through network as these CD-ROMs will be of high use to all users irrespective of faculty.

15. Agrl. Engg. faculty tops in daily use of Online/ Internet with 16.08 per cent while it is as low as 1.88 per cent in Vety. Above 20 per cent respondents of Agri and Vety use this facility once in a week and twice in a week. In general the frequency of use of Online/ Internet has to be improved by providing more facilities including user education.
16. Difficulties in formulating the search strategy are experienced by 16.08 per cent teachers, about 47 percent U.G students, and 18 per cent P.G students. Faculty-wise analysis reveals that while 82 per cent of Agrl. Engg. faculty are familiar with formulation of search strategy, 36.25 per cent respondents of Agriculture faculty, 30.45 per cent of Vety faculty and 33.80 per cent of Fisheries faculty experience difficulties which warrants user education. Further, difficulty in formulation of search strategy by 18 per cent P.G students reveals that present user education at P.G level is not adequate and effective and has to be redesigned.
17. Regarding locating books and articles while 13.51 per cent are not able to locate the documents, 15.24 per cent could locate all the books/articles of interest and 71.24 per cent could trace it partially. Among U.G. students 13.04 could locate all necessary documents while it is only 10.00 per cent in the case of P.G. students, and 20.58 per cent in the case of teachers. Intensive user education is essential for better utilization.
18. Among teaching aids overhead projector is used by about 63 per cent respondents and slide projector and Liquid Crystal Display (LCD) are used by about42 and 18 per cent respectively. Teachers occupy the top most position in utilizing overhead projector with a high percentage of 83.60 followed by 66 per cent of P.G. students, 49.61 per cent U.G. students. Overhead projector is the top ranked teaching aid followed by slide projector and LCD. Preparation of slides for use in slide projector is more

expensive. Being less expensive all categories prefer transparencies than slide projector and LCD.

19. About 50 per cent U.G students 35 per cent of teachers, and 41 per cent P.G students use 'Library Bulletin' and 'Content of the Month' issued by the libraries. Vety attains the topmost position in the use (84.21 per cent) followed by Agriculture (31.60 per cent), and Agrl. Engg. (24. 00 percent). Respondents of Fisheries are not at all using this facility, as these publications are not issued from Library. High utilization of these materials in the available libraries is an indication that this service is very useful and is well accepted by the users and hence this facility has to be provided by all the libraries and it is better to provide this in the web page to increase its access.

20. Of the various services rendered by KAULIS, **photocopying service** was rated as always good by 39.55 per cent of the teaching community. Among the P.G. students 32 per cent opined that photocopying service is occasionally good, while it is always good for 26 per cent and frequently good for 41 per cent. At present the photocopying service is out sourced with the help of Students Union in Vety college @ of fifty paise per page as this is more beneficial which can save one manpower of library. **Inter library loan services** was graded as always good only by 4 per cent of P.G. students, 5.47 per cent of teachers and 2.92 per cent of U.G. students while 32 percent of P.G. students, 22.83 per cent of teachers and 41.63 per cent of U.G. students have never been able to avail these services. Faculty wise analysis shows that 12.08 per cent respondents of Agriculture faculty, 27.82 per cent of the Vety faculty and 14 per cent of Agrl. Engg faculty and 18.31 per cent of Fisheries faculty never get **reference services** while 39.22 per cent respondents of Agriculture faculty and 41.73 per cent of the Vety faculty and 42 per cent of Agrl. Engg. faculty and 36.62 per cent of Fisheries faculty rated it as frequently good. **Bibliographical services** have never been able to avail by 8.68 per cent of

teachers and 15.18 per cent of U.G. students, 12 per cent of P.G. students while these services were graded as always good by 25.40 per cent of teachers, 13.23 per cent of U.G. students and 27 percent of P.G. students. In the teaching community 44.05 and 8.04 percent have graded Internet services as frequently good and occasionally good respectively. U.G. students have opined that 35.99 per cent of them never get Internet services. **Internet services** was rated as always good by 13.50,16.34 and 15 per cent teachers, U.G. students, and P.G. students respectively. Among teachers, U.G. students, and P.G. students 14.15, 21.01 and 26 per cent have rated **E-mail services** as always good. In the teaching community 62.06 and 18.33 percent have graded E-mail services as frequently good and occasionally good respectively. Among U.G. students 25.49 per cent never get E-mail services. Vety faculty tops in providing this service followed by Agriculture, Agrl. Engg., and Fisheries faculty.

21. In general 64.22 per cent KAULIS users are not at all getting User Instruction/User Education facility as this is not regularly given to U.G students while P.G students are receiving it as part of their course curricula. User Education is received by more than 15 per cent of teachers, about 36 per cent U.G students, and cent percent P.G students. Faculty- wise analysis reveals that Vety with 40.60 per cent attains the topmost position in the User Instruction/User Education followed by Fisheries (36.62 per cent), Agriculture (34.20 per cent), and Agrl. Engg. (26.00 per cent). Well acceptance of User Education credit course by P.G students is an indication that this service is very useful and this has to be introduced for U.G students and to teachers in the form of Refresher Course.

22. While inviting opinion on helpfulness of user education course, about 78 per cent teachers, 75 per cent U.G students, and 80 per cent P.G students opined that the course is helpful while a total of 23.68 per cent answered

negatively. Faculty-wise analysis reveals that 80.48 per cent respondents of Agriculture faculty, 73.68 per cent of Vety faculty and 56.34 per cent of Fisheries 74 per cent of Agrl. Engg. faculty are favourable for the course being helpful. In general 76.32 per cent respondents, and in particular 80 percent P.G students, who are the recipients of this course opined this course as helpful and hence this course has to be extended to U.G students and teachers.

23. In general the first preference area of various groups for User Instruction is CD search (88.65 per cent) and the second and third preference goes to Internet search (85.30 per cent), latest Software (78.49 per cent) respectively. Other areas in the order of preference are Bibliographic tools and their rules (77.95per cent), Collection (63.46 per cent), Classification (57.84 per cent), Fundamentals of computer (57.08 per cent), ånd Cataloguing (54.38 per cent). Hence a well-structured user Education course incorporating all these topics is the need of the hour.

24. The order of preference of U.G. students and P.G. students regarding methods of library instruction are same and the order is credit course (84.69 per cent), introductory lecture (42.67 per cent), printed guide (36.64 per cent), informal programmed lecture/orientation (27.85 per cent), and occasional get together (12.21 per cent). Printed guide (45.98 per cent) was given the first preference by the teachers. Faculty wise analysis reveals that all the faculties give their first preference to credit course while the second preference was given to the printed guide by all the faculties other than agriculture. Occasional get together was given last preference by all the faculties.

25. National and International trainings were attended by about 14 per cent, more than 5 per cent and 16.00 percentage of teachers, U.G students, and P.G students respectively. Three teachers have undergone training at International level of which two are teachers of Vety and

one from Agriculture. Faculty wise analysis reveals that Vety tops in IT training of their professionals.

Important findings based on the analysis of data collected from Agricultural University Libraries in India are

26. State Agricultural University Libraries lag behind Deemed to be Agricultural University Libraries in the case of Library automation. Only 30 per cent libraries are completely automated out of 34 responded Agricultural universities and automation is in progress in 13.33 per cent libraries. There is no uniformity in the use of library software. The commonly used software is CDS/ISIS and its total use is 41.18 per cent along with other software. This software is exclusively used in 23.53 per cent libraries. LIBSYS attains the second position in the use with 29.41 per cent. Use of same software in all the libraries can improve efficient use and easy exchange of information and can reduce the manpower to a great extend.

27. Internet connectivity is possessed by 79.41 per cent university central libraries and 70.39 per cent open it completely for users. While 3.70 per cent permit partial use of the Internet, 40 per cent collect fee from the users. Punjab Agricultural University and West Bengal University of Animal and Fishery Sciences collect the maximum fee of Rs.25/- per hour. It is recommended to collect a normal fee for the sustainable utilization and maintenance of Internet browsing facility and to provide one system free of charge on first come first served basis for Internet use especially for poor students, the faculty which lack in fee based service providing Agricultural libraries as revealed in this study.

28. CD-ROM database facility is provided by cent percent Deemed to be Agricultural Universities while this is provided only by about 67 per cent State and Central Agricultural University Libraries. It is recommended that

ICAR may take immediate steps to have a consortium among Agricultural Universities for the procurement of CD-ROMs and journals, which can reduce the cost to many lakhs. ICAR should establish a CD-ROM network access facility among Agricultural University libraries without violating the IPR at the earliest. As a first step instead of providing fund for procurement of CDs by individual Agricultural library ICAR can enter into an agreement with CABI to provide required CAB CDs to all Agricultural Universities at a concession rate along with online access facility.

29. Library orientation is given to teachers only by 29.41 per cent libraries while orientation is given to undergraduates and postgraduates by 73.53 per cent each libraries. This low rate of orientation in the case of teachers may be under the presumption that teachers are prominent in the general procedures followed in libraries and in handling IT tools. But it is also essential to include IT application in libraries in the refresher courses / arrange at least one-day workshop for the continuous updating of knowledge in recent technologies and techniques by the teachers.

30. User education course is conducted by 63.33 per cent State and Central and 75 per cent Deemed to be Agricultural Universities responded. None of the responded Universities give user education credit course at U.G level while 58.82 per cent and 35.29 per cent universities respectively give it at postgraduate level and Ph.D. level. University of Agricultural Sciences Dharwad, which started a course in library information usage in 1992, was discontinued in 1994 as they consider it as irrelevant for the degree programme. This course is compulsory for Ph.D. students if the students have not taken the course during their master's level. This course is compulsory for all the universities other than Maharastra Animal and Fisheries University where it is optional. It is one credit at all the universities except in

Assam Agricultural university, TANUVAS, NDRI, KAU and PAU.

31. The venue of the course for user education is central library for all the students for 47.06 per cent State and Central Agricultural University and cent percent Deemed to be Agricultural Universities. This shows the importance attached to the programmes. Common uniform course content is recommended as 85 per cent and 95 per cent for U.G and P.G level respectively.
32. LCD is used for user education courses by only 11.76 per cent course teachers while slid projector and OHP are used by 73.53 per cent and 29.41 per cent respectively. Low percentage of use of LCD shows less use of computer technology, which may be either due to lack of proper training to the teachers in the preparation of PowerPoint slides and it's use or the absence of LCD. The tutor has to be well trained to utilize more IT gadgets as PowerPoint multimedia presentations can convey knowledge in more appealing manner and they have to train the trainers (i.e. users including teacher community and future extension workers) in using teaching aids.
33. The course content followed by the various Agricultural Universities is more or less the same. Out of twenty universities, which conduct user education course about 80 per. cent lacks updating of topics according to present IT advancements. Indian Agricultural Research Institute (IARI), Dr. Y. S. Parmar University of Horticulture and Forestry , two colleges of Kerala Agricultural University , Sher-e-Kashmir University of Agricultural Sciences and Technology Jammu etc have suitably revised and tailored their course contents by integrating computer and communication Technology topics such as networking, Internet and E-mail, CD-Rom Technology, Computerized search formulation, Global Information systems and centres, etc. There is no uniformity either in the case of course contents or in the number of credits of the course in the case of constituent colleges of Kerala Agricultural

University, which warrants immediate uniformity. Lack of evaluation and assessment of the existing course is the main reason for lack of updating of topics according to present IT advancements in most of the universities.

34. Professionally qualified Librarian, Deputy Librarian or Assistant Librarian are actively associated with teaching of the User Education course either independently or jointly with other specialists in all the universities except PAU and SKUAST, Jammu. Librarian is independently teaching course in five universities such as DPDKV, IGAU, MAFSU, MPKV and CIFE. In CCSHAU, NDRI it is taught jointly by Librarian / Deputy Librarian / Assistant Librarian while Librarian and Deputy Librarian carry out this course in IARI.

35. All the universities which are regularly conducting user education course has reported the status of the course as academic and this shows that user education has been accepted as part of the instructional programme in those universities.

36. User education course is conducted in the main central library for all the P.G students by 55 per cent of Agricultural universities while Indira Gandhi Agricultural university has not mentioned the venue and 40 per cent conduct the course separately in different faculties.

37. Some text books/reference books have been prescribed for the user education course by 35 per cent universities, while 40 per cent of them have not prescribed any books and they are distributing in-house prepared course material during the course. This points towards the immense need of a uniform course material for the user education programme. This can bring out standardization of the courses and teaching methods and will help the students to use any of the libraries without difficulty.

38. The uniform course for user education at undergraduate level and postgraduate level was recommended by 85

per cent and 95 per cent each university respectively, while one university did not respond to the question, ten and five percent each responded negatively. Among them Indian Agricultural Research Institute has not recommended for U.G user education programme as it does not have a U.G course. All the universities other than Marathwada Agricultural University recommended the course for P.G. Although they are conducting scientific report writing course for P.G., they are of the opinion to conduct this course at the U.G level itself.

39. Internet and CD-ROM database facility is provided by 79.41 per cent and 70.59 per cent Agricultural Universities respectively. It is essential to teach it's contents, use and search strategy to the user category by including it in the user education course curriculum / refresher course of teachers.

10 DESIGN AND DEVELOPMENT OF USER EDUCATION PROGRAMME

Mission & Strategic Plan

User Education should be planned in concert with overall strategic library planning including the library's budgeting together with other members of KAU to participate in, support, and achieve the educational mission of University by teaching the core competencies, the abilities involved in identifying an information need, accessing needed information, evaluating, managing, and applying information, and understanding the legal, social, and ethical aspects of information use and research methodology.

The systematic delivery of instructional programes and services may also involve strategizing with other campus units to deliver collaboratively designed programming. It should be planned by recognizing the diverse nature of the learning community, including the varieties of learning theory, attitudes, educational levels, technology skill levels, and other learner variables such as proximity to the campus. User education should prepare learners not only for immediate curricular activities, but also for experiences with information use beyond the classroom-in work settings, careers, continuing education and self-development, and lifelong learning in general; and reflects changes in the institution and learning community through regular review and revision when appropriate.

The goal of user education

The goal of user education should be

1. To promote information empowerment as a key competency for lifelong learning, fundamental to the teaching, learning and research focus of the KAU community.
2. To ensure that KAULIS users are equipped with efficient methods of accessing, evaluating information from a variety of sources and synthesizing the information into a coherent whole ethically and legally, by organizing training based on level of difficulty of information and or users educational background.
3. To enable an individual to use computers, software applications, databases, and other technologies to achieve a wide variety of academic, work-related, and personal goals.
4. To improve the quality of users partly by their own spontaneous activity and partly through material set up for them and make them more creative and innovative for better research output for sustainable Agricultural development.

Objectives

The following may form the objectives for the proposed User Education Programme for Kerala Agricultural University Library and Information System (KAULIS).

1. To introduce users to facilities and the information resources available, both directly in the library and from external sources to meet their information needs and make them independent and self-sufficient users of library and information centres.

2. Educate users about various IT tools, information resources and how to exploit such resources-especially online resources- effectively and efficiently at the lowest cost.
3. To enable users to identify and locate up to date information from various information sources in ones own areas of interest.
4. To develop suitable search strategy.
5. To make users capable of writing research paper.
6. To develop a confidence in the user to use the Library and to seek the help of library staff.
7. To strengthen and sustain the quality and integrity of education and to improve transferability and marketability of students nationally and internationally.
8. To establish the library as the centre of academic activity by introducing credit courses for students and Refresher Courses for teachers for developing basic skills of users for lifelong learning.

The range of resources available to users becomes greater as new technology continues to be implemented in libraries and the tools used to find those resources are also constantly changing which in turn demands user education as critical as ever. The library recognizes that inherent pedagogical links exist between information empowerment and the development of other generic capabilities, such as resource-based learning, problem-based learning and the development of critical thinking. The programme must reflect the varied levels of skills of users and should become an integral part of the curriculum of the University in the case of students and refresher course in the case of teachers. A curriculum-integrated approach is one in which the development of skills and knowledge is integrated into the teaching curriculum content and where provision is made for developmental progression throughout the various years of the degree. It therefore differs from knowledge transmission through stand-alone or discrete subjects or by training programs offered outside the formal curriculum.[1] It must be delivered by various attractive but cost effective means. Each part of the programme has to be monitored and evaluated to ensure it's relevance to users' needs.

Major ingredients

The following ingredients have been taken into consideration while proposing 'Kerala Agricultural University Information Empowerment Course (KAU Inf Emp C)',(Fig.7.1) the user education programme for Kerala Agicultural University.

1. Proper understanding of the information requirements of users; their different levels;
2. Relevance: instruction has to be imparted at the time when it is most needed.
3. Attitude of users: the psychological complex of users have to be given due attention. A good number of users are contentedly confident of their ability to use the library while in reality they are blissfully ignorant of its manifold possibilities.
4. User education programme should have an integral relationship with key institutional curricula and initiatives.
5. Training Programmes must be developed around available resources including ATIC lab. An Information Empowerment package- "Info EmP"- an effective common multimedia courseware module - online as well as print - has to be developed in due course. Info EmP has to be designed as a multi-media program, which can be used in a variety of ways: as a component in formal courses in User education; as a unit for self-instruction and as a reference and access tool to information sources.
6. Expertise, fund, manpower, mode of instruction and evaluation methods are major determinants in effective teaching and learning;
7. Encouragement and recognition on the part of the authorities and dedication on the part of the staff are

essential for successful implementation of user education.

Hindrances that hamper user education

The major hindrances that hamper user education are expertise, fund, and manpower. At present libraries do not have any funding or the staff time to develop effective materials for user education programmes. Developing such programmes and materials is a massive task for which people not only need time and money but also expertise.

1. Expertise

Kerala Agricultural University Library Consultative Group (KAULCG) has to be constituted with Vice Chancellor as Chairman, Director / Head (KAULIS) as convener and members consisting of all Deans, Directors, and other subject specialists for extensive consultation about present and future user education strategy and to finalize the course outline of " KAU Information Empowerment Course" (KAU Inf Emp C). Those responsible for user education are expected to appraise and implement national and international developments, if they are appropriate to local needs.

2. Fund

The user education program should have adequate funds to cover all personnel costs connected with the programs such as supplies and materials; equipment or access to equipment; design, production, reproduction and revision of materials; promotion and evaluation of the instruction program as well as other identified costs. The budget allocation process should provide for training and continuing education of those involved in the instruction program and also allow charges for equipments and software replacement and enhancement. The budget allocation should entail sharing of budgetary responsibilities when appropriate for collaborative instructional projects with other Universities. As far as possible instructional personnel should use the expertise of development officers and those institutional staff persons with external fund raising responsibilities to further expand or enhance the program.

Indian Council of Agriculture Research (ICAR) / State Government / University Grants Commission have to provide sufficient fund.

3. Manpower

Staff responsible for the future management of the user education programme, should be of high academic caliber and will need to liaise closely with all academic areas, groups and individual users to ensure that it meets the increasingly diverse needs of users. The library should employ, develop, or have access to sufficient personnel with appropriate education, experience, and expertise

* to teach individuals and groups;
* to produce instructional materials using available media and electronic technologies responding to changing technologies, environments, and communities;
* to collect and interpret assessment data to evaluate and update instruction programs and services;
* to integrate and apply instructional technologies into learning activities when appropriate;
* to promote, market, manage, and coordinate diverse instruction activities; and
* to collaborate with faculty and other academic professionals in planning, implementing and assessing user education program.

One existing vacant post of Asst. Librarian in the UGC pay scale can be redesignated as Asst. Professor to engage the work of user education without any additional financial commitment on the part of the University.

Design of the course

The creation of a learning culture which produces graduates with a capacity and desire for lifelong learning in a rapidly changing, complex, and information over abundant environment requires a major shift in the educational paradigm and its resourcing.[2]

Levels of User Education

User education can take many forms depending on the specific needs of the users. This can include the

* first level of orientation of new users of the library;
* second level of teaching of library, information, computer and communication skills
* third level of teaching of specific information skills to help users with the resources available in their particular subject.

Based on the different levels of awareness on IT and library skills, status and effectiveness of existing user education programme revealed by different categories of users, three components are proposed for user education of KAULIS users (Figure). They are

I. Orientation for new users

II. Three credit compulsory course for Under Graduate and Post Graduate students namely Kerala Agricultural University Information Empowerment Credit Course (KAU Inf Emp CC);

III. Refresher Course for teachers- Information Empowerment Refresher Course (Inf Emp R C).

The second and third level can be consolidated and instruction can be delivered through the three credit compulsory course for students and Refresher Course for teachers. The criteria common to the entire above programme are Venue, Finance and Staff.

Venue

The location of the training programme can be the Central Library on having sufficient facilities and brilliant manpower and in its absence at the Agricultural Technology Information Centre (ATIC) / convenient faculty. Central Library offers the additional advantage of on spot demonstration of materials, processes and services.

Modes of Instruction

Wide range of methods are used to impart User Education. These include guides, videotapes, lectures and computer programs, Internet etc. Many universities have home pages on the Internet. The use of the Internet for user education has a lot of advantages as it allows information to be made available on a much larger scale than was possible, and that too also in multi-lingual format as is the case with the EDUCATE project. Users can access the information at their leisure and can exchange ideas easily. But Web based instruction is not likely to replace traditional methods completely, but it can be used to supplement and extend existing provision. The choice of teaching methods and the media depends on learning/ teaching situation, the subject material the students and the teachers. No single method can be suitable for all occasions.

Based on the knowledge and the wide variety of learning styles of individuals and groups different modes of instruction are suggested. They are

* group instruction in traditional or electronic classrooms;
* individualized instruction;
* electronic or print instruction aids (CD-ROMs, Guides);
* web tutorials and web-based instruction;
* asynchronous modes of instruction (e-mail, bulletin boards); and
* synchronous modes of instruction (chat software, videoconferencing).[3]

Asynchronous and synchronous modes of instruction are suggested as the constituent colleges of University are situated throughout Kerala and are not concentrated at the main campus at Vellanikkara.

1. Orientation

Orientation of new users is to be carried out at the time of their registering as members of the library. Orientation is "primarily concerned with ways of introducing the user to the general techniques of library usage and services available, and the organization, layout and facilities of a particular library."[4] It is suggested to give a basic orientation programme to first year students, in the first week of the term. User education has to be provided on a more selective basis to more homogeneous user bases.

Lecture to groups using overhead transparencies / LCD is suggested to provide basic information about the University, layout of the library, Library rules, membership privileges, working hours, issue system, library ethics, various sections and services, library collection and arrangement, classification scheme followed, call number and location symbols, OPAC its importance and how to use it, Reference tools, Info tech lab and facility for internet and CD-ROM search. The services available are to be detailed and users have to be provided with information on how to avail these services. They should be taught how to exploit library and resources with the help of library staff. The Library has to provide a basic fact sheet, Library Guide, Map Guides to the library, and Guide to the Online Public Access Catalogue for all new students / teachers along with membership form and library identity card while registration. There should have provision for Computer Assisted Instruction package (CAI package) for those students /members who had missed the orientation lectures to have the basic orientation information and also for reinforcement for the information already conveyed during the lecture.

The Library Guide could be used to supplement and reinforce the talks given to students in the first weeks of term / new users of the library at the time of membership. The Library Guide is very useful as it is available at the user's convenience and so can be used when it is most needed. The Library Guide has two-tier provision of user education such as the orientation user base and the instruction user base. Orientation information includes general information such as the library's telephone number, E-mail address, Website, library membership, Rules and regulations, more specific information about the holdings, and services of the Library, the physical layout of the library showing where subjects and services are located, instructional material about the OPAC etc. The aim of the instruction tier is to equip the student with the steps involved in carrying out a literature search, familiarize the distinction between abstracts and indexes, sources of information other than books and journals such as conference proceedings, theses, patents, government publications and standards etc., create an awareness of specialized library services such as Internet and the CD-ROM database., provide long term user education in the form of modules and to create a positive attitude among students towards the library and its staff.

Rice identifies three broad behavioural headings - affective, cognitive and psychomotor - under which the Library Guide's objectives can be grouped. **Affective objectives** are concerned with the feelings and attitudes of the readers and are thought to be of long term importance **Cognitive objectives** relate to the understanding of concepts and ideas which can be either abstract or concrete and **Psychomotor objectives** are concerned with physical activities. These objectives will determine the content of the user education and assist in the future evaluation of it's effectiveness.[5]

II. Kerala Agricultural University Information Empowerment Credit Course (KAU Inf Emp CC)

Time and Duration

The course is intended for Under- Graduate and Post - Graduate students including Ph. D. scholars of Kerala Agricultural University may coincide with the registration of new batch students. The course suggested is of three credits. Post Graduate students including Ph. D need to take up the three credit compulsory KAU Inf Emp CC only if there is a gap of more than three years after attending the same course previously. (Post Graduation/ after under graduate level). This course can be spread over 1st 2nd and 9th semester /last semester of UG programme. This course can be 'engaged along with first-year seminars, writing-across-the-curriculum programs; research methods courses in disciplinary majors; undergraduate research experiences/internships'.[6]

Course content

Theory

1. Introduction of the course- Information Empowerment concepts in the Information Age; the impact of technologies on information - Data / Information / Knowledge / Wisdom.
2. Overview of different types of libraries, both physical and electronic, includes Public, Academic, and Special.
3. Information sources - ephemeral and enduring sources - primary, secondary and tertiary sources, grey literature. Important sources - textbooks, abstracting journals, indexing journals, reviews, dictionaries, encyclopaedia, handbooks, manuals, glossary, thesaurus, lexicon etc.
4. Use of library for collection and collation of scientific literature - documentation — Various classification Schemes - DDC, divisions and sections and arrangement of resources in library.
5. Catalogue codes - Library catalogue / OPAC - entries on catalogues.
6. Use of Computers - familiarization Microsoft word, M S Office - Networking - Computer aided literature search - online and offline Information retrieval - use of CD-ROM.
7. Search strategies: Boolean operators, fields, controlled vocabulary - Research databases, bibliographic and full-text - E-Journals - free and fee based services - Uncover, CAPS, CCOD, NISCAIR -
8. The Web as an information tool - evaluation of Web- and print-based information - Web-based search strategies, Internet search engines and structure - important websites with agricultural focus such as Ag Bioforum, Agri Net and Agronomic links across the globe. Use of computers for agricultural research - electronic mail - use of "Power Point" for presentation - Photoshop, CorelDraw etc.

9. Bioinformatics and application of information technology for research and development - Biotechnology and Bioinformatics.
10. History of Research - Role of Research in scientific advancement- definition of research - objectives and characteristics of research - differences between science, technology and engineering - motives and benefits of doing research. Research methodology and research methods
11. Growth of agriculture as science - green revolution and after - agriculture research in world affairs. Agriculture research organizations in India and abroad - National and International Collaboration in Agricultural research - ICAR, FAO, CGIAR, CABI etc
12. Philosophy of research - science vs. philosophy - main concepts - empiricism - empirical methods - ockam's razor - reductionism - falsifiability - paradigm and paradigm shift pseudoscience and protoscience - scientific method - importance - advantages - steps
13. Hypothesis, theory and law - research hypothesis and statistical hypothesis - nature of research hypothesis - model of forming a hypothesis.
14. Chance of discoveries and exploitation of chance opportunities - serendipity - different type of chances - conditioned thinking and intuition - inductive and deductive reasoning - fallacies in reasoning - ethics in research - duties and qualities of researchers - fraud and misconduct in science - code of conduct for researchers.
15. Types of research - basic and applied - evaluation research, developmental research, action research - qualitative and quantitative - historical research, ethnographic research, descriptive research, correlational research, casual - comparative research.
16. Experimental research - experimental design - controlled experiments - natural experiments. Laboratory experiments and field experiments - farm trials -

multilocational trials - interdisciplinary and interfaculty approaches.

17. Surveys - attitude surveys - questionnaire - interviews (unstructured, semi-structured and structured interviews) case studies - identification of problems - prioritization of research projects.
18. Farmer participatory research - PRA and various participatory approaches.
19. Research projects - advantages and disadvantages of project system - project files and basic records - funding agencies for agricultural research.
20. Planning, developing and writing a research proposal - finding a research problem - questions to be considered while planning - different steps - proposal outline.
21. Study of model project proposal format - title - objectives - methodology - work programme - indicators - general considerations - reasons for rejection.
22. Research management - project management techniques - research management in Kerala Agricultural University - PC groups - thrust areas - FRC -monitoring and evaluation system.
23. Data collection - general principles scales of measurement - classification and tabulation - interpretation - presentation of data - diagrammatic and graphic representation.
24. Reporting search results - kind of reports to fellow scientists - extension workers, farmers and research management - project reports - thesis, dissertation, research notes, research papers, bulletins, popular articles, progress reports, annual reports, completion reports.
25. Preparation of research paper and thesis - IMARD structure - structure of a scientific paper - importance of the title, introduction, materials and methods, results, discussion, acknowledgements, references, abstract etc.

26. Citation of references and listing references - various styles - Harvard system and others - points to remember.
27. Choosing a journal - preparing a manuscript - submission - editing proofs etc. Parts of a thesis - general formatting requirements - Proof reading - Proof - reader's marks - things to check in proof practice in proof reading.
28. Hints for improving technical writing - distractions in writing - sentence checking - paragraphs - abbreviations - care with numerals - care with tenses - misuses of active and passive voice.
29. Carelessness in the use of verbs, nouns, articles, prepositions, adjectives, relative pronouns etc. Common errors in the use of compound sentences and conjunctions. Needless words and phrases causing verbosity - Punctuation.
30. SI Units - SI base units - units outside SI - prefixes - SI derived units - factors for converting non SI units to acceptable SI units.
31. Examples of preferred and alternative units for general use in agriculture and allied fields - SI unit and style conventions
32. Speaking at meetings - speaking vs. writing - planning a communication, causes of obscurity, delivery, technical problems, check list for a lecturer.
33. Workshop, symposia, colloquia, seminar, panel discussion and lectures - importance of handouts - guidelines for putting poster displays.
34. Teaching - guidelines for successful teaching - Illustrating talks and articles - writing the script for talk - preparation of slides, how to present data on slides, content of a slide - text, data, drawings, photographs.

Practical

Use of library - familiarization with various features of library, Preparation of index cards, Computer aided literature search - online and CD-ROM. Familiarization with Internet -

search engines - e-mail, Use of "Power Point" for presentation - Photoshop Coral draw. Presentation of scientific papers, discussion and critical evaluation of research papers -writing assignments- exercises on citing and listing references, preparation of a review article, exercises on processing of data and illustrations. Use of audio visual aids - Preparation of slides - Writing technical papers-Formulation of a research project - Proof correction, Preparation of a poster for display.

Evaluation of Course - Examinations (Total 300 marks)

Theory (200 marks)	*Practical (100 marks)*
Quiz 1	25
Record	20
Quiz 2	25
Class work	20
Midterm	50
Viva - voice	10
Final examination	100
Practical Examination	50

III. Information Empowerment Refresher Course (InfEmp R C).

Refresher Course for teachers

1. Introduction of the course- Information Empowerment concepts in the Information Age; the impact of technologies on information - Data / Information / Knowledge / Wisdom.
2. Use of library for collection and collation of scientific literature - documentation — Various classification Schemes - DDC, divisions and sections and arrangement of resources in library.
3. Catalogue codes - Library catalogue / OPAC - entries on catalogues.
4. Introduction to personal computers - classification of computers - generations - hardware - software - input,

output devices, external storage devices - MS Windows, MS Office.

5. Networking - Computer aided literature search - online and offline Information retrieval - use of CD-ROM.
6. Search strategies: Boolean operators, fields, controlled vocabulary - Research databases, bibliographic and full-text - E-Journals - free and fee based services - Uncover, CAPS, CCOD, NISCAIR -
7. The Web as an information tool - evaluation of Web- and print-based information - Web-based search strategies, Internet search engines and structure - important websites with agricultural focus such as Ag Bioforum, Agri Net and Agronomic links across the glob. Use of computers for agricultural research - electronic mail - use of "Power Point" for presentation - Photoshop, CorelDraw etc.
8. Bioinformatics and application of information technology for research and development - Biotechnology and Bioinformatics.
9. Growth of agriculture as science - green revolution and after - agriculture research in world affairs. Agriculture research organizations in India and abroad - National and International Collaboration in Agricultural research - ICAR, FAO, CGIAR, CABI etc
10. Project submission - presentation as part of the course work

Duration : 21 days

Methods

Methods suggested are lectures and informal discussion. Multimedia self instructional programmes can also be used. The training programme proposed above has to be augmented with the following.

* Self guiding course material in print/CD-ROM.
* Information guidance through informal individual meeting.

* Exhibition and film shows have to be organized to create an awareness, appreciation and love of library materials and services.

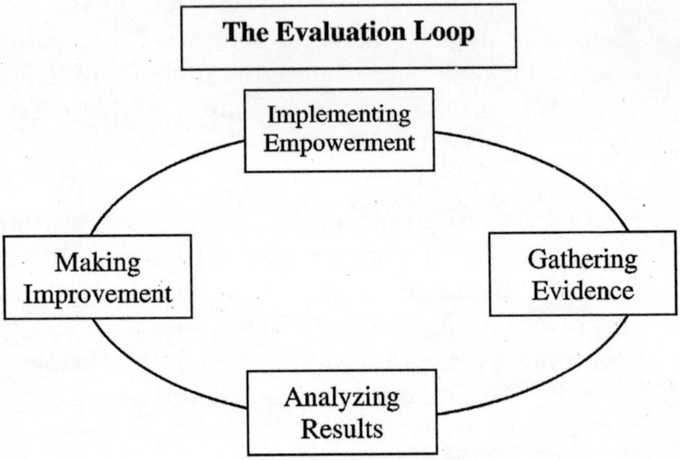

Improving the quality of users' learning experience and making them independent lifelong learners is surely the ultimate goal of evaluation of empowerment course. Gathering evidence, analyzing it and changing what we do as a result of conclusions drawn: this is the process of evaluation loop. Evaluation is also important to share examples of good practice, develop skills and justify the cost of service.[7]

The major factors that influence evaluation are lack of time, (director as well as users), resource, validity, reliability and purpose. The methods suggested for evaluation are observation, informal feedback from users, on - the - spot questionnaires, assignments and peer evaluation.

Standing Committee on Information Empowerment 'KAU-SCIE' has to be constituted to conduct utility survey, to ensure centralized, a more coordinated User Education Programme and to review, revise and propose new initiatives in the areas according to recent developments.

11 RECOMMENDATIONS

I. It is recommended to have the user education programme by integrating it in the course curricula of undergraduate and post graduate programme (compulsory for P G, if not taken up the course with in three years / during previous course) and to conduct at central library on having sufficient facilities including brilliant manpower and in its absence at the Agricultural Technology Information Centre (ATIC) / convenient faculty.

II. ICAR and IVC have to take immediate steps to integrate "Information Empowerment Course" (AU Inf Emp C), the user education course as a component of the Academic course curricula of all UG and PG programmes / Refresher course for teachers according to the degree of intention required considering the present IT scenario and in the light of this user education programme designed considering national and international information literacy scenario, based on major findings and views of officials of various Agricultural Universities in India, and information need of KAULIS users.

III. Agricultural University Library Consultative Group (AULCG) has to be constituted consisting of Administrators, librarians and other subject specialists to finalize the course outline of "Information Empowerment Course" (AU Inf Emp C) at national level.

IV. A project on Information Empowerment package- "Info EmP"- has to be taken up for the preparation of effective common multimedia courseware modules -online as well as print- for all Agricultural Universities for various categories with provision for local variation to avoid duplication of effort, men and material.

V. ICAR has to take immediate steps to publish a book, 'Handbook of Information Empowerment' for user education, for the standardization of the course.

VI. An Assistant/Associate Professor qualified as per UGC /

ICAR norms in Library and Information Science has to be entrusted with teaching of "Information Empowerment Course" (Inf Emp C) for various categories of users with the help of guest lecturers from other faculties. Librarian, Deputy Librarian **having prescribed qualifications as per UGC / ICAR norms** associated with the teaching of Inf Emp C both at undergraduate and postgraduate level has to be recognized as teachers.

VII. A Standing Committee on Information Empowerment (SCIE) for Agricultural Universities has to be constituted to conduct utility survey, to ensure centralized, a more co-ordinated User Education Programme and to review, revise and propose new initiatives in the areas according to recent developments.

VIII. Compulsory training in video conferencing is essential and KAU should provide 'Mobile video conferencing lab' under the control of ATIC for giving extension service to peasants in remote areas by the extension officers by accessing on spot advice from specialists in agricultural Centers of KAU as well as various Universities in spite of geographical location.

IX. College libraries have to be strengthened and networking among college and central libraries as well as web publishing is essential to meet the information requirements of KAULIS users as central library is not easily accessible and is not utilized by about 58 percent population.

X. A directorate of library and information science has to be established in all agricultural universities for smooth functioning of the constituent libraries and for conducting user education courses. A director in the status and cadre of Professor has to be posted instead of the designation University Librarian in the agricultural universities especially with decentralized and geographically distributed college and station libraries.

XI. With a view of imparting formal user education at

university level the students of librarianship has to be well trained in information empowerment during their M. Phil. programme by integrating these topics in the curriculum.

12. CONCLUSION

The main objective of the study was to design and develop user education programme suitable for various categories of users in the Kerala Agricultural University Library and Information System. In order to attain this goal six objectives were formulated

i. to assess the extend of use of library tools available in the Kerala Agricultural University Library and Information System by the user community.

ii. to assess the present use of information sources and services available in Kerala Agricultural University Library and Information System by users.

iii. to examine the information needs, use pattern and use behaviour of the various categories of users in the system.

iv. to examine user education programmes and facilities in Agricultural Universities in India;

v. to assess the existing user education programmes in Kerala Agricultural University Library and Information System; and

vi. to design and develop user based user education programme.

The survey results given in chapter entitled 'Kerala Agricultural University and Library and Information System' and 'Information Needs and Use Pattern of Users of Kerala Agricultural University Library and Information System: Analytical Study' substantiate the first, second third and fifth objectives. The survey results given in chapter entitled 'User Education Programmes in Agricultural Universities in India: Analytical Study' substantiate the fourth and fifth objective. The last chapter entitled 'Findings, Recommendations and Design of User Education Programme' substantiates the sixth objective by designing the User Education Programme.

The three hypotheses which led to the present study are

* The varied information needs of the students, research scholars and teachers are not adequately met by the KAU library and information system.
* The existing library tools especially IT tools and sophisticated information services available in the system are not fully utilized by the user community.
* The existing user education programmes in Kerala Agricultural University Library and Information System is not user based in the present IT environment.
* The results of the study mentioned above clearly substantiate the validity of hypotheses formulated in the study.

Areas of Further Research

The following areas may be considered for further research

I. Design and development of Information empowerment programme for farmers in Kerala.

II. Design and development of Web based Information literacy programme in Agriculture.

The era of globalization has made it imperative to improve the standards and quality of education. Common package of User Education is essential to strengthen and sustain the quality and integrity of education and improving transferability and marketability of students nationally and internationally. Indian Council of Agriculture Research (ICAR), in line with the National Assessment and Accreditation Council (NAAC) of UGC, has to take initiatives for assessment and to integrate user education programme into the course curriculum of all Agricultural Universities in India, to achieve life long perpetual education, to improve the level of efficiency of man power and to achieve the real goals of education. Remodeling and reorganizing the Agricultural Academic Curricula and Refresher Courses by integrating User Education programmes for students and teachers respectively is the need of the hour for their imparting perpetual knowledge and to train the extension functionaries and farmers and for evolving need-based and eco-friendly technologies for sustainable agriculture. The integrated IT based User Education as proposed can bridge the information access gap between the 'haves' and 'have-nots' and can boost the academic caliber of our students, teachers, scientists and technologists.

REFERENCES

1. McGurk, C. A Curriculum Integrated Approach to Comprehensive Information Literacies: Project Report, Working Party on Comprehensive Literacies, University of Woollongong, 1997. http://cedir.uow.edu.au/programs/literacies/information/report/00Rpts.html
2. Oliver, R. and Mc Loughlin, C. Using Web and Problem-based Learning Environments to Support the Development of Key Skills, ASCILITE Conference Proceedings. Queensland University of Technology, Brisbane, 1999.
3. Rice, J. Teaching library use: a guide for library instruction. Westport, Greenwood press, 1981.
4. Fjallbrant, N. & Malley, I. User education in libraries. 2nd ed., London, Clive Bingley Limited, 1984, p.13.
5. Rice, J. Teaching Library Use: a guide for library instruction. Westport, Connecticut, Greenwood Press, 1981, pp.37-38.
6. Guidelines for Instruction Programs in Academic Libraries, Chicago, Association of College and Research Libraries (ACRL) Board, June 2003.
7. Kirby, John et.al. Empowering the information user. London, Library Association Publishing.1998,p 62.

4

Information Requirements of Career Seekers and Information Resources and Services in Libraries

— Dr. Dineshan Koovakkai

1. INTRODUCTION

Information is a valuable input for social development. In the present information society, the quality of life as well as prospects for social change and economic development depend increasingly upon information and its utilization (Martin, 1995)[1]. It is a strategic resource in the modern society as capital is the strategic resources in the industrial economy.

The fortieth stanza of Jnana Yoga of Bhagavad Gita clearly states the need for knowledge (information) as:

... the man who is ignorant; who has no faith, who is of doubting nature perishes. For the doubting soul, there is neither this world nor the world beyond nor any happiness (Radhakrishnan, 1974, 172)[2].

Information generated from different activities is recorded in different forms such as books, periodicals, research papers, technical reports, conference proceedings, dissertations, patents, standards, microforms, electronic media and the like. Those who need information are expected to consult one or more of these sources to get the required information apart from gathering information from informal channels. A person's dependence for information on a particular source or information channel is influenced by human psychology as well as the environment (Lalitha, 1995)[3].

Customer oriented approach, design and evaluation are the founding pillars of any enterprise (Sridhar, 2002)[4]. Library and information centres as social institutions are ultimately meant to satisfy the information requirements of users. They are regarded now-a-days as high technology social institutions which have the responsibility of providing right information to the right clientele at the right time.

Providing information that a user wants, regardless of its format is the essential function of libraries. Hence, every library collection must be consciously developed and organized with its unique user community in mind. It does not simply mean the active user's persistent demand but the unexpressed demand of the potential customers as well (Faruqui, 1997)[5].

The user is the key component of any information system. The success of an information system depends considerably on how best the system design is based on close and accurate understanding of the users. (Sridhar, 1990)[6]. Persons visiting the library to receive any library service may be termed as users. The community of users may comprise of different categories depending upon their nature of information need and the class they belong to. It is however difficult to identify mutually exclusive category of users (Kawatra, 1992) [7].

The information needs, expectations, searching behaviour and methods of satisfying their needs are different among different user communities. The information activities of the users are determined by their socio-economic-educational background, their own characteristics, behavioural pattern, reading habit, approaches to information and the various kinds of limitations (Lahiri, 1988)[8].

Voigt (1961)[9] identified three types of information requirements. The workers in the field added a further type of information requirement later. Now it is commonly agreed by the information scientists that there are four types of information requirements which they call approaches to information. Current approach, everyday approach, exhaustive approach and catching up or brushing up approach are the four types of approaches to information.

The information requirement of a user to keep himself abreast of the current developments in his field of interest is known as current approach. Every day approach refers to the requirement for a specific piece of information. Exhaustive approach comes out of the need for all relevant literature or as much as possible on a subject and catching up or brushing up approach arises out of the need of users to have a brief but complete picture of a subject or topic (Guha, 1983)[10].

In a library or information centre, the users are the last link or the recipients of information in the communication cycle. Hence, understanding the user requirements is a fundamental pre-requisite for libraries which aim at satisfying the information needs of the users which vary from user to user (Devarajan, 1995)[11].

'Know thy customer' is the motto of any business enterprise. Accordingly, business enterprises conduct extensive market research for introducing a new product or to forecast the future demand of a product. However, library/information centre being a non-profit organisation is yet to accept this rule of business in its true spirit (Garg, 2000)[12].

The user being the key component of any information system, its prime concern will be user satisfaction. It is in turn related to user requirements which vary from person to person and according to the availability of resources and services in the right place, in the right time and in right amount. In order to serve the users in a better way by providing the required information in the least time, user requirements are to be understood by conducting thorough user surveys.

Even though the user is the most important component of the information communication system, information scientists had not given due consideration to this component (Guha, 1983)[10]. Systematic research and concern over the users and their information requirements are recent phenomena.

Those who contributed significantly to the field of user studies include psychologists, behavioural scientists and others (Sridhar, 1990)[6]. Though recently, library and information science researchers have also contributed to a great extent to the field of user studies.

In the library field, most of the earlier user studies were based on the indirect methods like citation counting and examining library issue and reference records. Such studies were inadequate to reveal the actual requirements of the users. As a result direct methods such as information use and information gathering habit surveys were started to study the user requirements (Guha, 1983)[10].

The late nineteen forties marked the actual beginning of user studies. Though some studies appeared in the fifties, the real large scale studies emerged in the sixties and seventies. Most of the earlier studies, however, were limited to United Kingdom and the United States of America. Only a very few studies were conducted in India before the eighties. The piecemeal studies conducted in India have been mostly local studies of a particular aspect of user behaviour. Though there have been some efforts to undertake user studies in the last twenty five years, the interest has been limited to obtain clues that will help to modulate present resources and services to meet the changing requirements of users (Kawatra, 1992)[7].

It is apparent that various studies have been conducted in the last few years to analyse the information requirements of users in different libraries and environments. However, no much studies have been conducted to analyse the information requirements of career seekers though they need great amount of information.

Going to work is like breathing to a great majority of people in the world. Employment forms a considerable part of one's self image and personal identity (Thomas and Madigan, 1976)[13]. The fifth stanza of 'Karma Yoga' of Bhagavad Gita clearly states the importance of work as:

... no one can remain for a moment without doing work;

every one is made to act helplessly by the impulses born of nature (Radhakrishnan, 1974, 133) [14].

Each society has its vocational tradition. The caste based Indian social structure was in turn based on vocation. The society was divided according to the vocation as: Brahmana, Kshatriya, Vaishya and Shudra. After the advent of democracy the number and types of profession increased. This coupled with increasing population created the problem of choice and competition (Sharma, 1997) [15].

In a state like Kerala where the educated unemployment problem is acute, choice and competition are of utmost importance. In such a state, it can be expected that there will be large demand for information about careers from the public at large. There is very little doubt that careers and related information will become an increasingly important resource.

Career seekers need information at various stages of their career search. They need information to know about the proper education and training for getting a job, to know about the job market, to find suitable employers, to know vacancy positions, to gain knowledge about preparing application forms and resumes, to prepare for various competitive examinations and to acquire interview / group discussion skills.

The agencies which provide career information in India to an extent at present include Pre-examination Training Centres (PETCs), University Employment Information and Guidance Bureaux, Specialised career guidance centres etc.

In the area of vocational guidance, the Employment Service through its vocational guidance units located in the employment exchanges and University Employment Information and Guidance Bureaux provides employment counselling / career guidance facilities to career seekers. The Employment Service also brings out various materials such as career literature, occupational information etc.

The Pre-examination Training Centres, which are promoted by the Social Welfare Department, aim at developing human resource among the weaker sections. These centres for various competitive examinations are arranging coaching programmes.

There are innumerable career guidance centres in the private sector. Most of them with their attractive advertisements try to make an impression that candidates are sure to get through the competitive examinations by attending classes conducted by them. There is no doubt that there are some reputed career guidance centres in the private sector. But most of them are concentrated in towns and cities which makes it impossible for the majority of the career seekers to get their service. Motivated by profit, most of these private centres charge very high fee for their services as well.

The above mentioned agencies, however, are not actually providing career information service to the fuller extent. They also suffer from poor information back up. It can be stated beyond doubt that no such centre can provide full fledged career information service as a library can. A library with its resources and professionally qualified personnel can provide information service to career seekers in a better way than any other agency (Turner, 1979)[16].

Libraries have a dominant role in assisting the career seekers by providing relevant materials and services at different stages of their career search. Information is required for the active job searching as today's labour market is highly complex. Well planned libraries will be in a prime position in the delivery of career and job sources and services which can help the stranded job seekers in the highly complex job market (Anderson, 1992)[17].

Libraries are the logical service providers and librarians are the logical resource persons to enhance the delivery of required career information. Librarians are in a better position of being aware of the career resources than any other career professional.

By understanding the labour market and the employment trends, libraries can develop strong collections in career sources to provide much of the information required by the career seekers. In the process of providing such information the library, as a social institution can enhance its reputation within the community (Anderson, 1992)[17].

Effective career information service requires that libraries have up-to-date material. Knowledge of the labour market, proper understanding about the exact user requirements and efficient system of imparting information are also of utmost importance in providing career information. It requires a combination of strong core collection of career information materials, knowledgeable library professionals and library sponsored programmes such as career guidance and marketing of services.

In the United States, Great Britain and other European countries, public and academic libraries consider career information service as one of their major services. Specialist career libraries function under many local authorities in the United Kingdom beyond the scope of their public library system. Experimental job libraries have been set up in high street locations such as East Bourne, Edinburgh and Wrexham (Turner, 1979)[16].

In the United States, Education, Job and Career Information Centres (EJICs) work in public libraries to serve the job seekers and career chargers. Many of these centres were started by the grants by the W.K. Kellogg Foundation. Ohio Public Library's InfoPLACE (Information Public Library Adult Career Education) is one of the most comprehensive EJICs in America (Durrance et al., 1993)[18].

Education, job and career information centres in America have sprung up in the places where unemployment, lay offs or other employment problems have had serious impact on society. Such centres have great importance in Indian situation also. Such services have much more importance in Kerala where the educated unemployment problem is very crucial.

2. NEED AND SIGNIFICANCE OF THE STUDY

The studies of user requirements and user satisfaction are of recent Origin. Various studies have been conducted, though recently, to analyse the information needs and seeking behaviour of different user communities especially in special library environment. However, no serious study was conducted especially in Kerala to analyse the information requirements of career seekers.

In a state like Kerala, where the problem of educated unemployment is very crucial, almost every one of the educated unemployed is engaged in the preparation of some kind of competitive examinations for acquiring a job. The traditional education system is creating more and more frustration among the majority of students who realise that the academic degrees are becoming worthless bits of paper in the present dynamic socio-economic scenario.

Despite the fact that Kerala has the highest rate of literacy in the country, the number of candidates coming out successful in all India tests like the civil service examinations is very low. The employment opportunities are very limited compared to the bulk of potential candidates in Kerala. As a result, the unemployed as well as the underemployed have to prove their mettle by competing with their counterparts having equal or even higher qualifications and capacity. Hence, it can be assumed that they are dependent on libraries more than any other group of users who have different information requirements.

However, most of the libraries are still to recognize the career seekers as a dominant group of actual as well as potential users. The information requirements and searching behaviour of this group are different from those of other groups who have definite and well-defined information needs.

Though still unrecognized, the career seekers are potential information seekers who need extensive library service (Anderson, 1992)[17]. The essential pre-requisite for providing relevant information services to career seekers is to understand the actual information requirements of this group. Thus, this study is of great importance as it aims at understanding the information requirements of career seekers.

Libraries which try to provide all the information needed by the career seekers require a lot of resources. Most of the agencies providing career information suffer from poor information back up (Turner, 1979)[16].

As the study aims at analysing the availability of materials and services in libraries to cater to the needs of the career seekers, it is expected to reveal the strength and weakness of the libraries in this area. This will help the library administrators to strengthen or modify the existing collection and services targeted towards these users.

Use of library resources and services is a true indicator of the user requirements. Libraries need to develop a strong service capacity for career seekers. The study is expected to bring out the extent of use of various documents and services in the library which in turn will reveal the relevance of the resources and services to career seekers in the library.

In order to satisfy the information needs of the users, the library collection must be adequate in terms of quantity, quality and currency (Sam, 1996)[19]. The study is aimed at revealing the adequacy of information resources and services in libraries. Thus the study will help the libraries to strengthen the collection and services where inadequacies are found, in order to provide better satisfaction to the career seekers.

The barriers to information access may prevent the career seekers from getting the required information in the right amount. As the study is aimed at understanding the barriers to information access, the study is expected to help the library administrators to reduce the barriers to give maximum satisfaction to the career seekers.

User satisfaction is of utmost importance in any library / information centre. The level of user satisfaction indicates the performance of the library. While measuring the user satisfaction of career seekers, the study is expected to bring out how well the library serves the career seekers. This will in turn help the libraries in making improvement in collection, services and the environment if necessary.

In providing comprehensive resources and services, libraries have to consider their space, budget, staff, administrative commitment etc. In India, libraries are always the last to get new investment in space, staff and equipment. At the same time they are the first when budgetary cuts are required to be applied (Haravu, 1988)[20]. It is a fact that without raising revenue on their own, most of the libraries cannot survive in the changing circumstances. Carefully designed information products which cater to the actual needs of the career seekers will be potential marketable products which can earn revenue to libraries. The study is expected to help the library authorities to design appropriate career information products / services which will earn them revenue.

Thus the study is of great importance in understanding the information requirements of one of the most significant groups in the society. It will help the library / information professionals to serve the community of career seekers in a better way. It will also be helpful to the library administrators in collection building and raising revenue to libraries.

3. STATEMENT OF THE PROBLEM

The problem of the present study is entitled as: INFORMATION REQUIREMENTS OF CAREER SEEKERS AND INFORMATION RESOURCES AND SERVICES OF LIBRARIES IN KERALA".

4. OPERATIONAL DEFINITION OF KEY TERMS

The key terms of the problem are:

Information requirements

Career seekers

Information resources

Services

Libraries

Kerala

Information Requirements

Longman dictionary of contemporary English (1978,

574)[21] defines information as "some thing which gives knowledge in the form of facts" and requirement as "something needed" (Longman dictionary of contemporary English, 1978, 940)[22].

According to Sridhar (1990, 65)[23] information requirement refers to "a look out for a sort of relevance of information to a given user and to his areas of concern and interests, likes and dislikes".

In the present study, information requirements refer to the seeking of materials and services which communicate necessary knowledge needed by the career seekers.

Career Seekers

The Oxford English dictionary (1933, 117)[24] defines career as a "course of professional life or employment, which affords opportunity for progress or advancement in the world" and seeker as "a searcher, an explorer, one who endeavours to find something hidden or lost" (The Oxford English dictionary, 1933, 390)[25]. Thus career seekers mean the persons who search for a profession or employment.

In the present context, career seekers mean, the unemployed people who search for some kind of employment.

Information Resources

The word resource means "stock or reserve upon which to draw when necessary". (The World Book dictionary, 1981, 1779)[26].

In the present study, information resources mean, materials printed or otherwise, which give necessary knowledge regarding career options and opportunities and which provide knowledge to career seekers.

Services

Longman dictionary of contemporary English (1978, 1016)[27] defines service as "an act or job done in favour of some one".

In the present study services refer to any kind of help given in libraries to career seekers at any stage of his/her search and preparation for employment.

Libraries

Harrod (1971, 378)[28] defines library as a place, building, room or rooms set apart for keeping and use of collection of books etc.

The definition holds good in the present study.

Kerala

The southern state of India which is known by this name.

5. OBJECTIVES

The following are the objectives of the study.

(i) To find out the level of requirement of career seekers for information resources and services.

(ii) To find out whether there exists any significant difference in the levels of requirements for information resources and services of different categories of career seekers on the basis of type of library using, gender, qualification and place of residence.

(iii) To find out the level of availability of information resources and services in libraries.

(iv) To find out whether there exists any significant difference in the levels of availability of information resources and services in different types of libraries.

(v) To find out the level of use of library resources and services by career seekers.

(vi) To know whether there exists any significant difference in the levels of use of resources and services of different categories of career seekers.

(vii) To understand the level of adequacy of resources and services of libraries.

(viii) To find out whether there exists any significant difference in the levels of adequacy of resources and services of different types of libraries.

(ix) To know the major barriers to information access.

(x) To know the level of satisfaction of career seekers with regard to the resources and services of libraries.

(xi) To find out whether there exists any significant difference in the levels of satisfaction of different categories of career seekers.

6. HYPOTHESES

The following are the hypotheses of the study.

(i) The level of requirements of career seekers for information resources and services is significantly high.

(ii) There exists significant difference in the levels of requirements of career seekers in different categories.

(iii) The level of availability of information resources and services is significantly high.

(iv) There exists significant difference in the levels of availability of information resources and services in different types of libraries.

(v) The level of use of library resources and services by the career seekers is significantly high.

(vi) There exists significant difference in the levels of use of resources and services of different categories of career seekers.

(vii) The level of adequacy of information resources and services is significantly high.

(viii) There exists significant difference in the levels of adequacy of resources and services of different types of libraries.

(ix) The level of satisfaction of career seekers in the resources and services of libraries is significantly high.

(x) There exists significant difference in the levels of satisfaction of different categories of career seekers.

7. METHODOLOGY OF THE STUDY

A brief description of the methodology of the study is given below.

Sample Used

The sample of career seekers for the study was taken from

five university libraries, twelve college libraries (three each from four affiliating university areas out of which one is a professional college) and six public libraries (two each from North Kerala, Central Kerala and South Kerala). The final sample is 1039 career seekers in Kerala.

Variables

The variables of the study are:

(i) Requirements of career seekers,

(ii) Availability of information resources and services in libraries,

(iii) Use of library resources and services,

(iv) Adequacy of information resources and services,

(v) Barriers to information access and

(vi) Satisfaction with regard to the resources and services of libraries.

The following are the classificatory variables.

a) Type of library,

b) Gender of career seekers,

c) Qualification of career seekers and

d) Place of residence of career seekers.

Tools Used for Data collection

The required data was collected using the following tools constructed by the investigator.

(i) Questionnaire on the Career Seekers' Sources of Information

(ii) User Satisfaction Scale for Career Seekers.

Statistical Techniques used for Analysis

The following statistical techniques are used to analyse the data to arrive at conclusions and to test the hypotheses.

(i) The percentage analysis

(ii) The z-test for significance

(iii) Chi-Square test (The level of significance was obtained by finding out the p-value).

(iv) The t-test for the difference between the mean score and the neutral value.

(v) The t-test for the difference between mean scores.

8. SCOPE AND LIMITATIONS OF THE STUDY

The present study is an attempt to explore the information requirements of career seekers in relation to information resources and services in libraries. The unemployed youths need to know about the educational opportunities available to them for getting employment and the various employment opportunities open to them. They should also prove their mettle in the competitive examinations and interviews as they are part of selecting candidates for different jobs. Hence the study aims at understanding the various information requirements related to the information resources and services.

Serious preparation for the competitive examinations and interviews / group discussions involves thorough library use. Thus the availability of library resources and services, their use, adequacy, different barriers to information access and user satisfaction come under the study.

The area of the study is limited to the geographical area of Kerala. This is because of the nature of unemployment in the state. The unemployment problem is crucial among the educated youths in this state.

Many posts in government, quasi-government and private sectors require a minimum qualification of graduation. Hence, those who have at least a Bachelor's Degree are included in this study.

The study is conducted on a sample of 1039 unemployed people. It is neither feasible nor possible to take all the unemployed in the state for this study. Thus a representative sample from all strata is taken.

The sample is selected from the unemployed graduate users of public, college and university libraries. Special libraries are excluded from the scope of this study since they have no much role in providing career related information.

9. ANALYSIS

The analysis of data involves critical examination of the data with the objectives in mind for determining the pattern of relationship among the variables. Social research most often requires quantitative analysis involving the application of various statistical techniques.

The term analysis refers to the computation of certain measures along with searching for patterns of relationship that exists among data groups (Kothari,1990).[1] The method and depth of analysis are determined by the type of the study and the complexity of the hypotheses.

In the present study, the statistical treatment of the collected data is made to find out the level of requirements of the career seekers, availability of information resources and services in libraries, use of library resources and services, adequacy of information resources and services and satisfaction of the career seekers in the resources and services of libraries. Comparison of the levels of these in various categories is also made based on classificatory variables. The barriers to information access also are analysed.

Percentage analysis is used to find out the level of requirement of the career seekers and the level of availability, use and adequacy of resources and services. To find out whether the levels are significantly high, z-test is used. To get the z-values for the level of requirement for resources/services, availability of resources/services and use of resources/services, the hypothesised value is 50 percent and for the level of adequacy of resources/services the hypothesised value is 75 percent (both adequate and moderately adequate taken together).

To find out whether there exists any significant difference in these levels among different categories of career seekers, Chi-square test is applied. The p-value is obtained to find out the level of significance of the difference.

The level of satisfaction of the career seekers in the resources and services of libraries is obtained by finding out the mean scores. To know whether the level of satisfaction is significantly high, t-value is obtained by comparing the mean score and the neutral point.

Comparison of mean scores of the career seekers in different categories also is done. The t-value is obtained to understand whether there is significant difference.

10. FINDINGS

1. The level of requirement of career seekers for information resources and services is significantly high.
2. No significant difference exists among the career seekers using different types of libraries and between the male and the female career seekers in the levels of requirement for the majority of the information resources/services taken for the study.
3. Between the graduate and the postgraduate career seekers and between the rural and the urban career seekers no significant difference in the levels of requirement for half of the resources/services taken for the study can be observed.
4. Higher levels of availability are observed in half of the resources/services taken for the study. The levels of availability of the other half are not significantly high.
5. The analysis of the response of the career seekers using different types of libraries shows that significant difference exists among different types of libraries in the case of availability of the majority of the resources/services taken for the study. The levels of availability of the majority of such resources/services are the highest in university libraries.
6. The levels of use of the majority of information resources/services of the career seekers are significantly high.
7. Significant difference exists among the career seekers using different types of libraries in the levels of use of the majority of the information resources/services in libraries.

8. There is significant difference between the levels of use of the male and the female career seekers in the case of the majority of the resources/services. The levels of use of the majority of such resources are higher among the female career seekers.
9. Significant difference exists between the graduate and the postgraduate career seekers in the levels of use of the majority of the resources/services. The levels of use in the majority of these cases are higher among the postgraduate career seekers.
10. No significant difference exists between the rural and the urban career seekers in the levels of use of the majority of the resources/services.
11. The levels of adequacy of a slight majority of the resources/services taken for the study are significantly high.
12. Significant difference exists among libraries in the case of level of adequacy of most of the resources/services. In the levels of adequacy of these resources/services, university libraries stand first.
13. The most important barriers to information access according to the career seekers are poor physical maintenance of library materials, inaccurate and outdated information and scatter of resources.
14. The level of satisfaction in the resources and services of libraries is significantly high among the career seekers.
15. Significant difference exists among the career seekers using different types of libraries in the level of satisfaction. Those who use university libraries are the most satisfied.
16. Significant difference exists between the level of satisfaction of the male and the female career seekers. The level of satisfaction is higher among the female career seekers.
17. No significant difference exists between the graduate and the postgraduate career seekers and between the rural

and the urban career seekers in the levels of satisfaction of the resources and services in libraries.

11. CONCLUSION

It is evident from the analysis that the requirement level of information resources/services is high among the career seekers.

The levels of requirement of the career seekers using different types of libraries and of the male and the female career seekers are not much different. The requirement levels of the graduate and the postgraduate career seekers and of the rural and the urban career seekers are not different in half of the cases taken for the study.

The availability levels of half of the resources/services taken for the study are high. At the same time the levels of availability of the other half are not high.

The availability levels of the majority of the resources/services are different in university, college and public libraries. University libraries come first in the availability of the majority of the resources/services taken for the study.

There is high level of use in the case of the resources and services of libraries. The levels of use are different among the career seekers using different types of libraries.

In the level of use of the majority of the resources/services, the female career seekers come first.

The level of use of the majority of the resources/services is high among the postgraduate career seekers as compared to the graduate career seekers.

The rural career seekers are not much different in using the information resources/services than the urban career seekers.

The adequacy rate is higher in the case of the majority of the resources/services. The responses of the career seekers show that university libraries stand first in the level of adequacy of comparatively larger number of resources/services.

Poor physical maintenance of library materials, inaccurate and out dated information and scatter of resources are the major barriers of the career seekers in accessing information.

It can be seen that the career seekers are satisfied in the resources and services of libraries. Among the career seekers using different types of libraries, those who use university libraries are the most satisfied.

Compared to the male career seekers the female career seekers are more satisfied in the resources and services of libraries.

12. TENABILITY OF HYPOTHESES

The tenability of hypotheses based on the results of statistical analysis is discussed below.

The first hypothesis states that 'the level of requirement of career seekers for information resources and services is significantly high'. The z- values indicate that the levels of requirement of the career seekers for the information resources and services taken for the study are significantly high. Thus the hypothesis is fully substantiated.

The second hypothesis states that 'there exists significant difference in the levels of requirements of career seekers in different categories'. The p- values indicate that no significant difference exists among the career seekers using different types of libraries and between the male and the female career seekers in the levels of requirement for the majority of the information resources/services. It can also be seen that between the graduate and the postgraduate career seekers and between the rural and the urban career seekers, no significant difference exists in the levels of requirement for half of the resources/services taken for the study. Hence, this hypothesis is not substantiated.

The third hypothesis states that 'The level of availability of information resources and services is significantly high'. The z-values show that the levels of availability of half of the resources/services taken for the study are significantly high. Thus the hypothesis is partially substantiated.

The fourth hypothesis states that 'there exists significant difference in the levels of availability of information resources and services in different types of libraries'. The p-values indicate that there is significant difference among libraries in the case of availability of the majority of the resources/services taken for the study. Hence, this hypothesis is fully substantiated.

The fifth hypothesis states that 'the level of use of library resources and services by the career seekers is significantly high'. The z- values show that the levels of use of the majority of the information resources/services of the career seekers are significantly high. Hence, this hypothesis is fully substantiated.

The sixth hypothesis states that 'there exists significant difference in the levels of use of resources and services of different categories of career seekers'. The p-values indicate that significant difference exists among the career seekers using different types of libraries, between the male and the female career seekers and between the graduate and the postgraduate career seekers in the levels of use of the majority of the resources/services. However, no significant difference exists between the rural and the urban career seekers in this case. Hence, this hypothesis is partially substantiated.

The seventh hypothesis states that 'the level of adequacy of information resources and services is significantly high'. The z- values show that the levels of adequacy of the majority of the resources/services are significantly high. Hence this hypothesis is fully substantiated.

The eighth hypothesis states 'there exists significant difference in the levels of adequacy of resources and services of different types of libraries'. The p-values show that significant difference exists among libraries in the case of the level of adequacy of most of the resources/services. Thus, this hypothesis is fully substantiated.

The ninth hypothesis states that 'the level of satisfaction of career seekers in the resources and services of libraries is significantly high'. The t- values show that the level of satisfaction of the career seekers in the resources and services of libraries is significantly high. Thus, this hypothesis is fully substantiated.

The tenth hypothesis states that 'there exists significant difference in the levels of satisfaction of different categories of career seekers'. The t-values indicate that significant difference exists among the career seekers using different types of libraries and between the male and the female career seekers in the levels of satisfaction. At the same time no significant difference exists between the graduate and the postgraduate career seekers and between the rural and the urban career seekers in the levels of satisfaction. Hence, this hypothesis is not fully substantiated.

13. IMPLICATIONS AND SUGGESTIONS

The analysis reveals that the level of requirement for information resources and services is high among the career seekers. This shows that the career seekers are eager to get various resources and services for their career seeking. The levels of requirement for the majority of the resources and services are not much different among the career seekers using different types of libraries. Between the male and the female career seekers also no much difference exists in the levels of requirement for most of the resources/services. Between the graduate and the postgraduate career seekers and between the rural and the urban career seekers no significant difference exists in the levels of requirement for half of the resources/ services taken for the study. This reveals that all categories of the career seekers highly require various resources and services which are helpful for their search for a career. This calls for the attention of the library administrators in the provision of career related information resources and services in libraries.

The availability level is high only in the case of half of the resources/services taken for the study. Hence, steps have to be taken to raise the level of availability of the resources/services which are not available to the required level by strengthening the collection and providing more services to meet the requirements of the career seekers.

On the availability side, university libraries are ahead of college and public libraries in majority of the resources and services taken for the study. This can be attributed to the strength of collection and services in university libraries. This points out that college and public libraries have to strengthen their resources and services targeted towards career seekers.

The level of use of information resources and services is high among the career seekers. This shows that career seekers are active library users.

When the levels of use of resources/services of the male and the female career seekers are compared, it can be observed that the levels of use of the majority of the cases are high among the female career seekers. The reason may be that the female career seekers are more keen in Kerala in getting a placement. The levels of use of the postgraduate career seekers are higher in majority of the cases as compared to the graduate career seekers. The reason may be that the postgraduate career seekers are more serious in the hunt for a career.

The adequacy rate of the majority of the resources/ services is high. However, some of the important resources/ services, career seekers require, are not adequate in libraries. Hence, steps have to be taken to ensure adequate provision of such resources/services especially career guidance, career planning guides, specific guides for each competitive examination, internet facility and personal assistance.

Poor physical maintenance of library materials, inaccurate and outdated information and scatter of resources are the major barriers of the career seekers in accessing information. Hence, steps have to be taken to reduce these barriers.

The analysis shows that the career seekers are satisfied in the resources and services of libraries. This shows that the libraries in Kerala are knowingly or unknowingly providing resources and services required by the career seekers. The high level of satisfaction of the career seekers using university libraries reveal that university libraries are providing more resources and services to career seekers.

The higher level of satisfaction of the female career

seekers over the male career seekers may be due to their high level of use.

14. SUGGESTIONS FOR FURTHER RESEARCH

The investigator wishes to suggest the following areas for further research to add to the quantum of knowledge in this area.

1. Study of the information seeking behaviour of the career seekers taking the sample of career seekers from those who attend coaching classes at different career guidance centres.
2. Evaluative study of libraries to understand the strength of collection and services needed for the career seekers.
3. Study on the impact of information on career choice.
4. Study on the marketing possibilities of career related information products/services.
5. Study among the employed persons on the role of libraries in providing information for acquiring a job.

REFERENCES

1. Martin, William J. (1995). *The global information society.* England: Aslib Grower.
2. Radhakrishnan, S. (1974). *The Bhagavad Gita: with an introductory essay, Sanskrit text, English translation and notes.* Bombay: Blackie, 172.
3. Lalitha, M. (1995). Information seeking behaviour of medical and engineering personnel: a comparative study with reference to their library use. *Library Science with a Slant to Documentation and Information Studies,* 32(2), 65-74.
4. Sridhar, M.S. (2002). *Library use and user research : with twenty case studies.* New Delhi: Concept.
5. Faruqui, Khalid Kamal. (Ed). (1997). *Development of collection in libraries.* New Delhi: Anmol.
6. Sridhar, M.S. (1990). *User research: a review of information behaviour studies in science and technology.* Bangalore: Biblio Infon Service.

7. Kawatra, P.S. (1992). *Library user studies : a manual for librarians and information scientists.* Mumbai: Jaico.
8. Lahiri, Ramansu. (1988). A study on the users of a university library. *IASLIC Bulletin,* 33(2/3), 81-91.
9. Voigt, Melvin. (1961). *Scientists' approaches to information.* New York: American Library Association.
10. Guha, B. (1983). *Documentation and information: services, techniques and systems* (2nd ed.). Calcutta : World Press.
11. Devarajan, G. (1995). *Library information users and use studies.* New Delhi: Beacon Books.
12. Garg, B. S. (2000). Information seeking patterns of users of engineering institutions in Rajastan. *Library Herald,* 37(4), 229-239.
13. Thomas, Brenda and Madigan, Chris. (1976). Unemployment and the unemployed-what types of people, what kind of problem?: a research note. *Journal of Management Studies,* 13(1), 76-83.
14. Radhakrishnan, S. (1974). *The Bhagavad Gita: with an introductory essay, Sanskrit text, English translation and notes.* Bombay: Blackie, 133.
15. Sharma, K.N. (1997). *Psychological bases of unemployment.* Jaipur: Print well.
16. Turner, Richard. (1979). Career information: a forgotten resource. *Assistant Librarian,* 72(7/8), 100-103.
17. Anderson, Byron. (1992). Delivering career and job information: a place for libraries. *Reference Librarian,* 36, 17-32.
18. Durrance, Joan C. et al. (1993). *Serving job seekers and career changers: a planning manual for public libraries: part of public library development program.* Chicago: American Library Association.
19. Sam, Joel. (1996). Adequacy of document collection and the satisfaction of information needs of agricultural policy makers and managers in Ghana. *International*

Information Communication and Education, 15(2), 176-185

20. Haravu, L.J. (1988). Marketing of library and information services. *IASLIC Bulletin,* 33(4), 139-147.
21. *Longman dictionary of contemporary English.* (1978). London: Longman, 574.
22. Ibid, 940.
23. Sridhar, M.S. (1990). *User research: a review of information behaviour studies in science and technology.* Bangalore: Biblio Infon Service,65.
24. *The Oxford English dictionary.* (1933). Oxford: Oxford University Press, 117.
25. Ibid, 390.
26. *The World Book dictionary.* (1981). Chicago: World Book Childcraft International, 1779.
27. *Longman dictionary of contemporary English.* (1978). London: Longman, 1016.
28. Harrod, Leonard Montague. (1971). *The librarians glossary of terms used in librarianship and the book craft and reference book* (3rd ed.). London: Andre Deutsch, 378.

5

Scientometric Analysis of the Research Productivity of University Teachers

— ***Dr. A. Gopikuttan***

1. INTRODUCTION

The whole World is today witnessing unprecedented developments especially in the field of science and technology. It is imperative for any country to evaluate its activity in science and take steps to direct it to the national objectives or development goals. "The basic research activities more or less accumulated in science and technology. The key to any effective improvement in higher education is the teacher, his vision, his motivation his determination, and his hard work. Systems, structures, syllabi, teaching methods, evaluation processes all have their value; but what counts in the enthusiasm of the teacher and his readiness to give of his best. The motivation that can give him such enthusiasm is not necessarily a function of his wages. Education can be reformed only through the efforts of the academic community, not by the politician."[1]

The reputation and credibility of a university is more or less based on the quality and quantity of new knowledge generated by it. The social role of University can be divided in to two. One is transmitting the accumulated knowledge to next generation; that is education. The second role is creating knowledge through research activity.

Teaching and research are the most important functions of a University. The achievement in the research fields takes a university the glorious positions. This is more true in the case of scientific research because it has become the life-breath of a progressive state. Science communication becomes more important in this context. The research output of the University needs to be effectively disseminated and distributed for its acceptance and timely application for social benefits. The research productivity of a University is usually indicated through the research publications that emanate from the various teaching and research departments. Scholarliness is revealed through many ways and academic publication is one of the major indicator to evaluate the scholarliness.

Harold Laski once observed that the true epochs in a University life are not marked by its building, its books or even the growth of its numbers they are marked by the great teachers it has possessed.[2]

The title of the present study is "Scientometric analysis of research productivity of faculty members in the science Departments of the University of Kerala". It deals with deals with the research output in terms of journal articles, conference papers, reports, books, chapter in books, produced by the teachers of science Departments, Faculty of Science, University of Kerala between 1980 and 1999 (twenty years) using scientometric techniques. There are ten Departments under faculty of science such as Aquatic biology, Biochemistry, Botany, Chemistry, Demography and population studies, Geology, Mathematics, Physics, Statistics and Zoology.

Scientometrics is a new branch of knowledge, which uses bibliometric measurements for the evaluation of scientrometric progress, level of scientific development, Social relevance and impact of the applications of science and technology. The term scientometrics is derived from the Russian term 'naukometrica' which means the study of the measurement of scientific and technological progress.[3]

Due to proliferation of knowledge and increasing tendency for research in the field of science and technology a number of scientific communications are being published in recent years. The availability of sophisticated computerised statistical software packages for data analysis has encouraged quantitative studies on information. The outcome of such efforts is the emergence of a new branch of science, whose prime emphasis is the application of the mathematical and statistical models and methods to study and measure the scientific communication. This science is being referenced to as scientometrics. It is devoted to quantitative studies of science and technology.

2. RELEVANCE OF THE STUDY

The University of Kerala has been placing great thrust on scientific research from its inception in 1937. In the preamble to the University act, special mention is made of the desirability for making greater and more systematic provision for the furtherance of original research in the various branched of applied sciences. The university has been adding new departments of science, both pure and applied, to cope with the tremendous development in the global scene of science and technology.

All these indicate that the research output of the University within the field of science and technology in remarkable. A quantitative analysis of the research output is most relevant in the present context.

3. OBJECTIVES OF THE STUDY

The study in intended to identify and determine the following with regard to the Scientific productivity of the teachers in the Science Departments of the University of Kerala.

1. To find out the relative contribution of scientific productivity in different science departments and the year-wise growth of literature.
2. To determine the authorship pattern in publication and identify the gender-wise distribution of publication
3. To identify the most productive journal selected by faculty members to publish the articles and their country-wise preferences.

4. To examine the faculty affiliation in publication.
5. To find out the individual research productivity and its characteristics
6. To examine the single authorship and principal authorship and their characteristics in publication.
7. To find out the characteristics of inter-publication difference with reference to research productivity in the following areas.
   a. Designation- wise difference.
   b. Gender-wise difference.
   c. Department -wise and time taken for the first publication and their characteristics.
8. To determine the most productive age group of the faculty members.
9. To find out the factors which influencing research productivity.

4. METHODOLOGY

The necessary bibliographic details were collected from the annual reports of the University of Kerala and created a database. Normal count procedure was followed. Full credit was given to each author (faculty member) regardless of who happens to be the first or the last name.

All forms of publications such as journal articles, conference papers, reports/working papers, Text books and chapter in books are analysed using scientometric techniques. The statistical tools such as SPSS and MS excel are used for data analysis.

5. HYPOTHESES

The following hypotheses are formulated.

1. Teachers from lab oriented Departments have more publications than non lab- oriented Department.
2. Female Teachers need more time to bring out research publication than male teachers.

3. There is a significant association between age and productivity
4. Multiple authorship is a common phenomenon in scientific publication.

6. LIMITATIONS

The data for the study is solely collected from the annual reports of Kerala University from 1980-1999 (20 years). Different forms of publications such as journal articles, conference papers, Books, chapters in book, Report/working papers etc. were considered for ranking the scientist. Further analysis is made only on the basis of the journal articles produced, since articles in scholarly journals are frequently considered to be the tangible end result of research activities.

7. FINDINGS AND CONCLUSIONS

The analysis revealed a number of fruitful findings in the area of research productivity of faculty members of the Science Departments in the University of Kerala. The major findings that have evolved from the discussions are summed up here under various heads.

Major forms of literature

A total number of 2500 items are identified under five categories of forms of publication produced by faculty members. Of this journal articles are the main vehicle of information transfer of faculty members, which accounts 1542 (61.68%), followed by conference papers 788 (31.52%) .Chapter in books are in the third position with122 (4.88%) items. Reports are 40 (1.6%) in number and text books are only 8 (0.32 %)

Department-wise distribution of research productivity

a. Conference papers

In the case of, conference papers Department of Zoology is in the first place by contributing a total of 158 (20.05 %) items. Out of which 29 (21.97%) papers are presented in International conferences. The second position goes to Department of Botany by producing 94 (11.93 %) papers. Out of which 12 (9.09%) papers are presented in International Conferences. The third position goes to Department of Statistics by contributing 92 (11.04%) papers out of which 12 (9.09%) papers are presented in International conferences.

b. Journal articles

In the contribution of journal articles, first position goes to Faculty members in Physics Department by producing 306 (19.94 %) articles .second position goes to Biochemistry Department by producing 288 (18.68%) articles of which 275 (20.93 %) articles are published in International Journals. The third position goes to Aquatic Biology by producing 258 (16.73%) articles out of which 190(14.46%) articles are published in International journals. It is seen that lab-oriented Departments have more publications, where as non-lab oriented Departments such as Statistics, Demography, Mathematics and Geology have less number of publication.

c. Reports

In the contribution of reports, Demography Department is placed in the first position by producing 29 (72.50%) reports .Geology Department produced 4 (10 %) reports and Botany and Aquatic biology produced 3 reports each during the period under study.

d. Text Books

Department of Aquatic Biology produced 3 text books (37.5%), Demography produced 2 (25%) books and Biochemistry, Botany and Zoology contributed 1 (12.5 %) book each.

e. Chapter in Books

In the case of chapter in books Zoology is in the first place by producing 24 (19.57%) items. Aquatic Biology is in the second position by producing 23 (18.85 %) items and Physics is in the third position by producing 22 (18.03 %) items.

Year-wise distribution of research productivity

The year 1989 has the highest number of conference papers, i.e. 65 papers (8.25 %). In the case of Journal articles 1981 recorded the highest number-138 (8.95 %). Reports are high in the year 1998. The year 1986 and 1990 share the top position in the category of text books. Contribution to chapter in books is in the top during the year 1990 and 98 (12)

A uniform growth or decline is not seen in the publication pattern of Faculty members during the period under study.

Authorship pattern

Two authors i.e. 55.77 % make majority of the contribution. It is followed by three authors contribution i.e. 22.89 %. Single author contribution is only 12.26 percent .

It seems that collaboration research is common in science. The reason for having more publication with two authored papers may be due to the fact that it may be an ideal combination in preparing the paper by the researcher and the supervisor.

a. Department-wise analysis of authorship pattern

Department -wise analysis of authorship pattern shows that two -authored papers are more in most of the departments. But, in the Department of Statistics 71.93 % of articles are contributed by single authors.

Gender-wise distribution of publication

In the case of Journal articles, significant difference is seen only in 1981,1982,1983,1984 and 1994 (5 years). In the case of contribution in regional journal there is no difference seen between Male and Female. In the case of conference papers, difference is seen only in the case of National Seminar. Significance difference is not seen in the cases of chapters in books, since the number of Research Reports and Text Books are less in number significance level is not tested.

Country-wise distribution of source journal

Out of 1542 articles, 964 (62.52 %) items are published in 169 Indian journals. The second position with182 (11.80 %) articles are published in 79 journals of US origin. The third position goes to UK with 153 (9.92 %) articles published in 54 journals.

Preference of journals for research reporting

Out of 408 journals, Proceeding of Indian Academy of Science has got top position with 73 (4.73 %) articles. Indian Journal of Chemistry scored the second position with 65 (4.21 5) articles and Indian Journal of Biochemistry and Biophysics scored the third position with 61 (3.95 %) articles each.

The Department preference shows that each Department has their own preference and there is no uniformity in selecting the journal for research reporting.

Faculty affiliation in publication

It is seen that only 171 (11.09%) articles have faculty co operation in producing the research papers. And also seen that the Department of Aquatic Biology is in the top in the case of Faculty co-operation. Department of Demography, Statistics and Mathematics have not produced even a single paper in this category.

Single authorship

a. Gender -wise analysis of single authored items.

Out of 189 single authored articles 167 (88.36 %) articles are contributed by male members and 22 (11.64%) articles are contributed by female members.

b. Department -wise analysis of single authorship

Department-wise analysis of single authored articles shows that Department of Statistics is in the first position with 41 (21.69 %) articles. Second and third position goes to Zoology and Physics with 32 (16.93%) and 29 (15.34%) articles respectively. Single authored items are very few in the Department of Biochemistry (5) Chemistry (10) and Mathematics (11)

Principal authorship

Out of the 1542 journal articles contributed by faculty members are found as principle authors only in 432 (28%) items. Department of aquatic biology is in the top position by producing 67 (15.5 %) articles in this category. The second position goes to the Department of Botany by producing 59

(13.66 %) articles and the third position goes to the Department of Physics with 57 (13.19 %) articles.

Professors contributed 194 (44.91 %) articles as principle authorship while Readers and Lecturers contributed 137 (31.71%) and 101 (23.38%) articles respectively. 377 (87.26 %) articles are contributed by male faculty members and 55 (12.73 %) articles are contributed by female members.

Productivity and time interval

This analysis is intended to know the time requirements of faculty members to bring out journal articles and its variations based on designation, gender difference and departments. Out of 1710 authorship, professors found in 973 (56.90 %) items, Readers found in 467 (27.31%) items and lecturers found in 270 (15.79 %) items.

a. Time interval by position

Mean year taken to bring out one article by a Lecturer is 0.915, Reader is 0.906 and Professor is 0.471.

A Professor may have more publications because; probably he will be in the author field in all publications by the scholar under his guidance. More over, the experience and knowledge gained by a professor may help to publish more.

b. Gender-wise analysis of time interval

The mean year taken by a male member, for the publication of an article is 0.607 where as a female member needs 0.944 mean year. The t test shows that there is a significant difference at 1 % level between a male faculty member and female faculty member. In the category of Lecturers a male member need 0.688 mean years and a female member need 1.631 mean years to bring out one publication. In the category of Readers the difference is male -0831 and female 1.369. But in the case of Professors a male member need only 0.480 mean years and a female member need 0.416 mean year to publish one article. Except in the category of Professors, there is a significant difference between male and female faculty members to bring out publication.

c. Time taken for the first publication after joining the University system

A Lecturer needs 2.222 mean years, A Reader needs only 1.771 mean years and a Professor needs only 0.708 mean years to bring out the first publication after joining the service. The t-test shows that there is a significant variation between these three categories. Professor is entirely different from the other categories of teachers who need only little time for the publication of the first article. This may be because of the experience he/she earned through the service and research guidance.

d. Gender-wise analysis for the first publication after joining the University service.

A male Lecturer working in the Science Department need 1.793 mean years for the publication of the first article whereas a female Lecturer need 3.00 years for the publication of the first article.

A male Reader need 1.750 mean years and a female Reader need 2.000 mean years to bring out the first publication.

e. Department -wise analysis of time interval for the Publication

Mathematics, Demography and Geology need 3.045, 3.143 and 1.911 mean years respectively, where as Physics and Biochemistry Departments need only 0.430 and 0.433 mean years respectively. Aquatic Biology need only 0.561 mean year for the publication of an article.There is a significant variation at 1 percentage level and it is seen that the lab oriented Departments such as Physics, Biochemistry, Aquatic Biology and Chemistry need less time to bring out one Publication than non lab oriented Departments such a Demography, Mathematics and Geology.

The Departments where theoretical nature of work is more naturally produce less number of papers than experimental nature of work like Departments of Physics, Chemistry, Bio-chemistry, Zoology, and Botany.

The position -wise analysis of publication shows that those who are working in a higher position need lesser time to bring out an article than lower level. How ever F test indicates that the significant variation is seen only in the Department of Physics, Botany, Biochemistry, and Aquatic Biology. The mean interval in the publication between two articles is much higher in the case of the Department of Demography and Mathematics. It is also seen that the female members need more time than the male members.

Age and productivity

Many studies are available using age as a factor, but conflicting results. Bland and Berquist (1997)[4] report that "the average productivity of faculty seems to drop with age, how ever, many senior faculty members remain quite active in research activities and their products are comparable those of younger faculty members." Einstein was twenty six when he worked out his special theory of relativity, and Darwin was twenty nine when he developed his theory of natural selection. The amount of important scientific research done by young scientist leads many scientists to believe that age is negatively correlated with scientific creativity and research productivity".[5]

In the present study the age group of faculty members up to 40 is the most productive group. This age group has an average productivity of 7.85 articles. The age group of 51-55 is in the second position with an average of 7.87 articles. The age group of 46-50 is the least productive group. i.e. an average of 5.17 articles. It seems that the initial enthusiasm in research productivity is not seen in the last years. Up to 40 may be the period of research work carried out by the faculty members leading to PhD .Early 50s may be a period of higher post with a supervisory capacity can produce more. After late 50s a senior professor may not able to concentrate on his research work due to administrative responsibilities.

Factors of productivity

The impact of variable such as sex, age, service and position to productivity was analyzed. It is seen that the above variables have only 4.6 % of influence in productivity. The selected variables have more influence on publication pattern of non lab oriented departments such as Geology, Demography and Mathematics. In lab oriented departments the influencing factors for research productivity may be the infrastructural facilities of the laboratory, library and funding etc.

8. SUGGESTIONS

The findings of the study may be useful to the University administrators and service level academician to formulate appropriate policies and strategies to improve research activities so as to achieve the objectives of the University. A few suggestions are given here which would be helpful to improve the mitigating research activities in the University system.

1. To formulate a research policy at the University level.
2. Specific steps to be taken for the enhancement of the research productivity of female faculty members, as a social measure since they need more time to bring out publication.
3. Facilities to be enhanced to undertaken major projects and to avoid unwanted administrative delays.
4. The tested variables such as age , sex, service ,designation have only 4.6 % of influence in productivity, especially in the lab oriented Departments. The major influence to productivity may be laboratory and library facilities for research publication. Hence it is necessary to enhance the laboratory and library facilities to improve research productivity.
5. The productivity rate is much higher in experimental research areas of the University Departments. New areas of such division to be identified and more facilities to be provided to such areas to promote research activities. The interdisciplinary research is a common nature of present day research. Hence a separate division is needed to formulate policies and strategies of research allocation at University level.

6. It is seen that there is no follow up after the publication of research findings. Hence a separate division of technology transfer is needed to co-ordinate further steps and develop liaison with industrial and commercial organization, so that it will encourage the faculty members to concentrate more in research activities.

9. CONCLUSIONS

The analysis has given a clear picture of the total Research productivity of teachers, during the period under study. Research productivity has been accepted as the most highly valued aspects of a faculty member's career, especially when University promotion, faculty evaluation and University goals are considered. The Science Departments of University of Kerala, vary considerably in respect to quantity of research and publication pattern. The study demonstrates that productivity has been linked to various factors such as age, position, service, sex and Department. It is expected that the study will be one of the driving forces that encourages faculty to publish profusely. It is found that scientific talent is highly concentrated in a limited number of individuals and most of the publication productivity is concentrated around the departments of Physics, Biochemistry, Aquatic Biology, Chemistry and Zoology.

REFERENCES

1. Chandy,P.T. (1983) Higher Education in Kerala. Ed.by. Alexander.P.G.Trivandrum, Juhanin Mar Thoma Study Centre . P.93.
2. Dongerkery,S.R.(1957) Quoted in "A history of University of Bombay (1857-1957)" University of Bombay. p.192.
3. Egge, Leoand Rousseau, Ronald (1990) Introduction to informetrics: quantitative methods in library, documentation and information science. Amsterdam, Elsevier.p2
4. Bland, C and Berquist W. (1997) The vitality of senior faculty members, snow on the roof- fire in the furnace (ERIC Document Reproduction No.ED 415733).

5. Levin, Sharon G and Stephen, Paula E (1991). Research productivity over the life Cycle: Evidence for Academic sScientists. The American Economic review, 81.p. 114-32.

6
Organisation, Administration and Utilization of DRDO Libraries

— Dr. M. Santhakumari

1. INTRODUCTION

India, ever since her independence in 1947, has been adopting a policy of relentless pursuit of self-reliance in all fields. With her metamorphosis as a new politically independent nation, conscious efforts were made to enhance and modernize the scientific infrastructure of the country by establishing a series of National Laboratories, Institutes of Advanced Technical Education, Universities and Research and Development (R&D) Institutions, covering all disciplines. As a result of these pragmatic policies and systematic exploitation of science and technology for socio-economic development, India has, today, successfully transformed herself from a largely agrarian society with virtually no industry at the time of independence to a highly industrialized one and from a food-starving country to a food-surplus nation.

World is in transition from the industrial age to the information age. The driving force behind this transformation is the tremendous growth in the output of literature due to R&D activities in all fields of human knowledge and the rapid development and diffusion of Information Technology (IT). Innovations in computer, microelectronics and communication technologies referred to as IT, has provided new dimensions to the handling and processing of information, which has brought information at global level, to the finger tips of users. The development in any field depends upon the adequate availability of relevant information. The output of scientific and technical literature is so high that no individual can go through all publications that may be relevant to him. This calls for an effective system for information transfer. Today, the state of perfection of any information system is determined by its capability to sort out the precise information that exactly suits the requirement of the user, from the entire ocean of information. The higher the quality of information accessed, the better the quality of the findings arrived at and decisions and policies made.

India is one of the leading countries in the field of basic research and her success in technology development in every field has been very significant. In pursuit of self-reliance in critical technologies relevant to national security, the Defence Research and Development Organisation (DRDO) of the Ministry of Defence (MoD) formulates and executes programmes of scientific as well as applied research in design, development, testing and evaluation of various systems, subsystems, devices and products required for the armed forces of the country. The defence R&D is multidisciplinary and interdisciplinary in nature. The DRDO with its large number of laboratories is engaged in scientific and technological research for end products necessary for defending the nation with its team of dedicated scientists and engineers.

The defence R&D has grown to embrace an ever-widening area. The defence science sector in India comprises of the research laboratories under DRDO, the Public Sector Undertakings of Government of India, the Defence Production Units under the Ministry of Defence Production, and other institutions under MoD. It differs only with regard to its limited clientele and restricted accessibility. There is also difference in the working environment where most of the research work is being conducted under the veil of secrecy and access to processed information is restricted due to security constraints. Surprise and secrecy are key elements in defence strategy. Protection of information about self and obtaining all possible information about enemy are vital for the success of every defence endeavour. Today it is not only the knowledge about immediate adversaries, knowledge about their direct and indirect allies is also equally important. The knowledge about ones own strength and weakness is as vital as the knowledge about the adversary. Those having better knowledge than their opponents succeed in their effort.

There is no difference of opinion regarding the importance of Science and Technology (S&T) information for defence. According to Sahi[1], over a period of time no information can be termed relatively modern, if it does not undergo a constant process of upgrading. Scientific information is of vital importance to a defence planner for acquiring knowledge about the latest developments to sharpen one's own arsenal and to deny information of such scientific development to hostile nations by adopting scientific counter intelligence methods. It is also necessary to obtain maximum possible know-how about scientific application of information of defence interest available with the adversaries to carry out research and development to devise means to offset the enemy's capabilities with the least possible loss of time.

Scientific information is the basic raw material for defence R&D activity. This would call for the establishment of a strong scientific base where data can be collected, evaluated, and supplied to the planners at the helm of defence matters as well as defence scientists. The R&D activities of DRDO cover important demarcated disciplines like aeronautics, missiles, electronics and instrumentation, combat vehicles, engineering system sciences, advanced computing, life sciences including high-altitude agriculture, physiology, food technology, nuclear medicines and allied sciences. Modern electronics and precision instrumentation are the eyes and ears of the defence system. Digital Signal Processing and advanced antenna techniques are essential elements on which the sophistication of the future radar would depend. The DRDO renders technical advice regarding formation requirements, evaluation of systems to be acquired, fire and explosive safety and mathematical/ statistical analysis of operational problems. The ambit of defence research is truly wide and highly specialised. Not only does it include the development of sophisticated weapon systems that must perform satisfactorily in the gruelling environment of the desert, snow, seas, etc. but also encompass modelling and simulation studies of operational problems, investigation of the psychological needs and physiological phenomena at high altitudes or at high speeds and a host of other analyses. Success in warfare is determined not by machines alone but also by the physical and mental efficiency of the men working under stress. To achieve the best results from the man-machine combination, extensive research is needed on all aspects of health too. The complexity of modern warfare in both methods and means demands correct analysis of the measures and counter-measures introduced at every stage. For this purpose, constant flow of scientific information on warfare is extremely essential. Latest information on new weapons, war materials, and battle tactics is necessary to gain self-confidence in fighting the adversary. With data available on the results of recent wars it becomes possible to study the operations in a qualitative and quantitative manner. Scientific analysis of the information regarding the performance of various weapons will indicate the advantages or deficiencies of those equipments and weapons and the tactics involved.

An effective Information System (IS) is indispensable since this sensitive area of defence relies on timely and reliable information for its efficient functioning. This responsibility is being thrust upon the information centres to function efficiently as active providers of up to date information to scientists for their R&D work. The Technical Information Centre (TIC) / DRDO library attached to the laboratories is the fountainhead around which all R&D activities in a DRDO laboratory revolve.

The TICs, established to serve the information needs of

the different R&D units, require to be coordinated and organised into an integrated system following uniform national and international standards to avoid or minimise wastage of resources through uncertainty and unintended reinvention, rediscovery, redevelopment and unfruitful decisions. The R&D work in the current era of high technology, calls for a highly efficient, effective and comprehensive information system network. The DRDO Information System is organised in the form of a number of libraries / TICs with Defence Scientific Information & Documentation Centre (DESIDOC) as the central coordinating agency. Each DRDO laboratory has a specific area of specialisation in defence research and has a well-organised and dedicated TIC to cater to the specific information requirements of the dependent scientists. The scientists of these laboratories simultaneously undertake various developmental projects in the respective fields of specialization. Bandyopadhyay[2] describes information requirements of the distinct phases of a complex project where concrete information is needed as follows:

1. **Preliminary project formulation** : In this phase, broad objectives are translated into preliminary practical alternative. For this pre-project study, the scientists require general information about the project. At this formulation stage they need review articles and state-of-the-art reports regarding the project. Any information of similar type of work conducted elsewhere is helpful to the scientists.

2. **Feasibility study and report** : Detailed information is needed in this stage. All the alternatives have to be studied and the basis of selecting the proposed one should be given. Exhaustive information is necessary for better reporting.

3. **Detailed project report** : The report contains (a) the general description analysing the environment to which the project belongs, (b) project descriptions giving analysis of alternatives and detailed description of the accepted one, (c) technological aspects covering

technology / process to be used and availability of know-how, (d) financial aspect stating the estimated cost including the foreign exchange, (e) manpower requirement, and (f) system plan. Detailed and extensive information covering all the aspects of the project is necessary at this stage.

4. **Progress of project work** : The progress is reported periodically. At this stage the scientists require specific information and data about the project.

5. **Final stage** : After completion of the project work, the research product, undergoes user trials. After successful trials the design characteristics are finalised and this information is sent for use in connection with production. Relatively less information is required at the final stage in comparison to the earlier stages. The scientists generate certain amount of data at all these stages. These are to be verified with available similar data. The information supplied has to be very specific and correct.

The prime function of the TICs, which are considered to be the reservoirs of knowledge and information, is to provide precise, reliable, and relevant information to the defence scientists without any loss of time, in a form most convenient for utilisation. The traditional tools and techniques have proved inadequate and slow to harness the information deluge. The availability of, or the access to a piece of valid information is all the more important rather than the ownership of documents. The information explosion has necessitated the TICs to act as an able link and bridge the gap between the producers of information and the seekers of information, with the aid of a highly capable information infrastructure.

2. THE RESEARCH PROBLEM

Any information system, to ascertain its potential fully and to identify the deficiencies if any, must undergo objective assessment of the present methods of handling information. A comprehensive investigation of the prevailing practices and situations is required. Therefore, it is imperative to study the availability of resources and the provision of facilities to assess how far the system is able to fulfill the objectives for which it has been established. The utilisation of the resources and facilities also should be examined to ascertain the requirements and expectations of the users.

The review of the research studies conducted so far on defence libraries reveals that a comprehensive study on DRDO libraries has not been attempted as yet. Hence it was decided that a survey to study the collection, organisation, administration and utilisation of the DRDO libraries / TICs attached to the DRDO laboratories be conducted.

The research work undertaken is titled "**Organisation, Administration and Utilisation of DRDO Libraries**"

3. RELEVANCE OF THE STUDY

Each DRDO laboratory has a unique area of specialisation in defence research and has a well-organised TIC, attached to it to cater to the information needs of its scientist community engaged in defence R&D activities. In every organisation a smooth and systematic flow of information is necessary and in its absence the organisation suffers through delayed decisions or decisions based on insufficient information. There is a definite need for an efficient database of information with a modular structure, having capability to integrate, disintegrate, and re-integrate according to the search needs, for achieving a purposeful information service. An up-to-date and efficient TIC is an amalgam of three basic elements namely - collection, organisation and dissemination of information. The collection must be built up keeping in view the aims and objectives of the organisation, the short range and long range information needs of the scientists, and the on-going and anticipated R&D activities of the organisation.

The information requirements of the clientele should be clearly understood by the information scientists and their interest profile should be kept up to date on the basis of which the library collection should be developed. Once a balanced information collection is built up, it must be processed and organised in an efficient manner. The concept of information dissemination is the foundation upon which an IS is built, and it is here that the effectiveness of collection building and organisation is translated into a reality. However good a collection may be, whatever means of processing might have been used, an information centre will not receive persistent support, if it is not equipped for effective dissemination of information.

The collection, organisation and dissemination of information are activities coordinated as well as balanced by administration. It provides the system the required management, leadership and direction. It supports the system by enabling to take decisions, fixing responsibilities of individuals and coordinates the joint efforts of all to achieve a common goal. It brings in order all the available means at its disposal to meet the desired ends for which the information centre exists. An efficient information scientist who runs the administration keeps the working of the information centre in tune with the organisational objectives.

This study which is intended to provide an in-depth analysis of the organisation, administration and utilisation of DRDO libraries endeavours to highlight the variations in the procedures adopted by the different DRDO libraries and identify the strengths and weaknesses in their organisational set up and administrative machinery. The study will have practical utility as it surveys the prevailing conditions with regard to their organisational and administrative set up, financial allocation and management, library resources and services and physical infrastructure. The study also aims at collecting opinions of the scientists regarding the documentary sources and the information services provided by the DRDO libraries, the analysis of which will enable to have a better understanding of the demands and expectations of the defence scientists. It will also analyse whether the resources and facilities of these libraries are responsive to the needs of the scientists and to find out how far the scientists are utilising the resources and services for productive output. None of the previous studies in India attempted to find out the variations and similarities existing among the different grades of defence scientists in their frequency of library use, purpose of visiting the library and the utilization of the resources and services. The study also examines the adequacy / inadequacy of staff, the major resources and services and the physical facilities of the DRDO libraries surveyed. The study will also help to understand the problems faced by the scientists with regard to the library facilities and of the library staff in their routine work and suggest effective measures to rectify them so as to provide better, smooth and efficient services. In addition, the findings will also enable to identify more areas for further research.

4. OPERATIONAL DEFINITIONS

The operational definitions of the key terms in the title of the study are:

Administration: Administration conveys the idea of group cooperation under executive direction, seeking fulfilment of goals through planning and organisation. It refers to the use of personnel and materials in the fulfilment of the objectives of the organisation.

DRDO Libraries: DRDO is the abbreviated version of "Defence Research and Development Organisation", under the Ministry of Defence. DRDO operates through a network of laboratories established throughout the country and is engaged in pursuit of self-reliance in defence technologies relevant to national security. Libraries attached to the laboratories to cater to the information requirements of the scientists engaged in R&D activities in the laboratories are the DRDO libraries. They fall under the category of special libraries.

Organisation: Organisation is a systematic arrangement for a definite purpose. It is the arrangement of personnel for facilitating the accomplishment of some agreed purpose through the allocation of functions and responsibilities. It is the relating of efforts and capacities of individuals and groups engaged upon a common task in such a way as to secure the desired objective with the least friction and the most satisfaction to those for whom the task is done and those engaged in the enterprise.

Special Library: A special library is one with the responsibility of building up a collection of specific documents and other materials that caters to the needs of the specific user community of the library. The services of these libraries lay emphasis on the dissemination of nascent micro thought to the specialist users of the library pin pointedly, exhaustively and expeditiously. Special libraries include libraries of science and technologies such as that of DRDO libraries that are distinguished from other libraries by some special characteristics like limitation of subject, special patronage and the smallness of collection, staff, clientele, etc.

Utilisation: Library utilisation means well-planned and deliberate attempt to make use of the library resources and facilities. It includes visits to the libraries, time spent in the libraries, documents consulted and borrowed, using the various information services offered by the library, etc.

5. OBJECTIVES

The present study was undertaken with the following objectives:

1. to examine the existing organisational and administrative set up of the DRDO libraries,
2. to assess the adequacy of the resources - materials, finance, and manpower of the DRDO libraries,
3. to assess the adequacy of different services offered by the DRDO libraries,
4. to evaluate the degree of utilisation of the resources and services of the DRDO libraries, and
5. to examine the existing infrastructure within the libraries.

6. HYPOTHESES

The study formulated the following hypotheses:

1. The existing resources in the DRDO libraries are

inadequate to meet the information needs of the scientists.

2. The services of the DRDO libraries are not satisfactory.
3. The physical infrastructure available in DRDO libraries is not adequate.

7. SCOPE AND LIMITATION OF THE STUDY

The present study endeavours to cover all the DRDO libraries of the country. Out of the fifty-two DRDO laboratories eleven do not have a library of their own. They are either field laboratories or are dependent on the rich nearby DRDO library. In addition, DESIDOC being the apex body is not included in the scope of the study. The remaining forty libraries spread across the country are included in the purview of this research study.

The user survey of the defence scientists, to study the information requirements and the utilisation of the resources and services of the DRDO libraries has been conducted only amongst the DRDO libraries in the State of Karnataka. The user survey is confined to scientists grade 'B' to 'G' only, and omits scientists 'H', Distinguished Scientists and other categories of users like technical officers, technical assistants, technicians, etc.

8. MEANS AND METHODS

The nature of the present study required the survey of various DRDO libraries, which are scattered through out the country. Data were to be collected from these libraries to examine the prevailing situations in them. A survey of library is widely recognised as the best procedure for the evaluation of its organisation, administration, and resources and services. According to Harrods's[3] glossary "Survey is an account of some research examination, or enquiry which has been done by scientific or organised method". It is one among the systematic methods of data collection, which involves questioning individuals on a topic or topics and describing their responses. With the help of a survey not only the past and the present conditions can be identified, but also the future requirements. The utility of the survey method has been pointed out by many social scientists. According to Moser[4], "Surveys have their usefulness both in leading to the formulation of hypothesis and at a more advanced stage in putting them to the test. Their function in a given research depends on how much is already known about the subject and on the purpose for which the information is required"

Sadhu and Singh[5] pointed out that "this type of research has the advantage of greater scope in the sense that a large volume of information can be controlled from a very large population. Survey research, no doubt, is more expensive but the amount and quality of information that is collected makes such investigation very economical. This information is also accurate, of course, within the range of sampling errors because trained and technically knowledgeable personnel are employed for the job". Taking into consideration the advantages and feasibility of the method, survey was decided as most appropriate for the present research study.

The study covers two major areas:

* Survey of the DRDO libraries and
* Study of the utilization of the resources and services of the DRDO libraries by the defence scientists engaged in research activities.

Methodology of the study is discussed under the following heads:

Data Collection

Survey method allows researchers to study larger groups more easily. In almost all cases it is not possible to survey the entire population. For the resuits to be meaningful, a representative group should participate in the study so that the findings can be generalised. The present study deals with the population of DRDO libraries and the population of the defence scientists.

All the forty DRDO libraries were approached for the required data to study their organisational and administrative set up. Out of the forty, only twenty-six libraries responded. Eight libraries out of the ten (80%) located in North India and eighteen libraries out of the thirty (60%) located in South India are represented in the study. Among the fourteen States and one field unit where the forty DRDO libraries are scattered, nine States are represented. Similarly libraries from all age groups and the various areas of specialisation except naval research and development have representation in the study.

The user questionnaires were sent to all the twenty-six libraries that responded to the librarians' questionnaire. Since the response was very poor even after repeated reminders the user survey was limited to the State of Karnataka only, and taken as a case study to examine the utilization of the resources and services of the DRDO libraries by the defence scientists. Within the chosen State all the ten DRDO libraries were included in the survey.

Sampling

According to Young[6] "case study is a comprehensive study of a social unit, be it a unit, a person, a group, a social institution, a district or community." For the user study of this research work, the DRDO libraries in Karnataka were selected, the results of which can be applied to other DRDO libraries also. The State of Karnataka has the maximum number (10) of DRDO libraries in a State, out of the total of forty libraries, which amounts to 25% of the total libraries and 38.46% of the twenty-six libraries under study. Hence, only the libraries located in Karnataka were taken as sample for the user study. It is also pertinent to note that for the scientist community of the DRDO laboratories, the geographical location is not a concern since they are transferable within the DRDO set up. Amongst the ten libraries the scientist group is quite large and hence a representative group had to be selected as sample for the study.

The details of the strength of scientists of various categories were obtained from the Seniority Roll of Scientists as on July 2000, published by DRDO Headquarters, New Delhi. The scientist population under study belonged to six different grades viz, 'B', 'C', 'D', 'E', 'F' and 'G'. In order to ensure that all the grades are fairly represented in the survey, proportionate stratified random sampling was considered as the most suitable technique. Accordingly the names of all 976 scientists from all laboratories in Karnataka were fed into the computer for proportionate stratified random sampling, keeping a target of 35% from each category from the overall list. The computer generated a list of 342 scientists. This list had to be rehashed a couple of times to generate fresh random sample list to cater for individuals who were away on other projects / long courses / long leave and those who retired / posted out / resigned. The researcher could collect 322 responses.

Table 1.1 gives the grade wise break up of the sample of the scientist population. For the convenience of analysis of data, the grades of scientists have been clubbed to form the Junior Scientists (JS) comprising of Scientists 'B' & 'C', Senior Scientists (SS) comprising of Scientists 'D' & 'E' and Eminent Scientists (ES) comprising of Scientists 'F' & 'G' categories.

Table 1.1. Category wise break up of the sample of scientists

Category	*Junior Scientists*	*Senior Scientists*	*Eminent Scientists*	*Total*		
Designation	Sc B	Sc C	Sc D	Sc E	Sc F	Sc G
Number	74	70	78	61	30	9
Total	144	139	39	322		
(Percentage)	(44.72%)	(43.17%)	(12.11%)	(100%)		

It can be observed from table 1.1 that the sample consists of 144 JS, 139 SS, and 39 ES. Out of the total of 322 sample scientists, Junior and Senior Scientists constitute 44.72% and 43.17% respectively, whereas Eminent Scientists constitute the remaining 12.11%.

Tools

As the information required included a great deal of qualitative and quantitative data it was decided to use the questionnaire as the most suitable research tool for data collection. A properly designed questionnaire is capable of extracting valuable and highly revealing data. The interview method could not be adopted as a tool because being defence research organisations it was difficult to get easy access to these organisations to conduct interviews. Hence, the only tools found useful for the present research work was questionnaire and personal observation. Two types of questionnaires were used for data collection.

Questionnaire I

Questionnaire administered to the personnel in-charge of the libraries of the DRDO laboratories was designed to extract maximum information on the organisation, administration and resources & services of the DRDO libraries. This questionnaire consists of thirteen parts as follows (Appendix-1):

1. General profile of the library
2. Infrastructure facilities of the library
3. Library Committee
4. Library budget and financial requirements
5. Selection and acquisition
6. Library collection
7. Technical organisation and maintenance
8. Library and information services
9. Computer applications
10. Manpower
11. Equipments
12. Auditing
13. Other information

Questionnaire II

Questionnaire administered to the defence scientists of the various DRDO laboratories in the State of Karnataka was structured to obtain information on the utilisation of the DRDO libraries. This questionnaire consists of five parts as follows (Appendix - 2):

1. Personal data of scientists
2. Library visits and use
3. Library resources and services
4. Library orientation
5. Suggestions

Personal Observation

All the DRDO libraries situated in Karnataka and a few others were visited personally to understand the existing organizational & administrative set up and to examine the infrastructure within the libraries. These visits also provided opportunity for discussions with the library professionals and scientists on the prevailing practices and conditions of the library.

Survey

Questionnaire I was administered to all the forty librarians through the Director of the laboratory, requesting permission to seek information from the librarians to collect data on the existing conditions of the DRDO libraries. Twenty-six librarians responded to the questionnaire, which amounts to 65% response.

Questionnaire II was administered to the 342 user scientists selected as per proportionate stratified random sampling, to study the degree of utilization of the library resources and facilities by the scientists. Questionnaires were distributed personally as far as possible and through the librarian. Scientists were very cooperative and the researcher could collect 94% response.

Method of Analysis

The data collected from the librarians were analysed manually while that from users were analysed with the aid of a computer. The data collected through questionnaires were supplemented with information obtained through observations and discussions with the librarian and staff of certain libraries. The collected data were analysed in view of the objectives. Simple statistical techniques such as percentages, mean score, chi-square test, t-test and one-way ANOVA tests were used for the analysis of data wherever applicable. Suitable tables and charts were also developed to facilitate interpretation of data.

9. ORGANISATION OF THE REPORT

The study is organized under the following chapters viz:

Chapter 1. Introduction:

This chapter presents the background, research problem, relevance, operational definitions of key terms, objectives, hypotheses, scope and limitations of the study and the methodology adopted in this study.

Chapter 2. Review of literature:

Related literature of previous studies conducted in India and abroad on the subject is reviewed in this section.

Chapter 3. Evolution of DRDO and its libraries:

This chapter broadly traces the origin and evolution of DRDO and its significant achievements. It outlays the role and importance of the libraries attached to the DRDO laboratories, the hierarchical organization of DESIDOC, etc.

Chapter 4. Institutional infrastructure:

A brief description of the profile of the laboratories, their areas of specialisation and some of their major achievements has been covered in this chapter. The important collections and services of the libraries attached to the laboratories have also been dealt with.

Chapter 5. Organization and administration of DRDO Libraries:

This chapter presents the analysis of the data collected from the librarians regarding the organization, administration, resources and services of DRDO libraries.

Chapter 6. Information requirements of defence scientists and the utilisation of DRDO libraries:

The analytical study of the data collected from the defence scientists for ascertaining their information requirements and the utilization of DRDO libraries is presented in this chapter.

Chapter 7. Findings and suggestions:

This chapter presents the results of the survey, suggestions and further areas for research.

10. FINDINGS AND SUGGESTIONS

The survey of DRDO libraries had revealed that no comprehensive attempt had been made earlier to study and evaluate the organisation, administration and utilization of resources and services of DRDO libraries. This survey, designed and executed as a descriptive and evaluative study of these aspects, analysed the data collected from the responses of the librarians of DRDO libraries and the user scientists working in the various DRDO laboratories, through the questionnaires sent to them. The analysis of the responses of the twenty-six librarians provided details of the organizational set up and administrative procedures of these libraries, while the analysis of the responses from the three hundred and twenty two user scientists provided details regarding their utilization of resources and services of DRDO libraries. The survey helped to identify the strengths and weaknesses of these libraries. It also revealed the views of the scientists regarding the various procedures followed in the libraries and pointed out wherever improvement is necessary. The information requirements of the scientists were also examined. the three categories of scientists namely the junior scientists, senior scientists and eminent scientists, selected by proportionate stratified random sampling, formed the sample of this study. Statistical tools were applied to study the difference among the three categories of scientists in utilizing the various resources and services of the library. The results were then subjected to inter group analysis wherever required to find out, among which categories the differences seen were statistically significant.

Inferences

The findings drawn from the analysis of the responses of the librarians in respect of the organization, administration and physical infrastructure of the libraries and of the defense scientists in respect of their information requirements and utilization of DRDO libraries are summarized under the following heads.

Organisation and Administration of DRDO Libraries

There are fifty-two (52) DRDO laboratories scattered through out the country, out of which eleven (11) laboratories have no library. DESIDOC is the apex body of the DRDO library system.

Ten (10) DRDO libraries are located in North and thirty (30) in South India.

The State of Karnataka has ten (10), the highest number of DRDO libraries in a State followed by Delhi, Maharashtra and Uttar Pradesh having six (6) each while Andhra Pradesh has five (5).

Each DRDO laboratory has a unique area of specialization.

Out of the twenty six (26) libraries covered in the study 96% of them were established prior to 1990 and one in 1994.

The organizational structure of the library varies depending upon the services offered by the library and the strength of the manpower in them.

In all DRDO libraries the Director of the laboratory is the supreme authority. He is assisted by an Associate Director (AD), Group Director (GD) and Coordinator (Coord) in organising, coordinating and supervising the library activities.

Even though the Librarian practically directs the various activities of the library in his capacity as the Head of the library, the librarian is accountable to the Director through the AD / GD / Coordinator for all the activities of the library.

All DRDO libraries have a Library Committee (LC) appointed by the Director of the laboratory. LC has a major role in the development of the library.

The periodicity of LC meetings varies among the laboratories. Most of them convene meetings on requirement basis. Emergency meetings are also held.

Books and book like materials, journals, CD-ROM products etc. are procured from vendors who are registered with DRDO libraries.

UDC is used for classification by 88% of DRDO libraries while the rest use DDC.

In most of the libraries, technical reports and standards & specifications are not classified. 77% of the libraries classify only books.

Loose journal issues and bound volumes of journals are arranged alphabetically and within the alphabetical arrangement, they are stacked in a chronological order.

All documents are catalogued using AACR in 92% of libraries, while the rest use CCC.

The Stock Verification Board in 81% of libraries does stock verification annually. Large libraries conduct stock verification within a gap of two to five years.

The mode of recovery and the rate of the handling charges vary among the different DRDO libraries in the case of loss of documents from user. Replacement of the lost book is the usual practice.

The Head of the laboratory has the power to write off lost documents up to a total value of Rs.5, 000/- per year.

Weeding out is resorted to by 77% of libraries. A Weeding Out Board is constituted for this purpose. The list of weeded out documents not mutilated or damaged is circulated among other DRDO establishments so that they can select required documents from this list. Documents not demanded, are sold at a price as fixed by the Weeding out Board to employees of the DRDO laboratories. The remaining documents are donated to social organisations / trusts / public libraries etc. in the best interest of the utilization of such weeded out documents.

Binding is outsourced, as most of the DRDO libraries do not have a binding section. Tendering is resorted to for getting the documents bound.

The range of expenditure of funds varied from Rs.2.60 lakhs to Rs.1.31 crores among the various DRDO libraries for the year 2000/2001. No specific criteria were followed for budgetary sanctions.

The amount spent on journals was enormously high when compared to books and book like materials. More than 65% of the libraries spend 60% to 80% of the annual library fund on subscription of journals.

Indian Journals are procured for a very meagre amount ranging from Rs 5000/- to Rs 50,000/-.

No library under study was found to subscribe journals by consortia.

Manpower of the library depends on the size of the various collections and the services offered by it.

Inadequacy of staff is reported by 58% of the librarians.

Great disparity is observed both in the proportion of professionals, semi professionals and non-professionals and also in the ratio of qualified professionals to scientists among the various DRDO libraries.

Staff are deputed for refresher courses / Continuing Education Programme (CEP) and other various courses by 81% libraries.

Equipments available in the library depend on the services offered and the type of resources held.

Quantum of reports, standards and specifications, bound volumes of journals, current journals and books on the subject of specialization of the parent laboratory are large in all DRDO libraries.

Only 31% libraries are found to have microform collection.

Full text CDs are held by 31% of libraries.

Growth of various collections is found to depend on the R&D activities undertaken by the laboratories than on the age of the libraries.

Steady annual increase in the collection of books during the last five years was recorded in only 12% of libraries. Rest of the libraries showed undulating figures.

The journal subscription for the year 2000/01, ranged from 31 to 235. Around 50% of the libraries were subscribing to up to 100 journals and the remaining subscribed to more than 100 journals. 12% libraries subscribe to more than 200 journals.

All the DRDO libraries follow open access. Only classified documents are kept under closed access.

The working hours span to eight hours plus a lunch break of 15-30 minutes. The working time of the library and the laboratory are the same, which is inconvenient and insufficient for the scientist community. 35% of libraries function on Saturdays to allow enough time to the defence scientists to frequent the library.

Membership is open to all regular employees of the laboratory without any membership fee. Membership is given at the discretion of the Head of the Laboratory to others as special cases for a specific period of time.

The loan period for the various reading materials are at variance among different DRDO libraries and are decided by the LC with the approval of the Director.

Inter Library Loan (ILL) facility is available in all the DRDO libraries.

Majority of libraries (96%) have photocopy service.

OPAC, circulation of accession list and CD-ROM search services are available in more than 60% of the libraries.

More than 50% of the libraries have Internet services, indexing, preparation of bibliographies, Selective Dissemination of Information and News Clipping service in their libraries.

Translation requirements of all DRDO laboratories are supported by DESIDOC.

Most of the libraries use Utility & User Survey and direct observation as their main collection evaluation methods. Very few libraries analyse the ILL statistics while some evaluate their collection based on compilation of statistics.

Only few libraries have designed publicity brochures. Others publicise their services through Intranet, web page, fixograph boards etc.

Primary means of communication are available with all the libraries.

Only 35% of the libraries are using Suchika, the integrated library management software developed exclusively for DRDO libraries. Rest of the libraries are found to use different software packages.

The library web page is available only for 19% libraries.

The LAN within library is available in more than half of the libraries.

The user orientation programme is offered by 46% of libraries only.

Many librarians (54%) are not satisfied with the location of the library.

Only 31% libraries have independent building. The rest are housed along with other divisions of the laboratory sharing the building. Many libraries do not have the provision for future expansion.

The average plinth area of the libraries under study is calculated as 7120 sq.ft.42 % of libraries have space below the average.

The average number of seats available in DRDO libraries covered in the study is 52. Many of the libraries (62%) have seating capacity below the average.

Only 46% of the librarians are satisfied with the physical infrastructure of their libraries. 38% of the librarians stated that the physical facilities need improvement.

Utilisation of DRDO Libraries

Scientists in general visit the library for books on specific subjects of interest to them and their parent organization, followed by reference books and current subject journals.

The Junior Scientists visit libraries more to consult reference books than the Senior and Eminent Scientists. The tendency to visit libraries to consult reference books is found to decrease with the increase in the grade or experience of the scientists.

Scientists visit the library to use the OPAC or Intranet, or to obtain photocopies of documents, or to avail the Internet facility more, when compared to the other services.

Junior Scientists tend to avail the Internet service more than the Senior and Eminent Scientists.

The Eminent Scientists use the Inter Library Loan service much more than the other two categories of scientists.

The information obtained from the library is used more to solve immediate technical problems, to keep abreast with the latest developments and to prepare for interviews and assessments, than for other purposes.

Junior and Senior Scientists seek information more to solve immediate technical problems while Eminent Scientists seek information mostly to keep up with the latest developments.

Junior and Senior Scientists seek information, also to prepare themselves for interviews and assessments.

Majority of scientists (98%) visit the library for information every week. More than 61% visit twice or more while 37% visit once a week. The pattern of weekly use of the library is almost identical by the three categories of scientists.

Daily visits by individual scientists are comparatively less (10%).

There are more than fifty users per day in 54% of libraries while 15% have more than hundred users. 46% of libraries have only below fifty users per day.

More than twenty-five issues per day are reported in 62% of libraries. 58% of the libraries have up to fifty consultations per day.

Greater percentage (52%) of scientists spend one to two hours a week in the library while 30% spend two to four hours. Senior Scientists spend more time in the library compared to Junior and Eminent Scientists.

With regard to the usefulness of the different reading materials scientists prefer books on specific subject, current subject journals and reference books, more.

With regard to usefulness among the services, the photocopy, indexing, OPAC / Intranet and the Internet services are preferred more than the rest of the services offered.

In the case of contributions of articles and conference papers during the period from 1996-2001 the maximum contribution is by the Eminent Scientists followed by the Senior Scientists. The contribution of Junior Scientists is much lower.

Personal contributions of scientists in the case of books and patents are negligible.

Participations in conferences and seminars are higher in the case of Eminent Scientists when compared to Senior and Junior Scientists.

The various reading materials of the library collection have been graded on an average as adequate by 39% of the scientist community. 49% has reported them as only partially adequate while 12% of the user community rated the reading materials as inadequate.

Reference books and current subject journals were graded as adequate by 47% of the scientists. 40% graded back volumes of journals as adequate while 36% rated books on specific subject as adequate. Only 28% of the scientists graded theses / reports / govt. publications as adequate. Standards and specifications were rated as adequate by 33% of the scientists.

Services like OPAC / Intranet, Internet, SDI / CAS, photocopy, inter library loan and news clippings service offered by the library were rated on an average as adequate by 26% of the user scientists only. 37% has rated the services as partially adequate while an equal percentage of scientists regarded the services of the library as inadequate.

OPAC & Intranet facilities were graded as adequate by 41% of the scientists while the Internet facility was graded as adequate by only 22% of the scientists. Photocopy and Inter library loan service were stated as adequate by 27% and 35% respectively, while SDI / CAS and News clipping service were graded as adequate by only a meager 19% and 14% of the scientists respectively.

Libraries other than parent libraries are visited by 34% of scientists for required information more than five times in a month.

Majority of the scientists (92%) got information available in the library in time.

More than 30% of scientists had to wait for more than two days to get the required information from CD and Internet searches.

Most of the libraries are not keen on getting the feedback from its clientele.

Reasons for not availing the various services were given by some of the scientists as 'not aware', 'do not know how to use', 'time consuming', 'no need' and 'not available'.

Many of the scientists do not receive initiation to the library activities and services.

More than 20% of the user scientists are not satisfied with the physical infrastructure of the libraries.

Tenability of Hypotheses

Data collected through the questionnaire from the librarians as well as the defence scientists were analysed with appropriate statistical tools and the results were drawn out which were summarized as the findings of the study. In the light of the major findings the tenability of the hypothesis framed for the study were tested. The following statements are the outcome of testing the hypothesis.

1. Analysis of the adequacy of resources of DRDO libraries namely, the collection of reading materials, finance, manpower and equipments, elaborately dealt with in chapter five, reveals that the resources are not sufficient. Analysis of the responses of user scientists in chapter six also confirms the finding and reveals their dissatisfaction with the adequacy level of the resources. Hence, the hypothesis that 'the existing resources in the DRDO libraries are inadequate to meet the information needs of the scientists' is substantiated.
2. Analysis of data in chapter five and six reveals that the services of the DRDO libraries are not sufficient enough to meet the requirements and expectation of the defence scientists. The library working hours and many of the information services offered by the library are found to be inadequate. The user satisfaction regarding the adequacy of information services is found to be negative substantiating the second hypothesis that 'the services of the DRDO libraries are not satisfactory'.
3. Analysis of the data on the physical infrastructure of the DRDO libraries obtained from the librarians as well as the user scientists dealt with in chapter five and six respectively, has revealed that it needs improvement. More than half of the libraries do not have independent buildings and many of them do not have provision for future expansion. Many of the librarians and users are not satisfied with the physical facilities of the libraries substantiating the third hypothesis also that the 'physical infrastructure available in DRDO libraries is not adequate'.

11. SUGGESTIONS

The survey helped to identify some of the drawbacks in the various aspects of functioning of the DRDO libraries, which need improvement. On examining the findings and the requirements put forward by the librarians and users, a few points could be singled out which need the attention of the authorities. They are presented in the following paragraphs.

The reference collection should be kept up-to-date by adding the latest editions of the most frequently used reference books and by weeding out obsolete books. One extra copy of the books on high demand must be procured and made available in the reference collection.

Reports of all national and international organisations and seminars of science and technology should be procured.

Latest versions of standards and specifications should be obtained regularly in the library and lists of the same should be circulated periodically to all the divisions of the laboratory.

Easy access to patent information on topics related to the research work of the parent laboratory should be provided.

DRDO library collection should be networked to enable all the defence scientists to access the resources of all the DRDO libraries.

CD-ROM products should be given more importance and developed into a good collection in view of its tremendous advantages.

Prompt replacement of returned and consulted books and periodic shelf rectification as well as proper labelling of the shelves and racks should be ensured to allow easy location of the information required.

Overdue charge should be levied so that books are returned in time.

All DRDO libraries should have a binding section of their own.

Irrespective of whether the establishment is small or otherwise, endeavour must be made to provide all the library services to the scientists, in an efficient way.

The facilities available in the library should be brought to the notice of the scientist community by conducting periodic awareness programmes. Periodical talks by library staff on the services offered, new services introduced, how to use the various facilities available etc. and regarding latest acquisitions should be conducted for optimum utilization of the library.

Publicity should be given to certain important services like SDI and CAS. The services not provided so far should be introduced without delay.

User orientation programmes for the newly inducted scientists should be arranged.

Working hours of the library should extend beyond the working hours of the laboratory and should function twelve hours a day so that scientists can utilise the library without any hindrance to their routine work. It is ideal if the service sections of the library functions for one shift during holidays.

It is necessary to use a standard library software package by all DRDO libraries, which would assist in networking of the DRDO libraries.

The existing database of the library should be updated on a regular basis and made available on the Intranet and on CD ROM if necessary.

Provision of online reservation and provision of technical news bulletins / newspaper clippings / latest publications should be made available through Intranet.

Adequate number of terminals should be provided for the users. OPAC should include information on issue status of books, like to whom the book is issued, its due date etc. also.

A dedicated Internet connection for the library with adequate computer terminals would enable the scientists to get the required information from Internet and CD searches without any time lag.

Microform reader / printer, audio / video facility etc should be made more efficient and easily accessible.

Feedback should be insisted, as it may contain fruitful suggestions which if implemented would lead to the overall development of the library and to the satisfaction of the clientele. The library should make deliberate efforts to obtain feedback from the user community through a structured questionnaire at regular intervals regarding the resources and services as well as other aspects of the library and endeavour to do the needful accordingly.

DRDO should have consortium approach for on-line resource subscription.

Library staff should be in proportion to the strength of the users, services provided and the working hours of the library. Qualified professionals supported by adequate staff should man all libraries.

All efforts must be made to fill up the shortage of manpower as per the DRDO staff formula. Additional staff must be provided for each new service added.

Library staff should be regularly detailed for in-service training and to attend various courses and education programmes to enable them to keep pace with the latest trends in the field.

The librarian with the consent of the management should organize periodic visits of the library staff in rotation, to the other major libraries in the region, which will enable mutual exchange of ideas and innovations on the resources and services of the libraries.

The DRDO libraries being special libraries of R&D establishments should have independent library buildings for their efficient functioning.

Libraries should have a modular structure in view of future expansions.

Libraries should be provided with ergonomically designed furniture.

Scientists should be provided with cubicles for reference without any hindrance.

Adequate space should be catered for the various sections of the library right in the planning stage itself anticipating its growth and development.

Library should have separate sections for bound volumes of journals, Internet / CD-ROM searches, reference services, reprography etc to enhance the functionality of the library.

Cleanliness cannot be compromised and necessary and stringent measures must be taken to ensure total cleanliness and provide a hygienic atmosphere.

12. AREAS FOR FURTHER RESEARCH

This research work, which endeavoured to study the organisation, administration and utilisation of DRDO Libraries, has identified a few areas for further research in future.

1. A comparative study of the organisation, administration and utilization of the services of the DRDO libraries with other R&D establishments in the country.
2. An in depth study of the resource sharing means of the DRDO libraries and other major libraries in a region to enhance the rate of information transfer.
3. A study on the standardisation of library software for DRDO libraries.
4. A study on consortium approach for on-line resource subscription for DRDO libraries.

REFERENCES

1 Sahi, SS. Importance of scientific information for defence. *National Conference on Scientific Information for Defence.* New Delhi, DESIDOC, 1986, pp. 76 - 79.

3. Bandyopadhyay, A et al. Information needs of defence scientists. *National Conference on scientific information for defence.* New Delhi, DESIDOC, 1986, p. 49.

4. Harrod, Leonard Montague. *Harrod's librarians' glossary and reference book, Ed. 5.* London, Gower, 1984.

5. Moser, CA. quoted by Thakur Devendra, in *Research methodology in Social Sciences.* New Delhi, Deep & Deep Publication, 1993, p. 45.

6. Sadhu, AN and Singh, Amarjit. *Research methodology in Social Sciences, Ed.5.* Bombay, Himalaya Publishing Home, 1992, p. 32.

7. Young, PV. *Scientific social surveys and research, Ed. 2.* Bombay, Asia Publishing House, 1960, p. 247.

7

Organisation, Administration and Utilization of University Libraries in Kerala : A Survey

— Dr.M.C.K Veeran

1. INTRODUCTION

The libraries are the informal institutions of education, which are the centres of global knowledge of all the times. Every educational advancement depends upon its resources and, in a large measure; the degree of advancement is proportional to the potential of the library to respond. The information infrastructure and modern library system are essential to aim at scientific, technological and economic progress and attain eminence. The role of university library is well recognized as a tool and an integral part of higher education to achieve quality education. The development of university libraries in the country has been parallel to the development of institutions of higher education. So it would be helpful to know the higher education scenario for studying the libraries of the universities.

HIGHER EDUCATION

Higher education provides an opportunity to reflect upon the social, economic, cultural, moral and spiritual issues facing humanity. It contributes to national development through dissemination of specialized knowledge and skills. It is indeed difficult to conceive a plan for building up a sustainable and prosperous society without the development of human resources, as the system of education and various socio-economic and cultural aspects, which influence national development, are inextricably linked with one another. In the present information age, new knowledge and technology are crucial for improving productivity of human and material resources. The green revolution in agriculture resulted in high productivity with the use of technology, a similar revolution in education that embraces information and communication technologies, that fosters the freedom and innovation and induces a market-oriented environment is vital for progress and prosperity of the country.

2. HIGHER EDUCATION: HISTORICAL BACKGROUND

"Higher Education in India has an unbroken tradition that can be traced back to ancient times, when the Guru would impart the principles of the Vedas to pupils selected from the priestly and ruling classes". It is said that Gurukula gradually expanded to include several Gurus and grew into a community of scholar parishads engaged in intellectual debate. These parishads established residential schools and centres with various faculties. Some historians are of the opinion that these centres mark the genesis of University education in India. Thakshashila in the north, Nalanda and Vikramshila in Bihar, Vallabhi in Kathiwad, Kanchi in the south and Nadia in Bengal were some of such centres. Nalanda was reputed to have had as many as 10000 students and taught subjects ranging from Metaphysics to Astronomy. Owing to the invasion from central Asia, institutions like Nalanda and Thakshashila began to wane.

By the dawn of the nineteenth century, British colonialism in India was firmly established and the question whether to develop traditional educational institutions or to promote modernization was a major issue that engaged the attention of colonial authorities. In 1835, Lord Macualay through the 'Macualay's minutes', for the first time stressed upon closure of institutions of oriental learning as they did not serve the educational purposes of Indians.

The objectives of Indian universities during the pre-independence period were to strive to achieve the goals that were set by foreigners to promote their own interests. In 1853 the British parliament for the first time instituted an enquiry in to the status of Indian education. This resulted in the famous educational document 'Woods Despatch' of July 1854, proposing the establishment of Universities at Calcutta, Bombay and Madras. Consequently in the year 1857, the Universities were established at Calcutta, Bombay and Madras. These were established not for the advancement of learning and research but to conduct examinations and award degrees as a hallmark of fitness for recruitment to the civil service of the country. These three universities served the needs of the entire country till 1881, when the University of Punjab (now in Pakistan) was set up followed by the University of Allahabad in 1887 to cater to the needs of North and Central India.

The first Indian Education Commission was appointed by Lord Ripon in 1882 with William Hunter as its Chairman to inquire in to the position of education in British India. As a result of various recommendations of the Commission, the progress of higher education was fast during last years of nineteenth century. Lord Curzon, the Viceroy of India had appointed the second Indian University commission under the chairmanship of Sir Thomas Raleigh on 27th January 1902. Based on the recommendations contained in the Report submitted in June 1902, the Legislative council passed the "Indian Universities Act" which came in to force on 21st March 1904." The Indian Universities Act 1904 was the first step towards reforms which stipulated that the Universities should assume more teaching responsibilities and offer research opportunities". The Higher Education in India expanded after the Education Policy of 1913, which proposed the establishment of new universities in each province. In 1915, Banaras Hindu University was established as a teaching and residential university without the power of affiliation. The University of Mysore in 1916, Patna in 1917 and Osmania in 1918 followed it. In 1917, the Calcutta University Commission headed by Sir Michal Sadler emphasized the need for residential universities, and within a decade or so several such universities were established. Those included Aligarh Muslim University (1920), Lucknow (1921), Delhi (1922) and Annamalai(1929).

The Simon Commission, appointed under the Government of India Act 1919 to inquire in to the working of administration including education appointed an auxiliary committee under the chairmanship of Sir Philip Hartog. In its comprehensive report on university education in India, which was submitted in September 1929, the Committee recognized the progress made particularly in research and pointed out certain glaring defects such as low standard of English language etc. Twenty-one universities were established in the pre-independence period and the last university was the University of Rajasthan in Jaipur in 1947.

The Government of India in November 1948, appointed the first University Education Commission under the chairmanship of Dr. S. Radhakrishnan to offer suggestions for enabling the Indian universities to meet the new responsibilities. The Commission felt that all universities should be constituted as autonomous bodies and they should be teaching institutions rather than affiliating types. It also suggested that the University Grants Committee be reconstituted and a University Grants Commission should be set up for allocation of funds.

The Second Education Commission was appointed by the Govt. of India in July 1964 under the chairmanship of Dr. D. S. Kothari to advise the Government on national pattern of education and on the general principles and policies for the development of education at all stages in all aspects. The Commission emphasized the expansion of higher education, enhancement of quality of higher education and research, and use of dynamic techniques of management and organization suited to the special functions and purposes. The National Policy on Education adopted in 1968 was based on the recommendations of Kothari Commission.

In June 1969, the University Grants Commission appointed a committee to consider the structures, functions, responsibilities, conditions of service of staff, students' participation and other allied matters for the Universities in India. Popularly known as Gajendragadkar Committee, among other recommendations, it strongly emphasized the need for better university- state relations particularly in view of the greater dependence of the universities on the state for funds.

It was in response to non-implementation of 1968 Education Policy that the Govt. of India adopted the new National Policy on Education (NPE) in May 1986. The Policy laid greater emphasis on the elimination of disparities in the educational system. The universal character of universities was under scored. The establishment of network arrangements between different institutions in the country to pool their resources and to participate in projects of national importance was emphasized. The policy further focused upon enhancing support to research in the universities.

The Government of India appointed a Committee on 7th May 1990 to review the National Policy on Education 1986 under the chairmanship of Ramamurthi. The Ramamurthi Cmmittee (1990) emphasized that the quality of higher and technical education is to be improved in real terms not only to make it relevant to the society but also to cater to the needs of industry.

With U.G.C efforts, higher education in free India has grown in leaps and bounds. "At present there are 213 University level institutions in India (including 52 deemed Universities). Of these, 162 are traditional universities (including 34 institutions for specialized studies in disciplines) while the others are professional/technical institutions". There has been commendable quantitative expansion in terms of students' enrolment, teachers, colleges, universities and increase in financial allocation. The perception about the development of higher education in India has not been entirely in line with the educational needs of masses. Some of the major issues confronting the higher education listed in the document 'New Education Policy' are the following:

1. "Problems associated with developing countries like scarcity of resources, dependence on and high competition from developed countries in the areas of high and specialized technologies etc and urgent need for faster development and progress put many constraints on teaching and research in higher education;
2. Pressure of a large number of students aspiring for higher education for personal, social and economic development;
3. Expansion of knowledge in its content and diversity and emerging of many new areas like computers, microelectronics, space, science, energy, biotechnology, communication etc;
4. Emergence and adoption of communication and microelectronics based technologies are transforming the industrial, social and cultural life of this country and the world;.
5. Non-homogenous student body can't be properly educated and trained by the existing educational system which was evolved on the principles of centralization and uniformity;
6. Grading and certification function of the Universities for admission to higher courses of study and for selection to various employment opportunities outside as well as inside pressures on teachers and educational institutions vitiating the entire teaching and learning process;
7. Dominant culture in the educational institutions is authoritarian and hierarchical;
8. Lack of motivation in the system has resulted in the limited success or often failure in many reforms based on sound principles and started with well-planned programmes and preparation;
9. Less importance often bordering on neglect given to the University system in Research and Development work has eliminated challenge from the system and resulted in falling standards;

10. Accountability is entirely absent in the system and good, bad and indifferent institutions, all get the same grant and support, and
11. Financial resources provided to higher education are not enough to carry out its responsibilities. Often the grant-in-aid and its controlling operation by the funding agency, is so restrictive and bound in long procedures and delay that it disheartens and dissuades those working for educational reforms and changes."

These are the problems faced by all Universities in India. The overall situation in higher education was summarized in the Ramamurthi Committee Report entitled "Towards an enlightened Humane Society (1990)". There are serious complaints at all levels about the lack of responsiveness in the system. Academic activities are at low ebb and the academic calendar itself gets seriously disrupted almost every year. The system of higher education continues to encourage memorization of facts and regurgitation rather than creativity. While the results in higher education are clearly determined by the foundation laid in school education, we cannot wait for the ills of school education to be remedied before bringing in meaningful improvements in higher education. We can not ignore the fact that we do not have many colleges today which can pride themselves of imparting undergraduate education of high quality, comparable to some of the well known institutions in the world"

In order to overcome the failure of the overall educational system, the problems of higher education should be properly addressed. In the midst of all these problems, the universities are forced to function for achieving objectives of higher education.

3. OBJECTIVES OF HIGHER EDUCATION

The university is an important agency for imparting higher education. Teaching, research and extension services are three major aims of a University. The University Education Commission, set up under the chairmanship of Dr. S.

Radhakrishnan (1948-49) gave an illuminating analysis of the aims of higher education at the university level. The Commission states: "Our educational system must find its guiding principles in the aims of social order for which it prepares, in the nature of civilization it hopes to build. Democracy depends for its very life on a high standards of general, vocational and professional education."

The Commission further adds the following objectives for the Universities to strive for:

1. "Great changes have taken place in the political and economic conditions of Indian society. The academic problem has assumed new dimensions. We have now a wider conception of duties and responsibilities of Universities. They have to provide leadership in politics, administration, profession, industry and commerce.
2. The aim of Universities should be to promote intellectual adventures.
3. Universities should be the organs of civilization. They should train the intellectual pioneers of civilization
4. Universities should produce such wise persons who may disseminate learning to make democracy successful and who may make an incessant research for new knowledge and unceasing efforts to plumb the meaning of life.
5. The content of education must accept the best of what modern advancement has to offer but without neglecting our cultural heritage from the past.
6. One of the main functions of the Universities is to bring about the spiritual development of the students.
7. Universities preserve culture and civilization of a country. If we want to be called civilized, we should sympathize with the poor, respect women, love peace and independence, and hate tyranny and injustice. The aim of the University education should be to infuse these ideals to youth.
8. Aim of education is to discover the innate qualities of a

person and to develop them through training. Universities should discharge both these duties towards their students.

9. A healthy mind is found in a healthy body. Hence in the Universities attention should be paid, not only to the mental but also to the physical development of students.
10. Literature deepens and enlarges the human feelings. Hence the Universities should give the most important place to the mother tongue in the general education.
11. We are engaged in quest for democracy through the realization of justice, liberty, equality and fraternity. Hence it is necessary that our universities should be the emblems of protections of these ideals."

The Radhakrishnan Commission thus makes both philosophical and practical statements on the functions of higher education. Keeping in view the then falling standards of education in India, which had aroused the consciousness of notable educators and scholars, compelled the Government of India to set up another Commission (1964-66) under the Chairmanship of Dr. D. S. Kothari, then Chairman of University Grants Commission. The Kothari Commission reviewing the entire educational system of the country, restated the objectives of higher education as follows:

1. "To seek and cultivate new knowledge, to encourage vigorously and fearlessly in the pursuit of truth, and to interpret old knowledge and belief in the light of new needs and discoveries.
2. To provide the right kind of leadership in all walks of life, to identify gifted youth and help them to develop their potential to the full by cultivating physical fitness, developing the power of the mind and cultivating right interests, attitudes and moral and intellectual values.
3. To provide society with competent men and women trained in agriculture, art, medicine, science and technology and various other professions who will also be cultivated individuals imbued with sense of social purposes.

4. To strive to promote equality and social justice and to reduce social and cultural differences through diffusion of education. And
5. To foster in the teachers and students, and through them in society generally, the attitude and values needed for developing the good life in individuals and society."

In addition to these broad functions common to all Universities, Indian Universities will have to shoulder some special responsibilities. The Commission envisaged that these institutions would turn out devoted and dedicated generations of students. The Commission suggests that:

1. "They must learn to serve as the conscience of the nation; and from this point of view they should encourage individually, variety and dissent within a climate of tolerance.
2. They should develop programmes of adult education in a big way and to that end, evolve a widespread network of part time and correspondence courses.
3. They should assist the schools in their attempts at qualitative self-improvement.
4. They should shake of the heavy load of their early tradition which gives a prominent place to examination and strive to improve standards all round a symbiotic development of teaching and research, and
5. They should create at least a few centres which would be comparable to those of their type in any other parts of the world, and thus help to bring back the centre of gravity of the Indian academic life within the country itself."

In the pre-independent India the objective of university education, which was concentrated in major towns, was restricted to teaching alone. The advent of freedom completely changed our concept of university education. It was agreed that the scope of university education should not be restricted merely to teaching, and advancement of learning and promotion of research. Instead it should meet the other obligations of the country, in the local, national, social and other contexts. The report of the Committee on Governance of universities and colleges records: "In order to improve the quality of instruction as well as to impart to it a social relevance, there should be greater contact between higher education and problems of life and society. No longer can we afford isolation between universities on one hand, and industry, agriculture, rural development, public administration etc on the other. The organization of the university should on the one hand, prevent the growth of an exclusive caste system of academic and administrators, and on the other encourage mobility between universities and various sectors of national life and economy". The Government soon realized the fact that higher education was the major investment in the development of human resources and felt the need for trained personnel in different disciplines and vacations.

Louis Round Wilson and Maurice F Tauber summarized the functions of the University under six heads namely, 1) conservation of knowledge and ideas 2) teaching 3) Research 4) publication 5) Extension and services and 6) interpretation.

Thus the basic functions of a modern university may be briefly summarized as follows.

1. "Conservation of knowledge and ideas amassed from time immemorial.
2. Dissemination and communication of this knowledge and ideas through teaching, publication and extension service.
3. Expansion and extension of boundaries of the existing knowledge by research through teachers and research scholars.
4. Production of manpower, for various professions by imparting technological and professional education
5. Transforming a student to mature as a person and as a student.
6. Interpretation of the results of research and investigation conducted by the university to the society in different ways."

University education in India is increasingly seen as an investment for economic growth, as a means to improve human values and to create integrated, modernized and egalitarian democratic society. In this light it can be concluded that the most formidable task facing the universities in India is to undertake research in as many branches of knowledge as possible and to produce an army of trained researchers committed to national service and development.

4. OBJECTIVES AND FUNCTIONS OF UNIVERSITY LIBRARY

A university library is established with the intention of aiding the successful accomplishment of the objectives of the university such as teaching, research and publication programmes. Keeping in view the multifarious objectives of a modern university, the university library has to shoulder onerous responsibilities. Sonal Singh states that, "The library performs a variety of functions, by way of helping students with text books, parallel studies, reference books and periodicals; by providing a large number of bibliographical tools and up to date literature on every subject for students, teachers and research workers; as well as by maintaining an efficient reference and information service."

The prime necessity for a university is a good library with a balanced and adequate collection, which can satisfy the needs of the university faculty, research scholars, and students and help promote advanced study and research programmes. The library in a University system occupies a significant and crucial place, because all the functions of teaching and research are served by it. Issac has rightly remarked about the present position of university libraries in India: "ever since the of University Grants Commission began to be directly involved in the development of university libraries, it has been possible to bring about significant improvement of these libraries both in respect of their book resources and organization. The position today is that the university libraries in the country are, by and large in the process of being adequately equipped for lending effective support to teaching and research programmes of the Universities."

The Radhakrishnan Commission (1948-49) has stressed the importance of libraries in higher education, thus: "Teaching is a cooperative enterprise. Teachers must have the necessary tools for teaching purposes in the shape of libraries and laboratories and also the right type of students. The library is the heart of all university's work, directly so as regards its research work and indirectly as regards its educational work. Scientific research needs a library as well as its laboratories, while for humanistic research; the library is both the library and laboratory in one. Training in higher branches of learning and research is mainly a question of learning how to use the tools, and if the library tools are not there, how can the students learn to use them".

Line is of the opinion that "The function of the university is to bring together information or knowledge on the one hand and human beings on the other. According to President Truman's Commission on Higher Education "The library is second only to the instructional staff in its importance for the high quality instruction and research. Both for humanistic and scientific studies, a first class library is essential in a university." The University Education Commission further states, "we have already indicated that lectures and tutorials must be supplemented by work in the library. The teacher gives the students some guidance as regards supplementary reading. But the reference assistant if he is properly qualified, will be in touch with the teachers and guide the students to the proper volume and proper page in each volume, which would be helpful. These reference assistants can be of help not only to the students, but also to the teacher in their special subjects of study."

Human knowledge is increasing at a pace never known before. This has a bearing on the university libraries in two ways: firstly, university libraries must collect and supply the right type of literature to the scholars and, secondly they must then endeavor to organize and give access to information and make selection and control as easy, acceptable and quick as possible.

The Kothari Education Commission (1964-66) has stressed the proper development of University library system in the country and observed: " A collection of books, even a collection of good books, does not constitute a 'library'. Given enthusiastic teachers who teach with books, and librarians who can cooperate with them in converting the library in to an intellectual workshop, even a comparatively small collection of sensitively chosen books may work wonders in the life of students. Without such staff the most luxurious building or extensive book collection may have no effect at all. The subject of library planning is not to build a collection of books unrelated to class work, laboratory research and conference room. The object is rather to relate book selection, organization of the books, conditions of access and all activities to the daily needs and activities of the academic community, both professors and students. The book selection should be oriented towards supporting instruction and research. The teaching and library staff should determine, the tittles and copies of books to be purchased and periodically work together to discard obsolete books."

The present education system expects a teacher to initiate the students in to new vistas of the Universe of knowledge. The faculty should give up the age-old textbooks centred and examination-oriented method of teaching and should encourage library-centred individual and group guidance method through tutorials, discussions, seminars, etc to make education really effective and worthwhile. The library can supply from its rich resources what the classroom has failed to. Ranganathan explains: "In the library each student will have the freedom to grow at his own speed along his own lines to his own fullness, with the help of books just suited to him under the guidance of the teacher and the librarian."

The objectives of university libraries as set by Kothari Education Commission are:

— "to provide resources necessary for research in fields of special interests to the university;

— to aid the university teacher in keeping abreast of developments in his field;

— to provide library facilities and services necessary for the success of all formal programmes of instructions;

— to open the door to the wide world of books that lie beyond the borders of one's own field of specialization; and

— to bring books, students and scholars together under conditions which encourage reading for pleasure, personal growth and sharpening of intellectual curiosity"

Wilson and Tauber have stressed that "1) resources for instruction, research and extension 2) competent library staff 3) organization of materials 4) adequate space and equipment 5) integration of library with administrative and educational policies 6) Integration of library with community, state, regional, national and international library resources 7) adequate financial support and 8) a workable policy of library government are essential and fundamental to the successful operation and development of a university library".

The observations of Paul Buck about the university library are as follows.

1. "The Library is the heart of education;
2. Methods and fashion in education change from generation to generation, but each generation uses the library as a mean of realizing its items; hence the library remains the great conservator of learning;
3. A quality education is impossible without a quality library.
4. You can't have quality faculty without a quality library;
5. A library is vital to proper exploitation of our intellectual resources;
6. The library is essential to maintenance of free access to ideas and to the functioning of the untrammeled mind."

To formulate a National Policy on Library and Information System, the Ministry of Human Resource

Development, Government of India, set up a Committee in October 1985 under the chairmanship of Prof. D. P. Chattopadhya. The Committee submitted its report titled 'National policy on Library and Information System: A presentation' in May 1986. As a follow up action, the Department of Culture set up an Empowered Committee in November 1986 again under the Chairmanship Prof. D. P. Chathopadhya. The Committee started functioning in March 1987 and completed its work in March 1988. The objectives of National Policy on Library and Information System formulated by the committee are as follows:

"Library and information system are vital for all sectors of national activity. The availability of information expeditiously and pin pointedly supports the decision making processes at all levels. Relevant information accelerates the pace of National development. An informed citizen is an asset to a democratic system of Government and proper utilization of information can improve the quality citizens. The Government of India, therefore realize the value of coordinating and upgrading the existing library and information systems and services and initiating new programmes relevant to our national needs taking advantage of the latest advances in informational technology"

5. PROBLEMS IN UNIVERSITY LIBRARY DEVELOPMENT

University libraries in India are in a parlous position in spite of the increased resources made available to them. As early as 1902, the University Commission appointed by the then Government of India observed: "of the present University libraries there is not much to be said. The library at Madras appears to be entirely neglected. Bombay has a good collection of oriental and other books but the library is little used by graduates and hardly at all by students. Calcutta has a library and money have been granted for the purpose of making it supplementary to other libraries in Calcutta. It is open to fellows and to persons permitted by the syndicate to use it, for purpose of literacy search". University libraries in India have a lot of imperfections. "The Madras University Library, a century old library, which incidentally has remained the beacon of modern Indian librarianship, has even today the smallest library expenditure, barely sufficient to meet its needs". "The Bombay University library, even now is more or less a reference library. Books are lent only at the discretion of the librarian on special request. This library has a closed access."

Paucity of funds is the problem generally faced by the university libraries. University libraries in India and other developing countries are confronted with several problems and obstacles in their course of development. Gelfand has pointed out the following obstacles faced by the university libraries in developing countries.

1. "Lack of clearly defined University and library objectives of co-operation and understanding from University authorities and faculties;
2. Severe import and currency restrictions;
3. Inadequate financial support;
4. Inadequate physical facilities;
5. Failure to appoint competent university librarian, to give him authority commensurate with his important responsibilities, and to recognize the educational and professional qualifications of librarians;
6. Unduly complex purchasing and other administrative regulations; and
7. The inhibiting enforcement of strict personal accountability for book losses. In addition to the specific obstacles, which are listed above, a number of factors may affect the development of university libraries. These may need to be considered in planning library development in the interests of the nation as well as the University. These include:
   a) number and type of specialized research institutions;
   b) the state of library service in the nation;

c) conditions in particular universities; and

d) the states of librarianship."

The notable attempts made at the national level by the Government to find out whether the university libraries were functioning to fulfill the aims and ideals of university education in India were the Indian Universities Act (1904), Government of India Resolution on Educational Policy (1913), University Education Commission (1964-66), U.G.C. Committee on Universities and Colleges (1957), Karl White's Survey of Delhi University Library (1965) and National Policy on Education (1986).

6. THE INFLIBNET

The Information and Library Network (INFLIBNET) aims at the establishment of a national network of libraries and information centres in universities, colleges, research and development organizations etc, in India.

OBJECTIVES OF INFLIBNET

The main objectives of INFLIBNET are :

1. "to evolve a national network, interconnecting various libraries and information centres in the libraries and information centres in the country and to improve capability in information handling and service;
2. to provide reliable access to document collection of libraries by creating on-line union catalogue of monographs, serials, and non-book materials (manuscripts, audio-visuals, computer media etc) in various libraries in India;
3. to provide better access to worthwhile bibliographic information sources, with citations and abstracts, such as periodical articles, conference papers, preprints, technical reports, standards and specifications, patents, monographs etc through indigenously created databases of the sectoral information centres of international databases held by international information networks and centres;

4. to provide document delivery service by establishing resource centres around libraries having a rich collection of documents;
5. to optimize information resource utilization through shared cataloguing, inter-library loan service, catalogue production, collection development and avoiding duplication in acquisition to the extent possible;
6. to implement computerization of operations and services in the libraries and information centres of the country, following a uniform standard;
7. to facilitate scientific communication amongst scientists, engineers, researchers, social scientists, academics, faculties and students through electronic mail, bulletin board, file transfer, computers/audio/video conferencing etc;
8. to enable the users disbursed all over the country irrespective of location and distance, to have access to information regarding books, monographs, serials and non-book materials by locating the sources where from available and to obtain it through the facilities of new communication technologies and union catelogue of documents;
9. to create database of projects, institutions and specialists for providing on-line information service;
10. to encourage cooperation among libraries, documentation centres and information centres in the country, so that the resources can be pooled for the benefit of helping the weaker resource centres by stronger ones;
11. to develop suitable professional manpower of appropriate quality to establish, manage and sustain INFLIBNET; and
12. to evolve standards and uniform guidelines in techniques, methods, procedures, hard wares and soft wares, service and so on and promote adoption in actual

practice by all libraries in order to facilitate pooling, sharing and exchanging resources and facilities towards optimization."

FOCUS OF INFLIBNET

INFLIBNET is a cooperative network. Its activities, outputs and services are directed towards promoting co-operative endeavors in resource development and utilization with a view to organize library service at macro level with an economical cost for maximum benefit. Through INFLIBNET the university libraries in the country are expected to co-ordinate their activities and avoid duplication to the extent possible. By doing so the total library funds of the country will go a long way in optimizing the resources and services. The main motivation of a library to participate in the network is to spread less than if it is to operate independently. The ultimate aim is to offer speedy and efficient services to users, academics and researchers all over the country through a well-articulated and versatile library and information network.

SERVICES OF INFLIBNET

INFLIBNET multifunction network will provide the following services:

Catalogue Based Services

— shared cataloguing of monographs, serials and non-book materials.

— union catalogue of books, serials and non-book materials

— on-line catalogue access for shared cataloguing and location identification.

— catalogue production in card, book, magnetic tape, floppy, CD-ROM, and COM form

Data Base Service

— Bibliographic data base services-Retrospective searches, SDI, Current awareness services.

— Database of non-bibliographic information such as on going and completed projects, institutions and specialists.

Document Supply Service

Inter-library loan request processing, Document delivery

A. Collection Development

Acquisition and assistance in selection and procurement

B. Communication Based Services

Referral Service

Electronic mail- transfer/receive messages, Bulletin based-view/update bulletin board, Academic communication through electronic mail, bulletin board, file transfer, computer/audio/video conferencing.

7. UNIVERSITY LIBRARIES IN KERALA

As the study aims at the assessment of organisation, administration and utilization of university libraries in Kerala, it is appropriate to give a brief account of the four university libraries in Kerala.

CALICUT UNIVERSITY LIBRARY

The Calicut University Library is situated in Tenhippalam, the head quarters of the University. It has a good collection of documents consisting of books, back volumes of periodicals, theses, dissertations, C-D-ROMS, Microfilms and Microfiches. On an average 500 to 600 students, research scholars, teachers and others visit the library daily.

The University of Calicut was established in 1968 at Tenhippalam, a hilly rural area in Malappuram District, 23 kilometers South of Calicut City, a historically well-known seaport on the Malabar Coast on the Mumbai-Kanyakumari highway. The university jurisdiction extends to five northern districts of Kerala. ie., Thrissur, Palakkad, Malappuram, Kozhikode and Wayanad excluding Mananthavady Taluk.

The university library started functioning from the year 1971 in a small building near the Administrative block. The first permanent building to be constructed in the Calicut University Campus was that of the University Library Building. The present library building, a two storied structure, has a total plinth area of 2056.70m^2. It started functioning in May 1974. The post of University Librarian was created in 1971 and Prof. M.N. Ramakrishnan Nair was appointed. He left the in 1973 and Prof. Anand P. Srivastava, took charge as Professor of Library Science and University Librarian. He also left the University in July 1975. Later Prof. (Dr.) M.Bavakutty joined the university as Deputy Librarian in charge and Head of the Department of library science and he became the University Librarian in the year 1987. He continued in that post till the year 2002. The Calicut University Library is named as C.H. Mohammed Koya Library in the year 1993 by a resolution of the University Syndicate.

ORGANISATION OF THE LIBRARY

For the functional convenience, the library is divided in to 8 sections. Acquisition Section, Technical Section, Circulation Section, Reference and Text Book Section, Maintenance Section, Information Technology Services Section and the Library Office.

ACQUISITION SECTION

Selection, ordering and acquisition of books are the main functions of this section. Acquisition of gift books, theses, dissertations, C-D-ROMS, bound volumes of periodicals etc. are also done in this section. Scrutinizing and passing of bills for payment are the other responsibilities of this section.

TECHNICAL SECTION

Classification, cataloguing and other technical processing of books and other reading materials are carried out in this section.

CIRCULATION SECTION

The circulation section is divided in to four divisions. i.e., Property counter, Security desk, Circulation counter and Membership desk.

The section collect books, renew books issued on loan, reserves new books and books issued on loan, collects overdue charges, enrolls members and issue clearance certificates to members. All these functions are computerized.

REFERENCE AND TEXTBOOKS SECTION

The Library has a good reference collection consisting of encyclopaedias, dictionaries, yearbooks, almanacs, gazetteers, biographies and various other reference volumes. The textbook section is also housed in the reference section. The members have the facility to get textbooks issued on loan for overnight use that will be issued after 7.PM and these are to be returned at the time of opening of the library on the next day. The reference books useful for various competitive examinations and civil service examinations are also available here. Previous years question papers of the university examinations and U.G.C. examinations are also available for reference and photocopying. Theses and dissertations collection form part of this section.

The university has recognized Calicut University Library as a centre for research in Library and Information Science and Sociology. Part time and full time scholars including full-time F.I.P. teacher scholars select the library as the centre of research. The Reference and Textbook section also handles matters relating to such research scholars.

PERIODICAL SECTION

Foreign as well as Indian periodicals are subscribed and displayed for use in this section. Presently the university library procures journals for all departments of the university. At present the library subscribes 36 foreign journal and 161 Indian journals. The bound back volumes of journals are also arranged here as a separate division. The newspapers are displayed for use on the right side of the entrance of the library.

MAINTENANCE SECTION (STACK ROOM)

The whole collection of the library for issue is displayed in this section. Books are arranged according to Dewey Decimal Classification scheme. Open access system is followed. Reading facility is also available in this section.

The catalogue of the entire holdings of the library is arranged in front of the maintenance section in card from as well as computerized form (OPAC). The card catalogue is prepared according to Anglo-American Cataloging Rules with slight variations. The card catalogue is arranged in two parts. ie., Classified part and Alphabetical part. There are separate catalogues for Malayalam and Hindi collections. The OPAC (Online Public Access Catalogue) can be used for searching the bibliographic records of all documents available in the library through any approach ie., author, title, subject, KWIC, Series, Publisher etc.

INFORMATION TECHNOLOGY SECTION

Computer based library services are provided from this section. All sections of the library have been connected through LAN. The database of the holdings of the library has been created using LIBSYS-4 software. The entire in- house activities are computerized and the circulation, reference, indexing and abstracting services. An Internet browsing centre with 16 terminals is functioning in the library.

The INFONET connectivity has been established in the University library through 1MBps leased line provided by ASIANET. This connection provides very fast access to E-resources and downloading speed is quite high. An exclusive centre is being set up for the facility where one server, 36 nodes and other necessary gadgets like C-D-writers, laser printers etc are to be provided. The service is provided to the university academic community without charging any fee and this has enabled them to acquire valuable study and research materials in the form of full text from major content providers of the world. The microfilms, microfiches and their readers are also provided in this section.

LIBRARY AND INFORMATION SERVICES

The Calicut University Library renders a variety of services such as document delivery service, inter-library loan service, reference service, bibliographical service, photocopying service etc. The library also conducts exhibitions, extension services and display of books to attract the users. The library has conducted four National Seminars in association with the Department of Library and Information Science on the topics of current interest, the details of which are given below.

Sl.	*Seminar Topic*	*Period*
1	Management of Libraries in the 21st century	May 1999
2	Organization of Libraries and information centres in the 21st century	May 2000
3	Library co operation in networked world	May 2001
4	Information access, Management and exchange in the technological Age	May 2002

LIBRARY RULES

The Calicut University Library is kept open from 8 AM to 8 PM on all working days. On Sundays and Second Saturdays, the library functions from 8.30 AM to 2. PM. The library remains closed on all public holidays. Membership of the library is open to the students, teachers, research scholars of the University and affiliated colleges, non teaching staff of the University, members of Senate, Syndicate, Academic Council, Faculties, Board of studies, Graduates of recognized Universities, oriental title holders of Kerala and staff of Government Offices functioning in the campus. The duration of membership for teachers in the University and affiliated colleges and non-teaching staff is three years renewable after submission of fresh application. The membership of students and research scholars continues through their period of study till the probable month and year of examination. The graduate members are required to renew their membership every year. Teachers are eligible to borrow 6 books and all other members are eligible to borrow three books at a time. The loan period for all members is one month. Books loaned may be renewed at the discretion of University Librarian for a further period provided a written request for the renewal of loan reaches the University Librarian within three days before/after the due date and no other member has reserved the book.

KERALA UNIVERSITY LIBRARY

The Kerala University Library is situated in the heart of the Thiruvananthapuram city, adjacent to University administrative buildings and Legislature hostel. It has a rich collection of documents consisting of books, back volumes of periodicals, theses, C-D ROMS, Microfilms etc. Being a major centre of study and research, on an average 1000-1250 users visit this library every day.

The Kerala University Library has a long history. The University of Travancore was established on 1st November 1937. Till the establishment of a separate library for the University, the Trivandrum Public Library which had been in existence for over 92 years also functioned as the University library. The Trivandrum Public Library was transferred to the control of Travancore University on 22nd August 1938 by a Government order. Then it had over 33356 books and was subscribing to 93 periodicals. About 20000 books, mostly of an advanced nature formed the nucleus of the University Library collection. The personal libraries of Diwan Bahadur Dr. S. Krishna Swami Aiyankar and Prof. P. P. Sastri were purchased and added to the collection. The library of University of Travancore (later renamed as Kerala University Library) was started in 1942. Four years later, the library was shifted to the new building, in the eastern side of the University College. The present library building a two-storied structure with a total plinth area of 53000 sq.feet started functioning on 8th September 1962. The post of University Librarian was created in 1959 and Prof. K. A. Issac was appointed to the post in the same year. He continued to be the University Librarian until 1980 and Sri K. C. John succeeded him. After his retirement the senior most deputy librarian is put in charge of the University Librarian.

ORGANISATION OF THE LIBRARY

For the functional convenience, the library is divided in to 11 sections. Circulation, Acquisition, Technical, Reference,

Periodicals, Documentation and information services, Information Technology. Kerala studies, U.N. and World Bank, Research and Maintenance section.

CIRCULATION SECTION

The circulation section at the entrance of the library is divided in to four divisions. 1. Property counter, 2. Circulation counter, 3. Membership desk and 4. Security Desk.

ACQUISITION SECTION

Selection, ordering and acquisition of books are the main functions performed by the section.

TECHNICAL SECTION

Classification, cataloging and other technical processing of books and bound volumes of periodicals that are added to the library are done in this section.

REFERENCE SECTION

The library has a good reference collection of national and international coverage. The textbook section is also attached to this section. The bibliography collection and books for the preparation of civil service examination and other competitive examinations are also available here. Previous year's question papers of various university examinations are also available for reference in the textbook section.

PERIODICAL SECTION

Foreign as well as Indian periodicals currently subscribed and received as gift are displayed for use here. Newspapers and popular magazines are also available here. At present the library is subscribing to 47 foreign periodicals and 245 Indian Journals. 175 periodicals are being received as gift.

INFORMATION TECHNOLOGY SECTION

Computer based library services are provided in this section. All sections of the library have been connected through LAN. Computer data bank of the holding of library has already been created using the library software LIBSYS-4. The database is available to the members through OPAC (On-line Public

Access Catalogue). Internet Services are provided through VSNL Dial-up access. An Internet Browsing centre with 10 computers is functioning in the library. A 64kbps leased line through Asianet cable and modem is made available for the purpose. E-journals and CD-ROM search facilities are also provided here besides the INFONET programme of INFLIBNET.

RESEARCH SECTION

Kerala University library is one of the important research centres of the university particularly for scholars in subjects for which there are no other research centres. This section deals with the requirements of the research scholars. A collection of doctoral theses of the university form part of this section where entry open to members from 10 AM to 5.PM on working days only.

DOCUMENTATION AND INFORMATION SERVICE SECTION

The bibliographies on important personalities and subjects are compiled in this section at regular intervals. One important publication from this section is the 'Kerala Index' which contains an index of articles of research value on topics relating to Kerala prepared from newspapers and magazines subscribed by the library.

U.N. AND WORLD BANK SECTION

Kerala University Library is the only repository for U.N. and World Bank publications in Kerala. Publications of other organs of UN are also received in the section. Documents are available for reference only. U.N. updates received on-line through Internet is also made available to the users.

KERALA STUDIES SECTION

This section started in 1973 is being developed as a specialized comprehensive collection comprising books on various aspects of Kerala such as history and culture, language and literature, religion, education, politics, economics, sociology etc. This collection is being built to meet the requirements of growing number of research scholars in the field of Kerala studies.

MAINTENANCE SECTION

The function of this section is the display and maintenance of books that are issued on loan. The whole collection is arranged on the shelves according to the colon classification scheme. Catalogue section also forms part of this section. The catalogue is designed as classified catalogue with classified part and alphabetical part. Separate catalogue for Malayalam section is also provided.

Photocopying services are provided from 8 AM to 6.30 PM. Two photocopying machines are available here.

THE LIBRARY RULES

The library works from 8 AM to 8 PM on all working days and from 2 PM to 8 PM on Sundays. The membership of the library is open to the following categories.

1. Students, teachers, research scholars of University and affiliated colleges.
2. Members of Senate, Syndicate, Faculties and boards of studies.
3. Non-teaching staff of the University
4. Graduates of recognized Universities residing in Kerala and
5. Recognized institutions.

Members eligible for borrowing books from the library is as follows.

a) Students -2 books
b) Teachers, Head of non-teaching departments and research students-6 books
c) Institutional members-10 books.
e) others –2 books

The students who are studying in Thiruvananthapuram corporation area should return books within 15 days. For students studying outside the corporation area and research scholars, the loan period is 30 days. All those entitled to borrow

6 books at a time can retain the books for 30 days. The loan period for all other members is 15 days.

MAHATMA GANDHI UNIVERSITY LIBRARY

Mahatma Gandhi University Library is situated at the Pryadarshini Hills, the headquarters Mahatma Gandhi University. It is the central facility to support the teaching and research needs of the University. It has a very rich collection of documents consisting of books, back volumes of periodicals, theses, dissertations, CD-ROMs, reprints, current contents etc.

The Gandhiji University renamed as Mahatma Gandhi University came in to existence on 2nd October 1983 by an ordinance issued by the Governor of Kerala. The ordinance passed into an Act in April 1985 by Kerala legislature. The University library was started functioning in 1989. Prof C.A. Augustine was appointed as special officer of the library. Later Sri.P.Ravindran was appointed as University Librarian. After his retirement in the senior most deputy librarian is given the charge of the library.

ORGANISATION OF THE LIBRARY

For the functional convenience the library is divided in to 8 sections. Those are: Acquisition, Technical, Maintenance, Periodical, Union catalogue, Documentation, Circulation and administration section. The traditional functions of these sections are as in Calicut University Library and in Kerala University Library.

LIBRARY AND INFORMATION SERVICES

The Library renders a variety of services such as document delivery service, inter-library loan services, reference service, bibliographical service, photocopying service, Internet service etc. The library also conducts exhibitions, extension services and display of books to attract users. The Library collection includes more than 35000 volumes of books, 200 current periodicals, over 50 popular magazines and 12 newspapers.

The Mahatma Gandhi University Library has provided

certain special services, which are in deviation from the traditional services provided by the University libraries. These are detailed here under:

REPRINT SERVICE

Reprints and Photocopies of journal articles, which are cited in the current contents and journals, are collected from the authors/institutions directly and issued to research scholars at nominal rate.

CURRENT CONTENTS SERVICE

The current contents of following subjects are provided on request.

1. Social Sciences and Humanities
2. Chemical and material science
3. Life sciences

The library also gets photocopies of articles from INSDOC, the cost of which is collected from the clients. A copy of all such photocopies collected is maintained as a separate collection called Reprint collection. A monthly documentation list is also published under the name "Mahatma Gandhi University Library Micro document index cumulated."

ON-LINE SERVICE

Library has access to about 200 on-line databases in science and technology.

LIBRARY RULES

The Library is kept open from 8AM to 7Pm, on all working days and from 10AM to 2PM on second Saturdays and Sundays. Library membership is open to teachers, students, and non-teaching staff of the University and teachers and post-graduate students of the affiliated colleges. Membership to any other category of users can be given only with the approval of Library Advisory committee. Research scholars and teachers of the university can borrow three books at a time. The students of the University departments, medical students and special categories of members can take two books at a time. Period of loan for all categories of members is 15 days, which can be renewed twice for the period of loan specified.

COCHIN UNIVERSITY LIBRARY

The Cochin University came in to being on July 10, 1971 by the Cochin University Act 1971(Act 30) for promotion of higher education and research in Greater Cochin area with emphasis on science, technology, industry and commerce. The Cochin University Library was established as a central agency for meeting the information requirements of the academic community of Cochin University of Science and Technology. It is located in a separate building opposite to the Administrative block of the university on its northeast side. Being the information centre of the technological university in the state, the university library has built up a balanced collection in all branches of science and technology, social sciences, humanities, languages and legal studies. At present the collection exceeds 70000 inclusive of several valuable reference books, doctoral theses, back volumes of periodicals, patents, CD-ROM databases etc.

Prof.A.B. George took charge as the first University Librarian. After his retirement Dr.C.V.Rajan Pillai joined the University as University Librarian. After his tenure Dr.M.D.Baby took charge as Deputy Librarian -in-charge and later on she became the University Librarian.

ORGANIZATION OF THE LIBRARY RESOURCES

Documents are classified according to Universal Decimal classification and indexed according to Anglo-American Cataloguing Rules with local variations. The Library offers computerized catalogue search service through the OPAC (Online Public Access Catalogue) interface of ADLIB software.

The University Library building is functional and is modular in construction. It has an area of 17000sq.ft. In four floors. The Ground floor houses the circulation counter, information desk, membership desk and display of new arrivals of books. The office of the Librarian, books on science and technology, reference collection, OPAC and Internet are also provided here. The books on humanities, social sciences and periodicals are provided in the first floor. A reading room for newspapers and periodicals are also housed here, facility for searching electronic information sources are also available in the periodical hall. The Administrative office, Acquisition and Technical section are located in the cellar of the building. The library has started a special collection section on the top floor of the building. It includes Theses, Patents, Art books, W.H.O and other U.N documents, Census reports, Planning Board publications and books on library and information sciences. The University library is the repository of Indian patents. About 28000 odd patents form an important part of this collection.

For the functional convenience, Cochin University Library is also divided in to different sections such as Acquisition, Technical, Circulations, Periodical, Maintenance, Information Technology etc where the conventional functions as in other University libraries are done. The library offers the following information services: Loan Services, Inter-library loan service, Literature search service, Reference service, Compilation of bibliographies, Reprographic service, Reprint service, Conference alert service, New Addition alert service, Patent information and Consultancy service.

The Internet access room has 15 fully functional Internet terminals and the service is free to the university community on first come first serve basis. Reservation of time slot in Internet service is also provided for students.

The library has a good collection of multimedia encyclopedias and dictionaries and a number of CD's of books on different subject fields. The library is subscribing chemical Abstracts in CD format. The users can copy the search results on floppies. A database of Current Contents Abstracts of ISI, Philadelphia is maintained to support the research needs of students.

The Library has been participating in the Information and Library Network of U.G.C (INFLIBNET) by contributing data to their database. With the financial assistance of from INFLIBNET, the library has acquired several PCs, printers and other computer accessories. The INFLIBNET database is accessible on-line through its website.

LIBRARY RULES

The library is kept open on all working days from 9am to 8pm. On second Saturdays and Sundays the library works from 10am to 4pm. Membership of the library is open to the students, research scholars, teachers and non-teaching staff of the university. Graduates of recognized Universities of three years standing who are residents in Greater Cochin area are also entitled for membership. Industrial and research institutions are admitted to institutional membership. The teachers can borrow 6 books at a time. The research scholars are permitted to take 4 books at a time while the post-graduates students and non-teaching staffs are permitted to borrow 3 books at a time. Graduates members can take only one book and institutional members are permitted to take 10 books.

8. THE PROBLEM OF THE PRESENT STUDY AND DEFINITION OF KEY TERMS

The study is entitled “A Survey of Organisation, Administration and Utilization of University Libraries in Kerala with Special Reference to Calicut University Library”.

The terms “Organisation and administration” as used in the study stand for the evaluation of University Libraries with respect to their organizational and administrative set up, staff, library collection, finance, services, automation and physical facilities.

The term ‘utilization’ stands for the use of the library resources by the, the students, the research scholars and the teachers with respect to the frequency of their library visits, the purposes of use, time spent in the library and the use of the library services.

By ‘University Library’ is meant the library or group of libraries established, maintained and administered by a

University to meet the needs of its students, research scholars and teachers.

The term 'Kerala' denotes the geographical area covered by the political map of the state under the same name.

The term 'Calicut University Library' is used to denote the C.H. Mohammed Koya Library, the Central Library of the university situated in the Calicut University Campus at Tenhipalam.

9. NEED AND SIGNIFICANCE OF THE STUDY

The importance of a university library in the process of higher education and in the promotion of research has been established and acknowledged for long. A well-established library with an all-round, adequate and up-to-date collection suitable for study and research is a *sine qua non* for modern higher education. No university can perform its academic objectives without a strong library at its centre. It is from the university library that all teaching and research activities should radiate. It is the central workshop of the university, which provides students, teachers and research scholars with the tools required for their overall advancement.

The functioning of a university library must be generally in conformity with the educational objectives of the parent institution i.e., the university. The library contributes to the realization of these objectives and supports the total programme by acquiring and making available the books, the materials, and the services, which are needed. The well organized and properly administered university library serves as an invaluable aid in the conservation of knowledge and ideas by acquiring and processing reading materials.

The importance of this study is that it is a survey to find out the existing state of the university libraries in Kerala with respect to their organizational set up, administrative efficiency, mode of financing, adequacy of the collection, efficiency of various types of services rendered by these libraries, adequacy of he physical facilities and utilization of these libraries by the academic community. The study also aims to investigate the existing staff pattern, method of book selection, technical processing and adaptation and utilization of information technology. Such detailed studies are very rare in India and no single work has so far been done in the state of Kerala. The problems faced by different university libraries in Kerala, with particular reference to Calicut University Library will be found out. The study will help to work out solutions for some of the crucial problems and will suggest an ideal system for the organization, administration and utilization of university libraries in Kerala. This should prove useful for the overall improvement of university library services in Kerala. It is hoped that the present study will be of great help to students, teachers, library personnel, educationists and also to the library and University authorities.

10. LIMITATIONS OF THE STUDY

The present study is only at the level of a region, i.e., the State of Kerala. A study at the level of a country is not feasible in a country like India because of the vast area and large number of university libraries. Hence the study is limited to the state of Kerala. There are seven universities in Kerala. This study covers only four university libraries. Calicut University Library, Kerala University Library, Cochin University Library and Mahatma Gandhi University Library. The Kerala Agriculture University Library is not included in the sphere of this study as the nature of its reading materials, equipments, source of finance, clientele etc are different, and hence the comparison with other university libraries will be difficult and unbalanced. The other two, namely Sri Sankara University of Sanskrit and Kannur University are new Universities where full-fledged university libraries are not yet functioning. As such these two universities are also kept outside the purview of this study. Even though the study is limited to the four university libraries, it is expected that it will bring to light problems common to other university libraries as well, and the conclusions will be useful not only to the university libraries in Kerala but also to other university libraries in the country.

11. ORGANIZATION OF THE THESIS

The report of the study is organized in six chapters, the details of which are given below:

Chapter 1 Introduction

1.1 Higher education

1.2 Objectives and functions of university library

1.3 The Inflibnet

1.4 University Libraries in Kerala

1.5 The Problem of the present Study and Definition of Key Terms

1.6 Need and Significance of the Study

1.7 Limitations of the Study

1.8 Organization of the Thesis

Chapter 2 Review of Related Studies

2.1 Organization and Administration of University Libraries

2.2 Library and Information Services

2.3 Use of University Libraries

Chapter 3 Research Methodology

3.1 Objectives of the study

3.2 Hypotheses

3.3 Methodology

3.4 Sources of data

3.5 Selection of the Sample

3.6 Statistical tools used

3.7 Analysis of the Data

Chapter 4 The University Libraries in Kerala; the State of the Art

4.1 University Library Management

4.2 Library Personnel

4.3 University Library Collections

4.4 Library Finance

4.5 University Library Services

4.6 Library Automation

4.7 Physical Facilities

Chapter 5 The Use of University Libraries

5.1 Frequency of Library Visits

5.2 Duration of the Library Use

5.3 Purposes of Visits in the University Libraries

5.4 Utility of Information obtained from the University Libraries

5.5 Ranking of Reading materials most used in the University Libraries

5.6 Sources to identify the Books and other materials

Chapter 6 Summary of the Findings and Suggestions

6.1 Summary of the Findings

6.2 Tenability of the Hypotheses

6.3 Suggestions

6.4 Suggestion of Areas for Further Research.

12. FINDINGS AND SUGGESTIONS

The analysis of the data collected through various sources, has revealed a number of findings with regarded to the organisation, administration and utilisation of university libraries in Kerala. The study provides the summary of the findings, suggestions for the proper organisation, administration ad utilisation of university libraries, tenability of hypotheses and suggestions of areas for further research.

The major findings that have evolved from the discussion in the previous chapters are summed up here under the heads Library Management, Library staff, Library finance, Library collections, Library services, Library automation, Physical facilities and use of university libraries.

SUMMARY OF THE FINDINGS

Library Management

1. The university libraries in Kerala are generally governed by the university authorities. However, in the Mahatma Gandhi University Library and the Cochin University Library have Library Advisory Committees with the Vice-Chancellor as chairman and University Librarian as convener. In other university libraries, in the absence of Library Advisory Committees, the policies are decided by the university authorities.

Library Personnel

2. The UGC scheme regarding scales of pay, career advancement etc. was implemented to qualified librarians in the university libraries in Kerala, but the anomalies are not rectified even today.
3. The library professional staff such as Junior Librarian/ Reference Assistant, Professional Assistant. Gr. I/ Technical Assistant (Library) and Professional Assistant Gr. II/Library Assistant are not brought under the purview of the UGC scheme. They get the scales of pay prevalent in the State of Kerala and promotions in the ratio of 3:5:4. Their scales of pay are also not uniform.
4. Presently the Cochin University alone has a University Librarian and in all other university libraries in Kerala, the senior most Deputy Librarians/ Asst.Librarian are put in charge of the University Librarians.
5. The number of library professional staff in the university libraries studied is substantially high.
6. The professional staff working in various sections of the Calicut University Library is much higher than the recommended formula of the UGC Library Committee.
7. The majority of users of Mahatma Gandhi University Library and Cochin University Library are of the view that the library staff are helpful to the readers, but, half of the users of Calicut University Library and majority of

users of Kerala University Library give a different opinion, i.e., the staff members are not helpful.

8. The majority of users from science and humanities departments and majority of research scholars, teachers and half of the students are of the opinion that the library staff in the university libraries are helpful to the readers. Whereas the majority of users of language background view that the staff members are not helpful.
9. The majority of users from humanities and languages and majority of research scholars responded that the staff in the Calicut University Library is not helpful to them. But, the majority of users from science, majority of the teachers and half of the students viewed that the staff are helpful.
10. The majority of users of Calicut University Library, Kerala University Library and Cochin University Library responded that the library staff are not cordial to the users. But the majority of users of Mahatma Gandhi University Library have a different opinion. i.e., staffs of the university libraries are cordial to the users. The majority of users of all subject groups and with different status responded that the staff members are not cordial to the users.
11. The majority of users from all subject groups and with different status from Calicut University viewed that the staff members are not cordial to the users.
12. The majority of users from all the University Libraries responded that the library staff in the university libraries are not prompt. The majority of users of all subject groups and with different status also expressed the same opinion.
13. The majority of users from all subject groups and status groups of Calicut University Library are of the view that the staff members are not prompt.
14. The majority of users of Calicut University Library and Kerala University Library viewed that the staff of these libraries are not capable of providing the required

information to the users. Whereas the majority of users of Mahatma Gandhi University Library and Cochin University Library opined that the staff members are capable of providing the required information to the users.

15. The majority of users from science departments responded that the staff members of university libraries are capable of providing the required information to the users, but the majority users of humanities and language departments and status wise groups gave a different opinion.
16. The majority of students, research scholars and teachers opined that the staff members of university libraries are not capable of providing the required information to the users.
17. The majority of users of different subject groups and the majority of students and research scholars from Calicut University Library expressed that the staff members are not capable for providing the required information to the users, but the majority of teachers have a different view.

Library Collections

18. The Good Offices Committee terms and conditions are followed in the purchase of books in all university libraries in Kerala except in Calicut University Library.
19. The Calicut University Library itself fixes the terms and conditions for purchase of books and other materials every year.
20. The University Librarians mainly select general and reference books and Heads of teaching departments are responsible for selecting subject books in the university libraries studied. In the Cochin University Library, the Library Advisory Committee also participates in the process of selection of documents.
21. All university libraries in Kerala procure periodicals directly from the publishers/their sole agents.

22. All university libraries in Kerala except Kerala University Library follow Kardex and serials control database for registration of periodicals. In Kerala University Library, the three-card system and serials control database are used for the purpose.
23. The Kerala University Library subscribes to more than 300 periodicals. The Mahatma Gandhi University Library and the Cochin University Library subscribe to 280 and 223 periodicals respectively, where as Calicut University Library subscribes to only 154 periodicals.
24. The collection of books, periodicals and other reading materials in the Calicut University Library is much less compared to other university libraries. Proper weightage for actual requirements of users are not seen considered in the process of collection development in the university libraries under study because of the financial constraints and interference of teachers, in the book selection process.
25. The majority of users of Calicut University Library, Kerala University Library. Mahatma Gandhi University Library and Cochin University Library responded that the library collection in their libraries are sufficient only to meet their requirements partially. The majority of users of different departments and of status wise groups also express the same opinion.
26. All the users from science departments and the majority from humanities and language departments and the majority of student's and all research scholars and teachers of Calicut University Library could not meet their requirements fully with the existing collection of Calicut University Library.
27. The majority of users of all the university libraries viewed that the books available in these libraries are not adequate for their study/research/teaching purposes. The majority of the users of subject wise categories and status wise categories also held this view.

28. The majority of the users of subject wise groups and status wise groups of Calicut University Library also expressed that the books available in this library are not adequate.
29. The majority of users of Mahatma Gandhi University Library and Cochin University Library viewed that the reference books available in these libraries are adequate for their purposes, where as the majority of users of Calicut University Library and Kerala University Library expressed that the reference books available in the university libraries are not adequate. The majority of subject wise and status wise groups of users of university libraries under study expressed that reference books in these libraries are not adequate.
30. The majority of subject wise and status wise groups of users of Calicut University Library opined that the reference books available in the library are not adequate for their purposes.
31. The majority of users of all university libraries responded that the subject journals and back issues subject journals available in these libraries are not adequate. The majority of subject wise and status wise groups of users of university libraries hold this view.
32. The majority of users of different subject groups and status groups of Calicut University Library also viewed that the subject journals and back issues of subject journals available in these libraries are inadequate.
33. The majority of users in all university libraries under study expressed that the indices, abstracts and bibliographies available in these libraries are not at all adequate. The great majority of subject wise and status wise groups of users of university libraries also hold this view.
34. The majority of users of different subject groups and status groups of Calicut University Library also expressed the same opinion about the adequacy of indices, abstracts and bibliographies.

Library Finance

35. The funds allocated from the University budget, State Plan Grants and grants from the U.G.C, constitute the major source of income for purchase of reading materials in all the university libraries in Kerala. The Kerala University, the parent university in Kerala could allot more funds to the university library during the last five years. The Mahatma Gandhi University and Cochin University also could allot more funds to their University libraries than the Calicut University.

36. The Calicut University Library, the Kerala University Library, the Mahatma Gandhi University Library and the Cochin University Library expend on an average of 1.53 per cent, 2.09 per cent, 2.91 per cent and 4.04 per cent respectively of the total university expenditure only to the library during the last five years, which is much lesser than the national and international norms prescribed. The Radhakrishnan Commission recommended 6.5 per cent and Kothari Commission recommends 6 per cent to 10 percent of total university expenditure for the library. As such the finance available for these university libraries is totally inadequate

37. The Calicut University, Kerala University, Mahatma Gandhi University and Cochin University had allotted on an average Rs.7986793/, Rs. 19667100/, Rs.13000000/ , and Rs.11465000/ respectively for the libraries during the last five years.

38. The Cochin University Library has spent more amounts for purchase of books and journals compared to other university libraries in Kerala. They spent on an average of Rs. 60 lakhs per year for this purpose, while Calicut University Library spent only on an average of Rs.8.25 lakhs for the same. The Kerala University Library and Mahatma Gandhi University Library spent on an average Rs. 45 lakhs and Rs. 38.6 lakhs respectively for the purchase of books and journals.

39. The Cochin University Library spent 51.95 per cent for books and journals, the Kerala University Library, Calicut University Library and Mahatma Gandhi University Library spent only 23.68 percent, 9.89 percent and 29.45 percent respectively for this purpose.
40. The percentage of expenditure on books and journals in Calicut University Library, Kerala University Library and Mahatma Gandhi University Library are much below the national and international standards. But the percentage of expenditure in Cochin University Library for this purpose is above the national and international standards.
41. The percentage of expenditure on salaries in Calicut University Library and Kerala University Library is much higher than the national and international standards. The Calicut University Library and Kerala University Library spent 83.71 per cent and 62.86 per cent respectively while Mahatma Gandhi University Library and Cochin University Library spent 48.01 per cent and 42.6 per cent respectively.
42. The Calicut University Library expend on an average of 1.53 per cent of the total university expenditure only to the library during the last five years, which is much lesser than the national and international norms prescribe.
43. The University library finance in Kerala reflects that the entire structure of financing needs extra support. The library resources in Kerala are not sufficient to meet the current as well as future requirements. It is also divulged that the amount spent by Calicut University Library for the purchase of books and journals in each year is much less, than that of other university libraries in Kerala.

Library Services

44. While the Calicut University Library and Mahatma Gandhi University Library use Dewey Decimal Classification scheme, the Kerala University Library follows Colon Classification and the Cochin University

Library use Universal Decimal Classification Scheme for classifying the documents. The Calicut University Library, Mahatma Gandhi University Library and Cochin University Library use AACR for cataloguing the documents. On the other hand, Kerala University Library follows Classified Catalogue Code of Dr.Ranganathan for this purpose. But, recently all university libraries in Kerala have started following the standard formats of computerized cataloguing.

45. The majority of users of Kerala University Library do not find the classification and cataloguing systems helpful for locating documents, whereas the majority of users of all other University libraries found them as helpful for tracing the documents. The subject wise and status wise groups of users also viewed that the classification and cataloguing system followed in these university libraries are helpful.
46. The majority of the users from science and humanities departments from Calicut University and the majority of research scholars and teachers opined that the classification and cataloguing followed in this library are helpful to locate the documents. But the users from language departments and majority of students viewed that the classification and cataloguing are not helpful.
47. It is found that Mahatma Gandhi University Library and the Cochin University Library regularly conduct weeding out programmes to make their collection up to date, but the other two university libraries do not conduct the same.
48. It is ascertained that the Calicut University Library is the only University Library in Kerala where the stock verification is conducted at least once in its lifetime.
49. The University libraries in Kerala have limited themselves to provide the traditional services, such as loan services, reference service, reprography service etc.
50. The reprographic service is available in all the university libraries in Kerala.

51. The documentation service is available only in Kerala University Library. The Calicut University Library has stopped this service, though the infrastructure to provide this service is available.

52. The majority of users of university libraries under study irrespective of subjects background and status groups require initiation in the 'library organization', 'library collection' and ' library services'. The majority of users of Cochin University Library are not in need of initiation in 'search of documents', whereas majority of users of other libraries do require this service. The majority of users from science departments do not want initiation in the 'search of documents', where as the majority of users from humanities and languages are in need of initiation in this area also.

53. The study revealed that most of the students and even research scholars and teachers of the universities under study are not aware of many of the modern library and information services. This is mainly because the university libraries under study do not provide several of these services.

54. The majority of users of all the university libraries except Kerala University Library are not aware about the 'Circulation of accession lists'. The 'indexing of articles' is familiar to the majority of users of Kerala University Library, Mahatma Gandhi University Library and half of the users of Calicut University Library, but the majority of users of Cochin University Library, are not familiar with this service. The 'Compilation of bibliographies' is familiar to the majority of users of Kerala University Library, but this service is not familiar to the majority of users of other university libraries. The majority of users of Kerala University library and Cochin University Library know about 'inter-library loan service', but the majority of users of other University libraries do not know about this service. The 'reprographic service' is familiar to the majority of users of all University libraries except Cochin

University Library. But the 'local abstracting service', 'routing of periodicals', 'contents page service', 'translation service' etc., are not familiar to the majority of users of all university libraries.

55. The majority of users of from science departments are aware of 'circulation of accession lists', whereas the majority of users of humanities and languages are not familiar with this service. The majority of users of all subject groups are familiar with the 'indexing of articles' and 'reprographic services'. The majority of users of science, humanities and language departments are not familiar with 'local abstracting services', 'routing of periodicals', 'contents page services', 'compilation of bibliographies', 'inter-library loan services', 'translation service' and the 'selective dissemination of information service'.

56. The 'circulation of accession lists', 'indexing of articles' and 'reprographic services' are known to the majority of research scholars and teachers, where as the majority of students are not aware of these services. The 'local abstracting service', 'routing of periodicals' and 'translation service' are known to the majority of teachers but these services are not known to the majority of students and research scholars. The 'contents page service' and 'compilation of bibliographies' are not familiar to the majority of students, research scholars and teachers.

57. The majority of teachers of Calicut University are familiar with the 'Circulation of access on lists', but the majority of students and research scholars are not familiar with this service. The 'indexing of articles' is known to the majority of research scholars and teachers of Calicut University, where as the majority of students do not know about this service. The 'local abstracting service', 'routing of periodicals', 'compilation of bibliographies', 'interlibrary-loan services' and 'selective dissemination of information service' are not familiar to the majority of

students, research scholars and teachers of this university.

58. The majority of users from humanities and language departments of Calicut University are aware about the 'indexing of articles', but the majority of science users are not aware about this service. The 'reprographic service' is familiar to the majority of all subject groups of users. The 'local abstracting service', 'routing of periodicals', 'contents page service', 'compilation of bibliographies', 'translation service' and 'selective dissemination of information service' are not known to the majority of subject wise groups of users of Calicut University Library.

59. The study /research/teaching works of majority of users of Calicut University Library, Kerala University Library and Mahatma Gandhi University Library irrespective of the subject background and status category are not adversely affected due to the lack of efficient library and information services in these libraries. But the majority of users of Cochin University Library expressed that their works are adversely affected due to the lack of efficient library and information services.

60. The majority of science users of Calicut University Library expressed that their studies are adversely affected due to the lack of efficient library and information services, but the majority of humanities and language users have given a different opinion. The majority of research scholars and teachers of Calicut University expressed that their research/teaching works are adversely affected due to the lack of efficient library and information services in Calicut University Library, but the majority of students viewed that their studies are not affected by the absence of efficient library services.

Library Automation

61. The retrospective conversion of bibliographic data is almost completed and these were done in house, in all university libraries.

62. The computerizations of library activities are mainly financed by the U.G.C. in all universities libraries expect Cochin University Library, where the funds are received from Netherlands.
63. All libraries have network connection with the INFLIBNET. The Mahatma Gandhi University Library and Cochin University Library have network connection with DELNET also.
64. The house keeping operations such as acquisition, cataloguing, serials control, circulation etc. are computerized in the Calicut University Library, the Mahatma Gandhi University Library and the Cochin University Library. On other hand, many of these activities are not fully computerized in the Kerala University Library.
65. The Internet search facilities and infonet service are available in all university libraries studied.
66. The computerized library services, such as current awareness service, S.D.I service, New additions alert service, computerized reference service, indexing of articles, online services, CD/DVD search service, computerized user education etc., are not provided in the University libraries in Kerala.
67. In Calicut University Library some of the manual procedures followed hither to are still continued partly or fully due to malfunctioning of outdated versions of computers every now and then.

Physical Facilities

68. The University libraries in Kerala in general, lack the essential physical facilities, which is pre-requisite for comfortable use of the libraries. Sufficient space is not seen provided for users, documents, staff and equipments. The lighting and ventilation are insufficient. The furnitures used in the libraries are outmoded and insufficient.

69. All users of Calicut University Library, Kerala University Library. Mahatma Gandhi University Library and majority of users of Cochin University Library irrespective of the subject background and the status of users are not satisfied with the location of libraries.

70. The majority of users of all university libraries irrespective of status of users are satisfied with the space available in the libraries.

71. The furniture available in the Calicut University Library, Mahatma Gandhi University Library and Cochin University Library are satisfactory, but the majority of users of Kerala University Library are not satisfied with the furniture available in that library. The majority of users of humanities, half of the users of language departments, majority of science users and students in general are not satisfied with the furniture. The majority of research scholars and teachers are satisfied with the available furniture in these libraries.

72. The majority of users from science, humanities and languages are not satisfied with the location of Calicut University Library building. The space available in this library is satisfactory to all subject groups of users. The majority of humanities, languages and half of science users are also satisfied with the available furniture. All the students, research scholars and teachers are not satisfied with the location of Calicut University Library building. The majority of research scholars and teachers are satisfied with the space available in this library, but the majority of students are not satisfied with this. The furniture available in the Calicut University Library is satisfactory to the majority of research scholars and teachers, where as the majority of students are not satisfied with the available furniture in the library.

USE OF THE UNIVERSITY LIBRARIES

Frequency of Library Visits

73. The frequency of use of university libraries in Kerala by

the academic community is not considerable. The maximum number of users of Calicut University Library and Cochin University Library visit the library 'twice or thrice a week', and the maximum number of users of Kerala University Library and Mahatma Gandhi University Library visit the University library 'once a week'. The maximum number of users of science and humanities departments visit the library 'twice or thrice a week' and the maximum number of users from language departments visit the library 'once a week'. The maximum number of students and research scholars visit the library 'twice or thrice a week', whereas the maximum of teachers visit the library 'once a week'. Generally the users of Calicut University Library, Cochin University Library, users of science and humanities and the students and research scholars visit the university libraries more frequently, than the users of Kerala University Library, Mahatma Gandhi University Library, users of language departments and teachers respectively.

74. The maximum of science and humanities users of Calicut University Library visit the library 'twice or thrice a week', where as the language users visit the library 'once a week'. The maximum of students and research scholars of Calicut University Library visit the library 'twice or thrice a week', but maximum of teachers visit the library 'once in week'. Generally the science and humanities users of Calicut University Library visit the library more frequently than the language users. The students and research scholars visit the Calicut University Library more frequently than the teachers.

Duration of the Library Use

75. The duration of library use in general by the academic community is insignificant, as good number of the users of the University Libraries in Kerala spent less than one hour only on an average per week in these libraries. A good number of users from different subject backgrounds and research scholars spent only 30 minutes to one hour

and 'one hour to two hours' on an average per week in the university libraries respectively. Generally, the research scholars and teachers spent more time in university libraries than the students. There is no significant difference in the duration of library use by the users of various subject groups in the Calicut University Library.

Purpose of the Library Visits

76. The majority of users visit the university libraries to 'read/borrow/return books on specific subjects', i.e., the first preference for readers visits it to the university libraries is for 'read/borrow/return specific subject books'. The second preference is to 'read subject journals' and to 'read/borrow/return general books'. The third preference of readers to visit the university libraries is 'to consult reference books'.

77. The majority of users in Calicut University also visit the library mainly to 'read/borrow/return specific subject books', then 'to read/borrow/return general books'. The third preference is to 'consult reference books' and 'consult theses/dissertations etc'. The majority is serious users as they visit the Calicut University Library for reading/ borrowing/returning books on specific subjects.

Utility of Information Obtained from the University Libraries

78. The majority of the clientele utilize the information obtained from the University libraries for 'study purpose' and 'research purpose' and secondly for 'teaching purpose' and 'writing of articles'. The users of Calicut University Library also ranked 'study purpose' as their first preference.

Reading Materials Most Used in the University Libraries

79. The majority of users ranked 'Books' as the most used material, then 'reference books', 'subject journals', 'Back issues of subject journals' in the order of preference. The 'Books' are the most used reading material by the users in the university libraries in Kerala and the main purpose of use is study/research/teaching. There is no major

difference in the ranking of reading materials most used by the users of Calicut University Library and other university libraries in Kerala.

Sources to Identify the Books and Other Materials

80. The majority of the academic community use 'Library Catalogue' to identify the documents from the university libraries. The 'Library Staff' and 'Books and Journals displayed in the library' are ranked as second and third respectively. In Calicut University Library also the 'Library Catalogue' is the most used source for selection of books and other reading materials from the university library.

13. TENABILITY OF THE HYPOTHESES

Hypothesis I

The Staff of the university libraries in Kerala in general and Calicut University Library in particular are not helpful, cordial and prompt to the users.

This Hypothesis has been partially proved by the findings 7 to 13.

The majority of users of Mahatma Gandhi University Library and Cochin University Library are of the view that the library staff are helpful to the readers, but, half of the users of Calicut University Library and majority of users of Kerala University Library give a different opinion, i.e., the staff members are not helpful. The majority of users from science and humanities departments and majority of research scholars, teachers and half of the students are of the opinion that the library staff in the university libraries are helpful to the readers. Whereas the majority of users of language background view that the staff members are not helpful. The majority of users from humanities and languages and majority of research scholars responded that the staff in the Calicut University Library is not helpful to them. But, the majority of users from science, majority of the teachers and half of the students viewed that the staff are helpful.

The majority of users of Calicut University Library, Kerala

University Library and Cochin University Library responded that the library staff is not cordial to the users. But the majority of users of Mahatma Gandhi University Library have a different opinion. i.e., staffs of the university libraries are cordial to the users. The majority of users of all subject groups and with different status responded that the staff members are not cordial to the users. The majority of the users from all subject groups and with different status from Calicut University viewed that the staff members are not cordial to the users.

The majority of users from all the University Libraries responded that the library staff in the university libraries is not prompt. The majority of users of all subject groups and with different status also expressed the same opinion. The majority of users from all subject groups and status groups of Calicut University Library are of the view that he staff members are not prompt.

Hypothesis II

The Staff of the university libraries in Kerala in general and Calicut University Library in particular are not capable of providing proper library and information services to the academic community.

This Hypothesis has also been partially proved by the findings 14 to 16.

The majority of users of Calicut University Library and Kerala University Library viewed that the staff of these libraries are not capable of providing the required information to the users. Whereas the majority of users of Mahatma Gandhi University Library and Cochin University Library opined that the staff members are capable of providing the required information to the users. The majority of users from science departments responded that the staff members of university libraries are capable of providing the required information to the users, but the majority users of humanities and language departments and status wise groups gave a different opinion. The majority of students, research scholars and teachers opined that the staff members of university libraries are not capable of providing the required information to the users.

The majority of users of different subject groups and the majority of students and research scholars from Calicut University Library expressed that the staff members are not capable for providing the required information to the users, but the majority of teachers have a different view.

Hypothesis III

The collections of the university libraries under study, particularly those of the Calicut University Library are not adequate to meet the requirements of the students, research scholars and teachers.

This Hypothesis has been substantiated by the findings 23 to 26.

The Kerala University Library subscribes to more than 300 periodicals. The Mahatma Gandhi University Library and the Cochin University Library subscribe to 280 and 223 periodicals respectively, where as Calicut University Library subscribes to only 154 periodicals. The collection of books, periodicals and other reading materials in the Calicut University Library is much less compared to other university libraries. Proper attention for actual requirements of users are not seen considered in the process of collection development in the university libraries under study because of the financial constraints and interference of teachers, in the book selection process.

The majority of users of all the university libraries in Kerala are of the view that the library collection in their libraries are sufficient only to meet their requirements partially. The majorities of the users from different departments and of all status groups also express the same opinion. All the users from science departments and the majority from humanities and language departments and the majority of students and all research scholars and teachers of Calicut University Library could not meet their requirements fully with the existing collection of Calicut University Library.

The majority of users of all the university libraries viewed that the books available in these libraries are not adequate for their study/research/teaching purposes. The majority of the users of subject wise categories and status wise categories also held this view. The majority of the users of different subject groups and status groups of the Calicut University Library also expressed that the books available in this library are not adequate.

Hypothesis IV

The financial resources available for the university libraries in Kerala in general and Calicut University Library in particular are not adequate.

The finding 36 has established this Hypothesis.

The Calicut Unversity Library, the Kerala University Library, the Mahatma Gandhi University Library and the Cochin University Library spent on an average of 1.53 per cent, 2.09 per cent 2.91 per cent and 4.04 per cent respectively of the total university expenditure to the library during the last five years, which is much lesser than the national and international norms prescribed. Among the four university libraries, the Calicut Unversity Library spent the least. The Radhakrishnan Commission recommended 6.5 per cent and Kothari Commission recommends 6 per cent to 10 percent of total university expenditure for the library. As such the finance available for these university libraries, particularly in the Calicut University Library is totally inadequate.

Hypothesis V

The allocation of library finance for reading materials in the universities in Kerala is not in accordance with any standard and hence insufficient.

This Hypothesis has been proved by the findings 39 to 41.

The Cochin University Library spent 51.95 per cent for books and journals, the Kerala University Library, Calicut University Library and Mahatma Gandhi University Library spent only 23.68 percent, 9.89 percent and 29.45 percent respectively for this purpose.. It is also divulged that the amount spent by Calicut University Library for the purchase of books and journals in each year is much less, than that of other university libraries in Kerala.

The percentage of expenditure on books and journals in Calicut University Library, Kerala University Library and Mahatma Gandhi University Library are much below the national and international standards. But the percentage of expenditure in Cochin University Library for this purpose is above the national and international standards. The percentage of expenditure on salaries in Calicut University Library and Kerala University Library is much higher than the national and international standards.

Hypothesis VI

The study / research / teaching activities of the students, research scholars and teachers are adversely affected by the lack of provision of proper and efficient library and information services in the university libraries in Kerala.

This Hypothesis has been partially substantiated by the findings 49 to 51 and 53 to 60.

The University libraries in Kerala have limited themselves to provide the traditional services, such as loan services, reference service, reprography service etc. The reprographic service is available in all the university libraries in Kerala. The documentation service is available only in Kerala University Library. The Calicut University Library has stopped this service, though the infrastructure to provide this service is available.

The study revealed that most of the students and even research scholars and teachers of the universities under study are not aware of many of the modern library and information services, as many of such services are not provided in these libraries.

The study /research/teaching works of majority of the users of Calicut University Library, Kerala University Library and Mahatma Gandhi University Library are not adversely affected due to the lack of efficient library and information services in these libraries. But, the majority of users of Cochin University Library expressed that their works are adversely affected due to the lack of efficient library and information services.

The majority of science users of Calicut University Library expressed that their studies are adversely affected due to the lack of efficient library and information services, but the majority of humanities and language users have given a different opinion. The majority of research scholars and teachers of Calicut University expressed that their research/teaching works are adversely affected due to the lack of efficient library and information services in Calicut University Library, but the majority of students viewed that their studies are not affected by the absence of efficient library services.

Hypothesis VII

The use of the university libraries under study by the students, research scholars and teachers is not significant.

This Hypothesis has been confirmed by the findings 74 to 76.

The frequency of use of university libraries in Kerala by the academic community is not considerable. The maximum number of users of Calicut University Library, Kerala University Library, Mahatma Gandhi University Library and Cochin University Library visit the library 'once a week' or 'twice or thrice a week'. The maximum number of users of science and humanities departments visit the library 'twice or thrice a week' and the maximum number of users from language departments visit the library 'once a week'. The maximum number of students and research scholars visit the library 'twice or thrice a week', whereas the maximum of teachers visit the library 'once a week'.

The maximum of users of science and humanities background of Calicut University Library visit the library 'twice or thrice a week', where as the language users visit the library 'once a week'. The maximum of students and research scholars of Calicut University Library visit the library 'twice or thrice a week', but maximum of teachers visit the library 'once in week'. Generally the science and humanities users of Calicut University Library visit the library more frequently than the language users. The students and research scholars visit the Calicut University Library more frequently than the teachers.

The duration of library use in general by the academic community is insignificant, as good number of the users of the University Libraries in Kerala spent less than one hour only on an average per week in these libraries. A good number of users from different subject backgrounds and research scholars spent only '30 minutes to one hour and 'one hour to two hours' on an average per week in the universities libraries respectively.

14. SUGGESTIONS

The findings of the study have brought out many facts, which are of interest and significance to the university authorities, the funding agencies, the university librarians, the users and the educationists. It is rightly realized that there must be qualitative improvements with respect to the university libraries in order to achieve the aims and objectives of higher education quickly and effectively. At present there are several bottlenecks for the proper development of these university libraries. The university libraries in Kerala are faced mainly with acute shortage of financial resources. It is fundamental that they are sorted out and the university libraries are empowered to perform their role efficiently and effectively. Though this study is limited to the university libraries in Kerala, the findings are equally applicable to the organisation, administration and utilization of university libraries in India as well. Long experience of the researcher in the area of study, discussion with experts and study of literature on the subject facilitated him to formulate a set of suggestions for the proper organisation, administration and utilization of university libraries in Kerala. They are:

1. Library Advisory Committee with Vice-chancellor as chairman and University Librarian as convener has to be set up in all universities to formulate policy decisions.

The powers of the committee have to be well defined.

2. The posts of University Librarian in all university libraries in Kerala have to be filled up at the earliest. The University Librarian has to be made an ex-officio member of all academic bodies.
3. The actual requirements of professional staff in different sections of the university libraries have to be assessed using national standard. The works of the sections and the professionals in the sections have to be specified and workflow has to be standardized.
4. The professional staff of the library should have academic status not only in the case of salary scales, but also in other service matters such as promotional avenues, retirement age, faculty improvement incentives, study leave etc.
5. The UGC scheme has to be extended to all professional staff in the universities and the existing ratio promotion scheme has to be abolished. The professional staff in the university libraries in Kerala has to be given regular refresher courses in computerization and modern library and information services.
6. The library staff has to strive to render quality service in the libraries and enhance the image of the profession with a view to merit the higher status held by them in the society.
7. Book selection has to be regarded as joint responsibility of librarians and teachers. The overall responsibility has to lie with the librarian aided by the teachers.
8. For efficient and balanced book selection with great economy the university libraries in Kerala should device some cooperative acquisition schemes for purchasing Indian books and other reading materials. An acquisitive programme may be undertaken in which all standard publishers in the country have to be invariably sent at least one copy of their latest publications to each

university library immediately after publication at a special discount rate. This programme has the following advantages.

i. All university libraries will get every new standard book on each subject published in the country.

ii. The books will be received in the university library as soon as they are published.

iii. Since the supply of books is on special discount rate, it will be profitable and economical for the university libraries, as there will not be any middleman.

9. For the selection and acquisition of standard foreign publications, the UGC may develop a programme to make available at least one copy of every standard book in every subject published outside the country to the university libraries similar to the UGC - INFONET service for subscription of online periodicals.

10. The university libraries in Kerala need to strengthen the primary sources such as periodicals, reports, standards, patents, theses, dissertations etc. essentially needed for research.

11. The State Government, the UGC and the university may formulate a policy based on judicious norms for funding university libraries which would ensure balanced growth of collection and effective library and information services.

12. The Universities have to accept Kothari Commossion recommendations of 6.5 per cent to 10 per cent of the total institutional budget for the library according to the stage of development of the library.

13. The extraordinary in balance between the expenditure on salaries in Calicut University Library and Kerala University Library and on the purchase of books and other reading materials has to be rectified by increasing the allocation for procurement of reading materials in these university libraries.

14. The university libraries in Kerala have to provide the modern library and information services such as circulation of accession lists, routing of periodicals, contents page service, indexing of articles, local abstracting service, interlibrary loan service, consultancy service, patent information service, user education service etc. to meet the various educational requirements of the users.
15. The university libraries in Kerala have to provide computerised services such as current awareness service, selective dissemination of information service, C.D/DVD search service, on-line database search service etc.
16. The university libraries in Kerala have to provide sufficient reading areas, space for stacking books and other materials, lighting and ventilation, furniture and equipments, drinking water and sanitation facilities etc. and care must be taken to increase these facilities proportionate to the increase in the documents and users.

15. SUGGESTIONS OF AREAS FOR FURTHER RESEARCH

The following are the areas identified for further research in this specific subject:

1. Evaluation of adequacy of various library collections for different categories of users.
2. Evaluation of the use of university libraries by different categories of the users with various subject backgrounds.
3. The study of time and cost involved in the processing of reading materials.
4. Attitudes of different categories of users towards the library and its services.
5. Academic status and job satisfaction among the library staff.
6. The problems in using the library catalogues.
7. Financial management of university libraries.
8. The effectiveness of library and information services.

9. The adequacy and functionalism of library buildings.
10. Extent and possibilities of resource sharing among the university libraries in Kerala.
11. Computer application in university libraries in Kerala

16. CONCLUSION

To sum up, the university libraries in Kerala have not been able to fulfill their obligations to fulfill the objectives of higher education because they have, insufficient financial support, inadequate book resources imeffective library services, poor physical facilities, outmoded furniture, lack of sufficient reading space and above all lack of dynamic leadership. An attempt is made by the researcher to study the state of the art of the university libraries in Kerala and the use made by the academic community. A set of suggestions and recommendations is also put forward to solve the hurdles faced by the university libraries and to make them most effective so as to serve as the nerve center of the academic activities. An earnest effort on the part of university authorities, funding agencies and state Government is urgently required for the proper development of the university libraries in Kerala.

REFERENCES

JOURNAL ARTICLES

1. Agboola, A.T, "Third generation Nigerian University libraries." *International Information and Library Review,* 25 (1), (March 1993), pp. 43-59.
2. Aguolu, C.C, "Staffing in Nigerian University Libraries." *Herald of Library Science,* 29(1-2), (January – April, 1990), pp.24-37.
3. Aina, Joseph O, "Use of Government documents at the University of Ilorin Library," *International Library Movement,* 17(2), (1995), pp. 52-60.
4. Akhidime, J.A. Fab "The training of non-professional staff in Nigerian University Libraries." *Annals of Library Science and Documentation,* 35(1) (March 1988), pp.11-19.

5. Alemna, A.A, and others "The role of libraries in the use of African published journals in African Universities", *International Information and Library Review, 33,* (2001), pp. 3-22.

6. Allen, G.G, "Resources, acquisitions and the viability of University libraries in developing countries". *Libri,* 43(3), (July-September 1993), pp. 234-244.

7. Amekuedee, J.O, "Barriers to successful University library automation in Ghana with particular reference to the Blame Library." *International Information and Library Review,* 27(2), (June 1995), pp. 171-181.

8. Amusa, O.I and Adekunnisi, S.R, "Collection development practices in a Nigerian third generation University library", *Library Herald* 41(1), (March 2003), pp. 38-49.

9. Ashoor, Mohammed Saleh, "Evaluation of the collections of Saudi University Libraries based on ACRL standards. *The International Information and Library Review.* 24(1), (March 1992), pp.3-14.

10. Atkins, Stephanie S and Weible, Cherie L, "Needles in haystack: using interlibrary loan data to identity material missing from library's collection," *Library Collections, Acquisitions, and Technical Services,* 27(2), (Summer 2003), pp. 187-2002.

11. Awogbani, Papoola A, "An analysis of instruction and orientation in the use of libraries by veteneriy medicine students in Nigerian universities", *Clis Observer,* XII (3-4), (July-December 1995), pp. 17-20.

12. Baba, Abdul Majid, "Measuring users' satisfaction with special reference to Kashmir University Library System." *Proceedings of the thirty-fourth All India Conference,* Calcutta (1988), pp. 292-298.

13. Banerjee, P. K. "Reflections on the University libraries of India". *Indian Librarian.* 19 (June 1964), pp. 23 - 27.

14. Banerjee, P.K. "Planning the University library". *Indian Librarian.* 13, (1958), pp. 240 - 247.

15. Barua, P and Tripathi, Tridib "An analysis of information seeking behaviour of research scholars vis-à-vis existing information sources and services of Burdwan University Library: A case study." *IASLIC Bulletin,* 32 (2-3), (June-September 1988), pp. 93-98.
16. Bashiruddin, S. "University libraries since independence". *Cultural forum* . 9, (1967), pp. 39 - 44.
17. Bernard, Bizimana. "Measures of library use and user satisfaction with academic library services". *Library & Information Science Research,* 18, (Summer 1996), pp.225-240.
18. Bhargava, C. D. "University libraries and educational set up of India". *Indian Librarian.* 14, (December 1959), pp 113 - 117.
19. Bii, Harison Kibet and Wangama, Patrick, "Automation and its impact an the job satisfaction among the staff of Margaret Thatcher library, Moi University", *Library Management,* 22(6-7), (2001), pp. 303-310.
20. Bonn, G. S. "State of Library Education in India". *Annals of Library Science.* 15 (1969) p.65.
21. Bose, Pramil Chandra. "The Story of Century Old University Library". *Library Herald.* 6 (1963). p.121.
22. Cannell, Sheila E and Mowat, Ian R.M. "Charges for on-line searches in University libraries: A report on a survey." *Journal of librarianship,* 14(3), (July 1982), pp. 176-203.
23. Chandraiah. "University Library Automation Scenario: A Study". Paper presented at the first International convention on Mapping Technology on Libraries and People, (CALIBER 2003) (13-15 February 2003), Ahmedabad. pp. 72-80.
24. Chang, Nai-Cheng and Perng, Jiin Huai, "Information searches habits of graduate students of Tatung University", *International Information and Library Review.* 33, (2001), pp. 341-346.

25. Cockrill, A. and Broady, J. "Opportunities and threats: the macro-economic environment of British and German University libraries." *Journal of Librarianship and Information Science,* 26 (2) (June 1994), pp. 83 -92.

26. Crawford, John C, "A survey of user of electronic services at Glasgow Caledonian University Library", *The Electronic Library,* 18(4), (2000), pp. 225-265.

27. Dabas, K.C and Sewa, Singh "Application of total quality management to University libraries of Pubjab: a study." *IASLIC Bulletin,* 45(3), (September 2000), pp. 119-128.

28. Dabas, K.C, and others. "Automation Scenario in University Libraries: A Study of Some Selected Libraries". Paper presented at the first International convention on Mapping Technology on Libraries and People, (CALIBER 2003) (13-15 February 2003), Ahmedbad, pp. 81-97

29. Dasgupta, R. K. "Some problems of University libraries in India". *Iaslic Bulletin,* 7 (December 1962), pp. 160 - 161.

30. Datta, B. K. "University libraries in India". *Indian Librarian,* 9 (3), (1954), pp. 102 - 103.

31. Deshpande, K. S. "Changing concept of library services with special reference to our university libraries". *I. L. A. Bulletin* 12 (3 - 4), (1976), pp. 158 - 168.

32. Deshpande, K. S. "University Library Service for a developing society". *I. L. A Bulletin,* 16 (1 - 2), (1980), p. 10 - 18.

33. Devarajan, G "An analysis and correlative study of the circulation data in relation to the users, collection and finance." *Proceedings of the thirty-second All India Library Conference,* Anantpur (1987), pp. 228-234.

34. Doraswany, M and Pullreddy, V. "Use of Photocopying services in S.V. University library: A study," *IASLIC Bulletin,* 40(4), (December 1995), pp. 157-164.

35. Dungaonkar, Dayanand. "Higher Education in India:

Varied dimensions". *University News*: Vol.42, (1), (May 24-30, 2004). p. 24.

36. Ekoja, Innocent, I. "The effects of austerity on collection development in Nigerian University libraries with particular reference to Usmania Danfodiyo university Library, Sokoto." *International Information and Library Review,* 24(2) (June 1992), pp. 173-187.

37. Elizabeth, Urbanik, "Sheet music cataloging for the non-specialist: the Templeton Collecton of Mississippi State University". *Library Collections, Acquisitions, and Technical Services*, 27, (Summer 2003), pp. 249-259.

38. Ethelene, Whitmire. "Academic library performance measures and undergraduates' library use and educational outcomes". *Library & Information Science Research*, 24, (2002) pp. 107-128.

39. Freeborn, Robert B. and Mugridge, Rebecca L. "The reorganization of monographic cataloging processes at Penn State University Libraries". *Library Collections, Acquisitions, and Technical Services*, 26, (Spring 2002), pp.35-45.

40. Ganesan, P and Pandian, N Murugesa. "Evaluating web resources, services and user attitude towards web based information services at University of Hydrabad Library: a study". Paper presented at the Second International CALIBER 2004 on Road Map to New Generation of Libraries Using Emerging Technologies. (11-13 February 2004), New Delhi. pp. 81-85.

41. Girija Kumar. "Academic status for university and college librarians", *I. L. A Bulletin*, 12 (1), (1976), p. 5 - 14.

42. Girija Kumar. "Planning and design of library building: Indian experience". *Library Horald,* 20 (2 - 4), (1981 – 82), p 59 - 71.

43. Gopinath, M. A. "Standards for use in the Planning of Library and Documentation System: Comparative data from India, U.K, U.S.A , and Canada". *Library Science*

with a slant to Documentation. 11(3-4), (1974) pp. 109-111.

44. Goyal, P. K and Anand, A. K. "Status of documentation activities in Indian Universities". *Annals of Library science and Documentation.*: 29 (4), (1982), p. 159 - 169.

45. Grewal, J.D. "A new approach to collection bias in academic libraries: The extent of corporate control in journal holdings". *Library & Information Science Research,* 19. (1997), pp. 359-385.

46. Hall, John, "Survey of information services in British University libraries." *Journal of Librarianship,* 7 (2), (April 1975), pp. 112-131.

47. Hass, Warren J. "Managing our academic libraries: Ways and means". *College and Research Libraries.* 40 (2), (1979), pp. 109 - 119.

48. Hingwe, K. S. "Indian University libraries: Need for cooperation", *Library Herald.* 6, (July-Oct. 1963), pp. 78 - 95.

49. Holdsworth, Harold. "University libraries in developing countries: standards and expectations". *Library Review.* 28, (1979), pp. 232 - 238.

50. Ibohal Singh and Others. "User's attitudes towards UGC-INFLIBNET SERVICES at Manipur University Library: An assessment". Paper presented at the Second International CALIBER 2004 on Road Map to Generation of Libraries Using Emerging Technologies. (11-13 February 2004), New Delhi. pp.49-60.

51. Issac, K. A. "Library systems for higher education". *University News,* 15 (12), (1977), pp. 321 - 323, 327.

52. Issac, K.A. "Need for an Academic Library System for Higher Education". *I.L.A. Bulletin.*, Vol. XIII,(1-4), (Jan-Dec. 1977). p.34.

53. Jolly, L. "Functions of the University library". *Journal of Documentation.* 18, (1962), pp. 81 - 88.

54. Juris, Dilevko and Lisa, Gottlieb. "Working at tribal college and university libraries: A portrait". *Library & Information Science Research*, 26, (Winter 2004), pp. 44-72.

55. Kanakachary, M. "Services of periodical section in Kakatiya University library: A survey." *Proceedings of the thirty-second All India Library Conference,* Anantpur (1987), pp. 186-192.

56. Kaser, David. "Modernising the University library structure". *College and Research libraries.* 31 (4), (1970), pp. 227 - 231.

57. Kaur, Amritpal and Nandan, Naresh, "Impact of I.T. and University libraries: a case study of Bhai Gurudas Library, Guru Nanak Dev University, Amritsar," *Library Herald,* 38(1). (April-June, 2000), pp. 124-128

58. Kavulya, Joseph Muema, "Marketing of library services: a case study of selected University libraries in Kenya." *Library Management,* 25(3), (2004), pp. 118-126.

59. Kawatra, P.S. "Attitudes of research scholars towards the resources and services o three university libraries in Rajasthan (India): A study." *Annals of Library Science and Documentation,* 35(4), (December 1988), pp. 171-177.

60. Khalaf, Nadim and Rubeiz, John. "Economics of American University of Beirut library ". *Libri,* 28 (1), (1978), pp. 58 - 82.

61. Khalid, Hafis Mohammed and Mahmood, Khalid, "Cataloguing Practice in University libraries: a comparison of three developing countries". *Asian Libraries,* 6(3-4), (1997), pp.155-165.

62. Khanna, J.K, "Participative management and its effectiveness: A study in University Libraries". *Journal of Library and Information Science* 6(1), (June 1981), pp. 18-28.

63. Kumar, Alok and Nath, P, "Barriers influencing information transfer in University libraries in North-eastern regions of India". *I.L.A Bulletin,* 34 (3-4), (October

1998 March 1999), pp.45-50.

64. Lahiri, Ramansu, "A study on the users of a university library". *IASLIC Bulletin,* 33(2-3), (June-September 1988), pp. 81-91.

65. Langstan, Mac, "The California State University E-book pilot project: implications for cooperative collection development". *Library collections, Acquisitions and Technical services,* 27(1), (Spring 2003), pp.19-32.

66. Lewes, Sussex. "British University libraries 1977 – 1987". *Journal of Documentation.* 44 (4), (1988), pp. 346-382.

67. Li lee, Hur, "Collection development as a social process". *Journal of Academic librarianship,* 29(1), (January-February 2003), pp. 23-31.

68. Liu, Lewis Guodo, "The contributions of library collections to prestige of academic programmes of universities: a quantitative analysis". *Library collections, Acquisitions and Technical services,* 25(1) (Spring 2001), pp. 49-65.

69. Majumdar, S and Taneja, K. K. "Role of Professional Assistants in Academic Libraries". *I. L. A Bulletin,* 20 (1 - 2), (1984), p. 63 - 77.

70. Mallaiah, T.V and Badami, K.K. "Library and information service facilities in Mangalore University Library from the research scholars' point of view". *Annals of Library Science and Documentation,* 40(4), (December 1993), pp. 155-165.

71. Mangla, P. B. "University libraries in India: Their development and proposals for the fifth five year plan". *International Library Review.* 6, (1974), p. 453 - 470

72. Maple, Amanda, and others, "Analysis of format duplication in an academic library collection". *Library Collections, Acquisitions and Technical Services,* 27(4), (Winter 2003), pp. 425-442.

73. Marc, Lanston. "The California State University E-book Pilot Project: implications for cooperative collection

development". *Library Collections, Acquisitions, and Technical Services,* 27, (Spring. 2003), pp.19-32.

74. Marchall, Nancy J, "Public relations in academic libraries: a descriptive analysis". *Journal of Academic Librarianship,* 27(2), (March 2001), pp. 116-121.

75. Marghalani, Mohammed Amin and Hafez, Abdul Rashid A. "On-line search service in the King Abdul Aziz University library, Jeddah, Saudi Arabia". *International information & library review,* 25(1), (March 1993), pp. 27-41.

76. Mittra, A. "Functional assessment of journal related services in the three university libraries of Orissa: Their inadequacies and suggested remedies" *Proceedings of the thirty-fourth All India Library Conference,* Anantpur (1988), pp. 172-176.

77. Mutshewva, A and Rao, K.N. "Enhancing access through electronic resources: the University of Botswana library experience". *Library Hi-tech,* 18(4), (2000), pp. 315-320.

78. Mutula, Stephen M, "The I.T. environment in Kenya: implications for libraries in public universities". *Library Hi-Tech,* 19(2),(2001), pp.155-166.

79. Neelameghan, A. "University library resources: some observations". *Library Herald*. 6, (1963), p. 87 - 95.

80. Obiagwu, Marcel C, "Library abuse in academic Institutions: A comparative study". *International Information and Library Review,* 24 (4), (December 1992) pp. 291-305.

81. Patil, P. K. "Mysore University library". *I. L. A Bulletin,* 4, (1968), pp. 27 - 36.

82. Prodhani, M.A, and Gautam, J.N, "Library services in Universities in North India". *ISALIC Bulletin,* 42(2), (December 1997), pp. 165-174.

83. Prodhani, M.A. and Gautam, J.N, "Study of current status of university libraries in North-east India". *Annals of Library science and Documentation,* 44(4), (December 1997), pp.126-139.

84. Ramesh and others. "Evaluation of IT based services on the basis of user requirements and satisfaction: a case study of University Libraries of Karnataka state". Paper presented at the Second International CALIBER 2004 ON Road Map to New Generation of Libraries Using Emerging Technologies. (11-13 February, 2004), New Delhi. pp.61-72.

85. Ranganathan, S. R. "Academic Library System: Then and now". *Library Herald.* 6, (1963), pp. 61 - 69.

86. Ranganathan, S. R. "Academic Library system: Fourth Plan period". *Library science with a Slant to Documentation.* 2, (1965) pp. 293 - 347.

87. Ranganathan,S.R. "Library Development Plan". *Library Science with a slant to documentation.* 2, (1965). p.300.

88. Raza, Mazoom, M and Anita Gupta, "Job satisfaction and job anxiety among library professional employees working in Delhi University library system". *IASLIC Bulletin,* 45(3), (September 2000), pp. 129-134.

89. Rick, Anderson and Steven, D. Zink. "Implementing the unthinkable: the demise of periodical check-in at the University of Nevada". *Library Collections, Acquisitions, and Technical Services,* 27, (Spring 2003), pp. 61-71.

90. Roberts, Norman. "Aspects of British University Librarianship". *College and Research Libraries.* 38 (6), (1977). pp. 460 - 474.

91. Rosamma Joseph, "An assessment of the procurement of periodicals through agents and by direct subscription". *Proceedings of the thirty fourth All India Library Conference,* Calcutta, (1988), pp. 162-171.

92. Rowena, Cullen and Philip, Calvert. "New Zealand University libraries effectiveness project: Dimensions and concepts of organisational effectiveness". *Library & Information Science Research,* 18, (Spring 1996), pp. 99-119.

93. Sahai, S. N. "Development of University Libraries in India

Since Independence". *I. L. A Bulletin.* 12 (1), (1976), pp. 37 - 42.

94. Sahi, S.S. "Evaluation of reference service provided by the Jammu University library: A user's survey". *Proceedings of the thirty-second All India Library Conference,* Anantpur (1987), pp. 280-288.

95. Sajjad-ur-Rahman and Shabeena Basheer, "Comparative measurement of book availability in academic libraries". *International Information and Library Review,* 25(3), (September 1993), pp. 183-193.

96. Sardana, J. L. "University and college libraries during fourth plan 1966 – 1971". *Herald of Library science.* 5, (January 1966), pp. 53 - 60.

97. Satyanarayana, M "Utility of periodicals in the Andhra university library: A case study". *Annals of library science and documentation,* 40(2), (June 1993), pp. 59-63.

98. Sehgal, Premchand and Navlani, K, "Growth and development of Punjabi University library, Patiala". *I.L.A. Bulletin,* XXXV (3-4), (October 1999 March 2000), pp. 46-53.

99. Seigliano, Marisa, "Consortium purchases: a case study for cost benefit analysis". *The Journal of Academic librarianship,* 28(6), (November-December 2002), pp. 393-399.

100. Sewa Singh, "Role of users in collection development in University Libraries in India: A study". *Proceedings of the thirtieth All India Library Conference.* Jaipur (1985), pp. 154-163.

101. Shalini, R, "Measuring book availability performance in Mysore University library". *Proceedings of thirty-fourth All India Library Conference,* Calcutta (1988), pp.390-400.

102. Sharma, C. D. "Problems of university libraries in India". *I. L. A Bulletin.* 10 (3 - 4), (1974), p. 89 - 97.

103. Sharma, Lokesh "Frustration and extraversion introversion: An inferential study of professional staff in

Jamia Millia Islamia Library and Delhi University library system". *Library Herald* 23 (2-3), (July-October, 1984), pp.114-123.

104. Shokeen, Ashu and Kaushik, Sanjay K, "Information seeking behaviour of social scientists of Hariyana Universities". *Library Herald,* 40(1), (March 2002), pp. 28-35.

105. Siddiqui, Asif Fareed, "Use of library collection in the Jawaharlal Nehru University Library". New Delhi, *IASLIC Bulletin,* 46(4), (December 2001), pp. 184-196.

106. Sigh, Dev Raj, "Career pattern of University library professionals in India". *Journal of Library and Information Science,* 18 (2) (December 1993), pp. 154-176.

107. Singh, Dev Raj, "Library Professional's response towards need for enhancing qualification: An analysis". *ILA Bulletin,* XXVIII (3-4) (October. 1992-March 1993) pp. 61-73.

108. Singh, Dev Raj "An evaluative study of services provided by Delhi University Library System". *Proceedings of the thirty-fourth All India Library Conference,* Calcutta (1988), pp. 25-40.

109. Singh, Harishchandra Kumar. "Development of University libraries in India". *National Librarian,* 5 (1), (1980), pp. 17 – 18.

110. Soma Raju, P, "Information and Research scholars in Andhra University Library". *Proceedings of thirty-fourth All India Library Conference,* Culcutta (1988), pp. 339-350.

111. Srivastava, Anand P. "Need for NationaL Level Planning on certain areas for University libraries in India". *Indian Librarian,* 29, (1974), pp. 107 - 109.

112. Suriya, M and Kalavathi, M.S. "Measuring the effectiveness of a University library in Tamilnadu". *Annals of Library Science and Documentation,* 35(2), (June 1988), pp. 77-83.

113. Suriya, M and Malathi, N, "Cost effectiveness of library and information services: A case study of marine biological center of Annamalai University". *Proceedings of the thirty-second All India Library Conference,* Anantpur (1987), pp. 256-270.

114. Surya, M and others, "Evaluation of collection effectiveness in University libraries: A case study" *Proceedings of the thirty fourth All India Library Conference,* Calcutta, (1988), pp. 141-161.

115. Unomah, J.I, "Student utilization of academic libraries in Nigeria: An assessment". *Journal of Library and Information Science,* 10(2), (December 1985), pp. 170-182.

116. Vijayalakshmi, N and Maheswarappa, B.S, "Information user pattern of post graduate lady students of Gulbarga University, Gulbarga". *Annals of Library and Information Studies,* 48(3), (September 2001), pp. 93-106.

117. Viswamohan, V and others. "A study of collection maintenance in select University libraries in Hyderabad". *Proceedings of the thirty second All India Library Conference.* Ananatpur, (1987), pp. 208-219.

118. Vyas, S.D, "Application of Information Technology in University Libraries of Rajasthan: a survey report". Paper presented at the first International convention of Mapping Technology on Libraries and People, (CALIBER 2003) (13-15 February2003), Ahmedabad. pp. 134-139.

119. Vyas, S.D. "Management of backlog cataloguing in University Libraries in Rajasthan". *Annals of Library Science and Documentation,*44 (1),(March 1997), pp.1-17.

120. Whitemmire, Ethelene, "Cultural diversity and undergraduate's academic library use". *Journal of Academic Librarianship,* 29(3), (May 2003), pp. 148-161.

121. Woodhead, P.A and Martin, J.V "Subject specialization in

British University Libraries". *Journals of Librarianship,* 24(2), (April 1982), pp. 93-108.

122. Yang, Zheng Ye (Lan), "University faculties perception of a library liaison programme: a case study". *Journal of Academic Librarianship,* 26(2), (March 2000), pp. 124-128.

123. Yasar, Tonta. "Collection development of electronic information resources in Turkish university libraries". *Library Collections, Acquisitions, and Technical Services,* 25, (Autumn 2001), pp. 291-298.

BOOKS, THESES AND REPORTS

124. Association of Indian Universities (New Delhi). New Education Policy. New Delhi: Association of Indian Universities, 1985. pp.5-7.

125. Association of Indian Universities (New Delhi). Universities Handbook. 26th Ed. New Delhi: Association of Indian Universities, 1995. p.IX.

126. Bavakutty, M. Libraries in higher education. New Delhi: ESS ESS Publications, 1988.

127. Bryan, Harrison. University libraries in Britain: A new look. London: Clive Bingley, 1976.

128. Buck, Paul, Libraries and Universities. Harvard: Harvard University Press, 1964.

129. Chandrakant Sharma. Management and organisational pattern of university libraries in Madhya Pradesh (Ph.D Thesis), Ravishankar University, 1977.

130. Cowley, John. Libraries in higher education. London: Clive Bingley, 1975.

131. Danton, J.P. Book selection and collection: a comparison of German American University Libraries. New York: Columbia University Press, 1963.

132. Deshpande, K. S. University library system in India. New Delhi: sterling, 1985.

133. Devarajan, G. Resource allocation in University Libraries.

New Delhi: ESS ESS Publications, 1993.

134. Devarajan, G. Resource development in academic libraries. New Delhi: ESS ESS Publications, 1992.

135. Ellsworth, Ralph.E. Academic Library Buildings. Colorado: Associated University Press, 1973.

136. Fiepal, Louis N, and Browning, Earl. Library Binding Manuel, Chicago: A.L.A, 1951.

137. Gelfand, M. A. University libraries for developing countries. Paris: Unesco, 1968.

138. Ghosh, D. K. University library system in India, Jabalpur: Rahul Publications, 1983.

139. Gupta, O.P. Development of University libraries in India, after independence. New Delhi: Concept Publishing Company, 1992.

140. Heartsills, Young, Ed. A.L.A.Glossary of Library and Information Science. Chicago: A .L .A, 1983, p.139.

141. Higham, Norman. The library in the University: observations on a service. London: Andre Deutsch, 1980.

142. Hingwe, K. S. Management of University libraries in India. Calcutta: World Press Private Ltd, 1982.

143. Inamdar, N. B and Ramaiah, L. S, Ed. National Policy for University libraries in India: problems and perspectives. New Delhi: Concept Publishing Company, 1989.

144. India, Education Commission (1964-66) (Chairman: D.S.Kothari) Report: Education and National Development. Delhi: MOP, 1966. p.288.

145. India, University Education Commission (1948-49) (Chairman: S. Radhakrishnan), Report. Delhi: MOP, 1949. p.452.

146. Jayaswal, P.K. Indian Academic libraries. Delhi: Kalinga Publications, 1988.

147. Jenkins, Clare and Morley, Mary. Collection Management in Academic Libraries. Bombay: Jaico Publishing House, 1996.

148. Jolly.L. Australian University Libraries. In University and Library Studies. Ed by W. L. Saunders. London: Pergamon Press, 1968. pp.37-38.

149. Jugal Kishore. Motivational dynamics and work efficiency in the university libraries. (Ph.D Thesis), Punjab University, 1979.

150. Kaula, P. N. Plan for the Development of B. H. U. Libraries. New Delhi: Vikas, 1971.

151. Khanna, J.K. Manual for administrating academic libraries. New Delhi: Beacon Books, 1997.

152. Krishna Kumar. Research Libraries in Developing Countries. Delhi: Vikas, 1973.

153. Line, M. B. The functions of the University library. University and research library studies, by W. L. Saunders. Oxford: Pergamon Press, 1968 p.148.

154. Mathew, Raju M, Allocation of resources in recently started University libraries in developing countries with special reference to some Indian University Libraries, (University of Kerala; Doctoral Dissertation, 1990).

155. Metcalf, Keyis Dewitt. Planning academic and research library buildings. Chicago: American Library Association, 1987.

156. Mukerjee, S.K and Sengupta, B. Library Organization and administration. Culcutta: The World Press, 1977.

157. Murali Krishna, C. Manpower Planning in University libraries. New Delhi: ESS ESS Publications, 1993.

158. Ojha, D. C. University libraries in India. Jodhpur : Latesh Prakashan, 1980.

159. Oloumi, Tacherch. Library Administration. Tehran: SAMT, 1998.

160. Panda, B. D. Growth of academic library system. New Delhi: Anmol publications, 1992.

161. Prasher, R.G. University Libraries in India: 1980's and Beyond. New Delhi: Medallion Press, 1991.

162. Raffel, J.A and Shisko, Robert. Systematic analysis of university libraries. Cambridge: MIT, 1969.

163. Rajwant Singh, University library buildings in India. New Delhi: Academic Publications, 1984.

164. Rajwant Singh. University library buildings in India: a critical appraisal (Ph.D Thesis), Rajasthan University, 1983.

165. Rastogi, Umesh C, Changing dimensions in academic libraries. Lucknow: Lucknow Christian college, 1989.

166. Rogers, Rutherford D and Weber, David C. University library administration. New York: H.W. Wilson Company, 1971.

167. Saini, B. S. Library Organisation for Higher Education: The status and role of university librarian. New Delhi: ESS ESS Publications, 1976.

168. Saunders, W. L. University and Research Library Studies. Oxford: Pergamon Press, 1968.

169. Sharma, C.K University library: its management and organisation. Delhi: Metropolitan, 1977.

170. Shukla, K.H. University Libraries in India: Some Observations and Suggestions. Jaipur: RBSA Publications, 1994

171. Singh, Sonal. University Libraries: A current appraisal. Jaipur: RBSA Publications, 1997.

172. Somaraju, P. Role of University Library in Promoting Research Activity in Universities (Ph.D Thesis), Andhra University, 1984.

173. Stockham, K. A. The Government and Control of Libraries. London: Andre Deutsch, 1968.

174. Tejomurthy, A . University Library Finance in Madhya Pradesh (Ph.D Thesis), Vikram University. 1982.

175. Tejomurthy, A University Libraries in M.P (Ph.D Thesis), University of Rajasthan, 1985.

176. Tejomurthy, A, Studies in Academic Librarianship. Jaipur:

Print well, 1987.

177. Thompson, Godfrey. Planning and Design of Library Buildings. Ed.2, London: Architectural Press, 1977.

178. Thompson, James. An Introduction to University Library Administation. Ed. 2. London: Clive Bingley, 1970.

179. U.G.C, U.K. Capital Provision for University Libraries: Report of the working party. London: H.M.S.O, 1976. p.5.

180. University Grants Commission (1957). (Chairman: S. R.Ranganathan). Report: University and College Libraries. New Delhi: U.G.C, 1965. p.141.

181. University Grants Commission (India). Report of the Committee on Governance of Universities and Colleges. Pt.1.New Delhi: U.G.C, 1971. p.7.

182. Venketaramana, V. Pattern and Development of University Libraries. New Delhi: ESS ESS Publications, 1995.

183. Walia, Paramjeet Kaur, Use of Government publications by political scientists in Delhi University and Jawaharlal Nehru University, In Sardana, J.L. Libraries and Information studies in Retrospect and Prospect, New Delhi: Concept Publishing Company, (2002), pp. 562-570.

184. White, Carl.M. A survey of University of Delhi Library, Delhi: University of Delhi, 1965.

185. Wilson, L. R and Tauber, M. F. The University Library. 2nd ed. New York: Columbia University Press, 1956.

8

IT Applications in Church Libraries in Kerala

— *Dr.Merciamma Mathew*

1. INTRODUCTION

As a world religion Christianity has its growth and development for the last 21centuries and is still continuing. These periods have witnessed admirable changes happened in the socio, economic and religious fields. As a religion Christianity has got its origin, development, doctrine and history. Christianity is spread in almost all parts of the world. This is made possible through the teaching and preaching mission of the church. The church played an important role in the fields of education also. It is believed that only through education one can grow in social, moral, economic, and political levels and it is only through education one can realize one's identity and dignity. The schools, colleges, monasteries and seminaries are the agencies, which impart education to the public. Several studies have been conducted in different parts of the world on the role of such institutions and their libraries. John Harvey conducted a study on scholarly and popular religious libraries in 1987. "Religious libraries provide service on all populated continents, with Europe and North America having the predominant numbers. The growth of religious libraries led to the organizations of several international and scholarly religious library associations. Certain national and international religious denomination's head quarters maintain popular level library departments, which provide educational advisory and public services"(Harvey, 1987)[1]. John F Harvey on "World Survey of

Popular Church and Synagogue Libraries in 1986" has conducted similar studies. The primary objective of the study was to obtain information about popular Church and Synagogue libraries outside United States. Jean M Wood on religious libraries in UK conducted another study in 1985. A study was conducted by Trevor Zweck on "Religious body libraries" in 1991.

Education is one of the missions of the Church. The priest and religious act as an ambassador to this education process. They are trained in seminaries, where scholarships on various subjects are gained. The subjects include Logic, Metaphysics, Psychology, Anthropology, Philosophy, Theology, Sacred Scripture, study of various other religions etc. These knowledge available in the seminaries and religious houses are not available to the common public due to various constrains. If there is a situation to share these stored knowledge it will enable the outside world to have a deep understanding of the hidden knowledge available in these seminaries and formation houses.

2. SIGNIFICANCE OF THE STUDY

Today the services rendered by the libraries become more significant than ever for the survival and growth of modern societies. Libraries and information centres are institutions concerned with the collection, storage, processing, organizing and dissemination of knowledge recorded in documents. The advent and advance of democracy, the extension of the horizons of education, the new methods in research and the virtual explosion of knowledge and information have necessitated the service of well organized, properly staffed and updated libraries.

Christian Congregation and seminary (CC&S) libraries have a rightful place in the category of special libraries. Special library, according to J.E. Wright, "is a library which is concerned almost exclusively with literature of a particular subject or a group of subjects, to serve the needs of the personnel of a parent organization". CC&S libraries are special libraries because they have special subject collections and special collections organized for and used by special clientele.

Usually CC&S libraries are attached to seminaries, churches, monasteries, theological centres, formation houses and other Christian institutions. The term seminary means a college for the training of priests and ministers for conducting religious ceremonies. They impart education as dogma of the church, ministerial training (sacramental formation), and exposure programmes to its candidates. The theological education primarily aims at forming leaders who are positively responsive to the needs and problems of the people and uplift them from the bondage of injustice and slavery and educate with moral values. Archives and manuscript collections are available as special items in these libraries. These libraries are well equipped with books, periodicals, national and international journals and other non-book documents. Each and every seminary functions like a college with all the activities such as learning, teaching and experimenting, along with research studies.

In the academic field, IT plays a vital role. Here the people make use of IT for their learning, teaching and research. Learning and teaching are two main activities, through which information generation is made possible. Hence IT should be provided to the academic community, as it becomes an integral component of the present day study and search for knowledge and information.

This study, which includes the evaluation of organization and services of the CC&S libraries in Kerala, is the first of its kind. Descriptive and evaluative studies on this category of libraries are there in Library and Information Science literature, but they are mostly with reference to European and American situations. Systematic studies on the libraries of the Christian churches in Kerala have not been conducted so far. This is what the investigator is attempting. Hence the present study becomes relevant and significant.

3. STATEMENT OF THE PROBLEM

The title of the study is stated as *"THE IMPACT OF IT ON THE ORGANIZATION AND SERVICES OF THE LIBRARIES IN*

CHRISTIAN CONGREGATIONS AND SEMINARIES IN KERALA".

OPERATIONAL DEFINITION OF KEY TERMS

The key terms of the study are:

Impact

Impact means "the act of an object hitting or colliding with another object, a collision, strong effect or force of. It is a continuing, powerful influence." (New International Webster's Comprehensive Dictionary, 2001).[2]

By 'impact' the investigator means the overall influence, control, after effects and challenges that are put forward by the presence and interaction of something.

Information Technology (IT)

The term ' Information Technology' (IT) is commonly used to mean combination of computer and communication technologies used for information storage, retrieval and dissemination.

According to ALA Glossary 'IT' "is the application of computers and other technologies to the acquisition, organization, storage, retrieval and dissemination of information. 'IT' is a product of information science and technology." (Bhargava,2002).[3]

Moll defines 'IT' as various means of obtaining, storing and transferring information using computers, telecommunications and microelectronics.

However, it is clear that the convergence of three technologies computer, microelectronics and communications constitute the information technology.

Organization

Organization "is a systematic arrangement for a definite purpose; the way in which something is organised."(New International Webster's Comprehensive Dictionary, 2001)[4]. By the term Organization the investigator means for a systematic arrangement of the different functional parts of an institution for a definite purpose. The library as an institution has several functions like collection, building, technical organization, circulation, maintenance etc.

Services

The term service means " the act of serving, a man who performs services of maintenance, supply, and repair etc." (New International Webster's Comprehensive Dictionary, 2001)[5]. By the term 'Service' the investigator means the library services; the various ways in which the library is made useful to its clientele. The traditional services of a library are lending, reference etc. Modern libraries have developed various sophisticated services like OPAC, Current Awareness Services, Selective Dissemination of Information, Online searching etc.

Library

"Library is a public institution or establishment charged with the care of collection of books and the duty of making them accessible to those who require the use of them and the task of converting every person into a habitual library goer and reader of books" (Ranganathan, 1961) [6]. However, the term library generally conveys the notion of a collection of printed books and the services and operations connected therewith. But in the special context of this study the term library is meant to include also archives and manuscripts besides printed books and the electronic media documents.

Christian Congregation

Christian congregations are communities where monks and nuns live in great austerity, observing the vows of poverty, chastity and obedience. The members of these congregations normally lead a religious life having been separated from their own family and domestic backgrounds and those who adopt this manner of life are called monks, nuns, brothers or sisters or simply the religious. Congregations are found in all denominations of the Christian church.

Seminary

Seminary "is a school for training clergymen. It is also called Theological Seminary." (The World Book Encyclopaedia, 2000)[7].

By the term seminary the investigator means is a school for training priests of the various Christian denominations. It is also called theological seminary, as it is the place where theological and religious formation is imparted to the potential priests and other members of the religious ministry. Also it is common to use the term 'formation houses' in the case of women. However in the present study the term 'seminary' is used to mean both the categories.

CHRISTIAN CONGREGATION AND SEMINARY LIBRARIES

The term Christian congregations and seminary libraries are those which are attached to Christian theological centres, churches, seminaries and religious congregations, having special collection of Christian literature including the works on various aspects of theology, divinity, religion, spirituality, ecclesiology, church history, sociology, philosophy etc. Modern seminaries have very comprehensive collections covering almost all subjects.

4. OBJECTIVES

The following are the major objectives of the study.

1. To investigate the existing state of the CC&S libraries i.e., collection, organizational set up, computerization, services, finance and physical facilities.
2. To find out the quality and quantity of the library personnel in the CC & S libraries.
3. To assess the information requirements of various categories of users such as students and teachers of seminaries i.e. priests and nuns of religious congregations.
4. To assess the degree of utilization of existing library resources and facilities by the different categories of users in Christian congregations and seminaries.
5. To find out the extent of the availability and use of IT in library such as computer, Internet, E-mail, audio-video, CD-Rom, Multimedia and Online search.

5. HYPOTHESES

The following are the working hypotheses formulated for the study.

1. The CC&S libraries have not been organized properly in modern scientific lines.
2. The quality and quantity of the library personnel in the CC&S libraries are totally inadequate to provide the expected library services.
3. The library resources and facilities in the CC&S libraries are under utilized.
4. The application and use of IT in CC&S libraries have not reached an optimum level of satisfaction by the users.

6. METHODOLOGY

A survey of a library is widely recognized as a wise procedure for the evaluation of library services, the creation of a basis for planning library development and determination of the degree to which a library is achieving its goals. The present study is based on a survey on the libraries of seminaries and the various Christian congregations belonging to the major Christian denominations in Kerala. It examined the existing conditions and possibilities for developments of the CC&S Libraries. It has been designed as a descriptive study based on the primary data collected by the investigator through various means.

7. SELECTION OF SAMPLE

There are 385 CC&S libraries in Kerala, which are attached to the major Christian churches such as Roman Catholic, Orthodox and Protestant. Out of 385 CC&S libraries 327 are Roman Catholic, and 59 are Orthodox or Protestant. Out of 327 Catholic libraries 158 are Generalate and Provincialate libraries. The district wise distribution of these libraries are given in the following tables: table 1.1, 1.2,1.3, and 1.4 respectively.

Table 1.1. District Wise Distribution of Catholic Seminaries and Formation House Libraries

Collection	TVM	KLL	PTH	ALP	KTM	IDY	EKM	TCR	PLA	KZH	MAL	WAY	KAN	Total
Below 5,000	7	4	1	1	16	2	14	18	2	6	1	20	5	97
5,000- 10,000	4	–	–	2	20	–	5	6	–	3	1	6	6	53
10,000 -15,000	–	–	–	–	1	–	–	–	–	–	–	–	–	1
15,000 -20,000	–	–	–	–		–	2	1	–	–	–	–	–	3
20,000 - 25,000	–	–	–	–	1	–	3	2	–	–	–	–	–	6
25,000 - 30,000	1	–	–	–	2	–	–	–	–	–	–	1	–	4
30,000 - 35,000	1	–	–	–	–	–	–	–	–	–	–	–	–	1
35,000 - 40,000	–	–	–	–	–	–	–	–	–	–	–	–	–	–
40,000- 45,000	–	–	–	–	–	–	1	–	–	–	–	–	–	1
45,000- 50,000	–	–	–	–	–	–	–	–	–	–	–	–	–	–
Above 50,000	–	–	–	–	1	–	1	–	–	–	–	–	–	2
Total	**13**	**4**	**1**	**3**	**41**	**2**	**26**	**27**	**2**	**9**	**2**	**27**	**11**	**168**

TVM – Trivandrum KLL – Kollam PTH – Pathanamthitta
KZH – Kozhikode KAN – Kannur ALP – Alleppey
KTM – Kottayam IDY – Idukky MAL – Malappuram
KAS – Kasargode EKM – Ernakulam TCR – Trichur
PLA – Palakkad WAY – Wayanad

Table 1.2. District Wise Distribution Of Orthodox And Protestant Seminary Libraries

Collection	TVM	KLL	PTH	ALP	KTM	IDY	EKM	KZH	MAL	Total
Below 5,000	3	6	8	2	4	3	2	4	2	34
5,000- 10,000	-	1	4	1	3	2	-	1	-	12
10,000 -15,000	1	2	1	-	-	1	-	-	-	5
15,000 -20,000	1	-	-	-	1	-	-	-	-	2
20,000 - 25,000	-	1	-	-	-	1	-	-	-	2
25,000 - 30,000	-	-	1	-	2	-	-	-	-	3
30,000 - 35,000	-	-	-	-	-	-	-	-	-	-
35,000 - 40,000	-	-	-	-	-	-	-	-	-	-
40,000- 45,000	-	-	-	-	-	-	-	-	-	-

Collection	***TVM***	***KLL***	***PTH***	***ALP***	***KTM***	***IDY***	***EKM***	***KZH***	***MAL***	***Total***
45,000- 50,000	-	-	-	-	-	-	-	-	-	-
Above 50,000	-	-	1	-	-	-	-	-	-	1
Total	**5**	**10**	**15**	**3**	**10**	**7**	**2**	**5**	**2**	**59**

TVM – Trivandrum KLL – Kollam PTH – Pathanamthitta
ALP – Alleppey KTM – Kottayam IDY – Idukky
EKM – Ernakulam MAL – Malappuram KZH – Kozhikode

Table-1.3. District Wise Distribution of Generalate Libraries

Collection	***TVM***	***PTH***	***ALP***	***KTM***	***IDY***	***EKM***	***TCR***	***PLA***	***KZH***	***MAL***	***WAY***	***KAN***	***Total***
Below 5,000	2	2	-	5	1	4	4	2	1	2	2	1	26
5,000- 10,000	-	-	1	4	-	10	5	-	-	-	-	-	20
10,000 -15,000	-	-	-	-	-	-	-	-	-	-	-	-	-
15,000 -20,000	-	-	-	-	-	-	1	-	-	-	-	-	1
20,000 - 25,000	-	-	-	-	-	-	-	-	-	-	-	-	-
25,000 - 30,000	-	-	-	-	-	-	-	-	-	-	-	-	-
30,000 - 35,000	-	-	-	-	-	-	-	-	-	-	-	-	-
35,000 - 40,000	-	-	-	-	-	-	-	-	-	-	-	-	-
40,000- 45,000	-	-	-	-	-	-	-	-	-	-	-	-	-
45,000- 50,000	-	-	-	-	-	-	-	-	-	-	-	-	-
Above 50,000	-	-	-	-	-	-	-	-	-	-	-	-	-
Total	2	2	1	9	1	14	10	2	1	2	2	1	47

TVM – Trivandrum PTH – Pathanamthitta ALP – Alleppey
KTM – Kottayam IDY – Idukky EKM – Ernakulam
TR – Trichur PLA – Palakkad MAL – Malappuram
KZH – Kozhikode WAY – Wayanad KAN – Kannur

Table-1.4. District Wise Distribution of Provincialate Libraries

Collection	***TVM***	***KLL***	***PTH***	***ALP***	***KTM***	***IDY***	***EKM***	***TCR***	***PLA***	***KZH***	***WAY***	***KAN***	***Total***
Below 5,000	4	1	-	2	17	2	10	10	4	9	7	6	72
5,000- 10,000	3	-	2	-	6	-	16	6	-	1	-	-	34
10,000 -15,000	-	-	-	-	-	-	-	2	-	-	-	-	2
15,000 -20,000	-	-	-	-	-	-	-	-	-	-	-	-	-
20,000 - 25,000	-	-	-	-	-	-	-	-	-	1	-	-	1
25,000 - 30,000	-	-	-	-	1	-	-	-	-	1	-	-	2

Collection	TVM	KLL	PTH	ALP	KTM	IDY	EKM	TCR	PLA	KZH	WAY	KAN	Total
30,000 - 35,000	-	-	-	-	-	-	-	-	-	-	-	-	-
35,000 - 40,000	-	-	-	-	-	-	-	-	-	-	-	-	-
40,000- 45,000	-	-	-	-	-	-	-	-	-	-	-	-	-
45,000- 50,000	-	-	-	-	-	-	-	-	-	-	-	-	-
Above 50,000	-	-	-	-	-	-	-	-	-	-	-	-	-
Total	7	1	2	2	24	2	26	18	4	12	7	6	111

TVM – Trivandrum KLL – Kollam PTH – Pathanamthitta
ALP – Alleppey KTM – Kottayam IDY – Idukky
EKM – Ernakulam TCR – Trichur PLA – Palakkad
KZH – Kozhikode WAY – Wayanad KAN – Kannur

These libraries are scattered in the 13 districts of Kerala except Kasargaud. The largest number is in Kottayam district with 82, Eranakulam comes next with 73 and Thrissur comes third with 55 libraries. Number of libraries in other district is less.

As it was inconvenient to collect data from all the CC&S libraries the investigator selected samples from the three denominations and religious congregations representing each zone of Kerala - North, Central and South and libraries having different collection and number of users. Thus representative samples were selected from libraries having a collection of below 5000; 5000-10000; 10000-20000; 20000-40000; above 40000 and having more than twenty five users.

The sample of 50 CC & S libraries selected for the study consists of 15 Orthodox and Protestant seminary libraries, 18 Catholic seminary libraries and 17 Generalate and Provincialate libraries.

Table 1.5. Distribution of questionnaires among users

Type of libraries	Total No. of users	No. of Questionnaires distributed	No. of Questionnaires received	%
Orthodox & Protestant Seminary Libraries	2175	216	195	89.8
Catholic Seminary Libraries	2914	301	195	96.67
Generalte & Provincialate Libraries	754	80	60	75
Total	**5843**	**597**	**545**	**91.28**

There were a total of 5843 users of which 2175 were from OPSL, 2914 were from CSL and 754 were from GPL. Questionnairés as seen in appendix II and III were distributed to 10% of total number of users in each category. A total number of 216 questionnaires were distributed to OPSL, 301 to CSL and 80 to GPL.

Out of 216 questionnaires distributed in OPSL 195 (89.8%) were received back, out of 301 distributed in CSL 290 (96.67%) were returned and out of 80 distributed in GPL only 60 were received duly filled in.

Altogether 597 questionnaires were distributed to the users of 50 CC&S libraries to examine the degree of utilization of library resources and facilities of which 545 (91.2%) were received duly filled in.

A total number of 326 questionnaires were distributed to the under graduate (UG), 53 to the postgraduates (PG), 38 to the research scholars (RS) and 180 to the staff members out of which 310 (95%) were duly filled up from the UG students 40 (75%) from the PG students, 25 (65%) from the RS and 170 (94%) from the staff. Break up of the respondents are given in table1.2. The largest category is UG.

Table 1.6. Break-up of the respondents

Respondents	***F***	**%**
UG	310	57
PG	40	7.3
RS	25	4.5
STAFF	170	31.1
TOTAL	545	99.9

Questionnaires were distributed to the librarians of 50 CC&S libraries to study the existing state of the libraries such as collection, organization, computerization, service, personnel, finance and physical facilities.

DATA SOURCES

The investigator under the guidance of the supervising teacher prepared the questionnaire. Before preparing the questionnaire, similar previous studies were consulted as the first step. A rough draft of the questionnaire was prepared, consulted with the experts and made corrections.

The investigator then made necessary arrangements with the authority of the CC&S libraries to meet the students in person for administering the questionnaire. The investigator then made sufficient number of copies of the questionnaire and met the students in their classrooms and distributed the questionnaire individually. The subject was introduced to the respondents in a simple, brief and succinct manner with a view to eliciting all relevant data. Personal details such as, age, name of the institution and subject of specialization were asked in the questionnaire. Necessary instructions were given to the respondents to fill up the questionnaire. Users were given sufficient time to go through the questionnaire and record their responses and the filled up questionnaires were collected. Users showed very interest and co-operation in filling the questionnaire. As the investigator personally visited the CC&S libraries, the data collection was completed without much delay.

In the present study the investigator has made use of the following sources for data collection.

Questionnaire administered to the personnel in charge of the CC&S libraries (librarians) under study in Kerala to collect data on the organization, services, collection, computerization, mode of financing, Questionnaire administered to a representative group of members of faculty, research scholars, students of the seminaries and priests and nuns of the religious congregations to collect data regarding the information requirements and use of the library resources and facilities.

Personal observation of the organization and administrative practices, functions, facilities, resources and the extent of the utilization of the CC&S libraries under study.

Examination of the relevant files and records maintained in the CC&S libraries.

All these enabled the preparation of the questionnaire in a comprehensive manner covering almost all the details of the organization and services of the CC&S libraries in Kerala.

QUESTIONNAIRE TO THE LIBRARIANS

Questionnaire as seen in APPENDIX II to the librarians mainly consisted of three parts: part A, part B and part C.

Part A – Institutional profile meant to obtain information about the fifty CC&S libraries with regard to their year of establishment, location and address.

Part B – Aimed to gather information relating to the collection of books in the library, classification and cataloguing, computerization library facilities, services, personnel and finance.

Part C – Intended to obtain suggestions for improving the organization, services and facilities of the CC&S libraries.

QUESTIONNAIRE TO THE USERS

The Questionnaire as seen in APPENDIX III for users consisted of three parts: part A, part B and Part C.

Part A – User profile meant to gather information about

the age, qualification and the course of study of the respondents.

Part B – Intended to obtain data on information requirements, information sources, information use, adequacy of reading materials and library effectiveness.

Part C – Aimed to obtain suggestions for the improvement of the library facilities and services.

DATA ANALYSIS TECHNIQUE

For analysis, users were categorized into four groups such as UG, PG, RS and Staff. Percentage, Average Score and Chi-square Test analysis wherever it was appropriate have been used to represent the data in the tables. Tables and Figures also used to present the data.

8. ORGANIZATION OF THE THESIS

The thesis is in six chapters. The first chapter entitled "Introduction" provides a general view of the content of the thesis under the major headings: significance of the study, statement of the problem, operational definition, objectives, hypothesis, methodology, analysis and interpretation of data, and the organisation of the thesis.

The second chapter entitled "Review of Literature" presents the studies done previously on this problem. An earnest attempt is made to locate books and articles published on this area for the period from 1977 to 2003.

The third chapter entitled "Profile of the study area" contains brief sketch of the 50 CC&S libraries selected for the study. The investigator has visited all the 50 libraries to collect the data required and spent two weeks per library for this purpose.

The fourth chapter entitled "The impact of IT on CC&S libraries" presents under the following headings. The introduction, definition of IT, automation of libraries, need for library automation, merits of library automation, areas of automation, IT scenario in church library system, integrating it in church libraries, impact of electronic media and storage system, networking of church libraries and conclusion.

The fifth chapter entitled "Analysis and Interpretation of Data" contains analysis of data collected through questionnaires, interview, observation and examination of relevant registers.

The sixth chapter entitled "Conclusion" contains findings and suggestions emerged out of this study. There are a few recommendations to the higher authorities to improve the conditions towards automation of libraries. Finally it identifies the areas for further research.

The thesis ends with a general bibliography listing alphabetically the books and articles consulted by the investigator for the preparation of the thesis.

9. FINDINGS AND CONCLUSION

The present study has been designed and executed as a descriptive and evaluative study of the functioning of libraries attached to the Christian congregations and seminaries in Kerala. The study was conducted with a set of hypotheses relating to (a) the organization and functioning of CC&S libraries with respect to collection, services, personal, finance and physical facilities and (b) utilization of information sources and facilities in CC&S libraries by the users and (c) the application and use of IT. The data required for testing the validity of the hypotheses were collected through the following sources:

(i) Questionnaires administered to 545 users in the select CC&S libraries under study.

(ii) Questionnaires administered to 50 CC&S librarians / person-in-charge of the libraries in CC&S libraries under study.

(iii) Relevant records, registers and files available in the CC&S libraries under study.

(iv) Personnel observation of organizational practices, functioning, resources and facilities of the CC&S libraries and their utilization by users in the CC&S libraries under study.

This was supplemented by discussions with the librarians or person in charge of the libraries and users.

HYPOTHESES TESTED

The following are the hypotheses tested for the study:

(i) The CC&S libraries have not been organized properly in modern scientific lines.

(ii) The quality and quantity of the library personnel in the CC&S libraries are totally inadequate to provide the expected library services.

(iii) The library resources and facilities in the CC&S libraries are under utilized.

(iv) There are only very few CC&S libraries with wide application of IT.

The hypotheses tested above facilitated the pinpointing of specific issues to be investigated, and the methods to be followed for obtaining data needed for resolving each of these issues. The analysis of data discussed in detail in chapter V, helped to answer the basic questions raised in the study and test the tenability or otherwise each of the hypotheses.

The study on the whole, substantiated hypothesis (i). The analysis of data in chapter V has revealed that the resources available in the CC&S libraries have not been organized properly on modern scientific lines and this hinders proper functioning, fruitful use and efficient services. Fast and efficient retrieval of information is not provided to the users due to the absence of systematically organized information services.

Hypothesis (ii) is substantiated. The study revealed that CC&S libraries are facing the shortage of professional and non-professional staff. Further, qualifications, both general and professional possessed by the librarians are inadequate to discharge professional responsibilities and duties effectively. The study provides sufficient evidence to substantiate the hypothesis that, in the absence of professionally qualified library personal and adequate number of supporting staff, the libraries are not able to function effectively and provide modern library services.

The analysis of data substantiated hypothesis (iii). Examination of the library resources and facilities of the CC&S libraries revealed that information obtained from the library resources and facilities of the CC&S libraries are utilized by the users for writing an article or book, writing assignments, theses, or dissertations and also for acquiring general knowledge. The study provides clear evidence to substantiate the view that the resources of the CC&S libraries under study are adequate but the computer facilities that exist in the CC&S libraries are inadequate to meet the users' requirements.

Hypothesis (iv) is substantiated. The study revealed that the number of CC&S libraries with wide application of IT is very limited. Only 14 percent of CC&S libraries are fully computerized and 48 percent are in the process of computerization. Although eighty four percent of CC&S libraries have computer, internet and e-mail facility, application of computers in library operations are there only in a small percentage of libraries. This is because they have a collection of less than 10,000 books.

OBJECTIVES

The study was conducted with the following objectives:

(i) To investigate the existing state of the CC&S libraries, i.e., collection, organizational setup, computerization, services, finance and physical facilities.

(ii) To find out the quality and quantity of the library personal in the CC&S libraries.

(iii) To assess the information requirements of various categories of users such as students and teachers of seminaries, i.e., priests and nuns of religious congregations and seminaries.

(iv) To assess the degree of utilization of existing resources and facilities by the different categories of users in Christian congregations and seminaries.

(v) To find out the extent of the availability and use of IT in library such as computer, internet, e-mail, audio-video,

CD-ROM, Multimedia and online search.

The culmination of the study resulted in the formulation of certain number of findings correlating to the objectives of the study. They are epitomized as given below.

FINDINGS

Summary of the answers to the questions posed as the 6 objectives of the study is presented below under the appropriate headings.

LIBRARY COLLECTION

1. The collection of books in all major seminary libraries is adequate.
2. The available books are old and outdated even the reference books in these libraries are of very old editions.
3. In the CC&S libraries under study 54.8 percent users reported that the subject books are adequate and 69.5 percent opined that the reference books are adequate.
4. Majority of users reported the adequacy of the current issues of periodicals (91.3%), back volumes of periodicals (83.6%) and newspapers (94.3%).
5. The reading materials such as maps, charts, photographs, rare books and manuscripts, ancient and continental language books etc. are not adequate and not preserved carefully in majority of the minor seminaries, generalate and provincialate libraries and in some major seminary libraries.
6. The CC&S libraries under study do not follow a regular system for procuring books.
7. The selection of books in most of the CC&S libraries is done by the faculty on consultation with the rector and librarian.
8. The latest books on different subjects are regularly bought in all the major seminary libraries under study.

Technical processing

9. All libraries except one follow DDC for classification and CCC for cataloguing.

10. Card- catalogue is commonly used in all libraries.

Library Services

11. Among CC&S libraries, except one provide open access system.
12. In majority of the GPL, there is access on a self-service basis and they do not put any restrictions on the use of reading materials by the users.

Borrowing of books

13. The books are issued to students in all the CC&S libraries and the maximum number of books issued per student is five in majority of the libraries.
14. No limit is put on the number of books issued to teachers at a time.
15. The period of loan in the CC&S libraries varies from two weeks to one month and this is found sufficient by the readers.

Working hours

16. The number of hours the library kept open varied from 2 to 12 hours. About half of the libraries (48%) are kept open for less than 8 hours. Most of these libraries are minor seminaries, generalates and provincialates. Thirty two percent of libraries are kept open between 8-10 hours and 20 percent of libraries are kept open between 10-12 hours. Majority of major seminary libraries are kept open for more than 8 hours.
17. All the CC&S libraries provide reference service; inter library loan service, photocopying service, current awareness service, and display of latest arrivals.
18. Thrissur Major seminary library provides translation service also.
19. All major seminary libraries organize special functions connected with seminaries like display of books, book exhibitions, group study, and projects.
20. All the major seminary libraries have a collection of paper clippings.

21. All these libraries have computer, internet, e-mail, OPAC and CD-ROM facilities.
22. One library (GFA) has Bar coding facility.

Library Budget

23. Many of the CC&S libraries have no regular source of income.
24. Many of these libraries depend on the meager amount received from the institution or church to which the library is attached.

Library Personnel

25. All the CC&S libraries have a librarian / person in-charge of the library.
26. Supporting staff and students are provided for assisting the librarian in majority of major seminary libraries.
27. The 83%of the CSL librarians do not have professional qualifications but majority of them (78%) have higher general qualifications such as PG and Ph.D.
28. Ten librarians (67%) of OPSL, 3 (17%) of CSL and 2 (12%) of GPL possess bachelor's degree or diploma in library science and only one librarian has master's degree in library science.

Physical Facilities

29. Almost all the CC&S libraries have separate space for reading, reference, periodicals and archival sections. The OP SL and CSL have more facilities compared to GPL libraries.

USE OF INFORMATION FACILITIES

30. In general users visit the library more often to read newspapers and magazines, to update knowledge, to prepare seminar paper, and speeches.
31. The staff and UG visit the library more to read newspapers and magazines while PG and RS make use of the library more for consultation of reference books.
32. In general use the information obtained from the library

for writing assignments, writing article / book.

33. The staff and RS use the information mainly for writing an article or book and theses or dissertation respectively while UG and PG use it mainly for writing assignments.

Information Sources

34. "Books" are found to be the most important source for information followed by journals and periodicals, faculty members, TV/Radio/Internet and seminar/workshops.

35. Among the different categories of users, UG find 'Books' as the most important source while PG, RS and Staff mainly depend on journals/periodicals and seminar/ workshop.

36. The users of CC&S libraries also rely on "personal collection" for their information requirements. Staff and RS have a good collection of books in their personal library and they have ranked "personal library" as the next important source other than the seminary library while UG and PG ranked "other Christian seminary libraries" as the next important source.

Use of reading materials by users

37. Among the different reading materials, theses and dissertations are given a comparatively lower rank by all categories of users except RS.

38. The subject on which the reading materials are required often are Philosophy, Theology, Bible (Scripture), Psychology and Church History.

Information Use

39. A larger percentage (64%) of users visit the library daily while 8.4 percent visit the library 2-3 times in a week and 19.6 percent visit the library 'once in a week' and 8 percent occasionally.

40. Among the four categories of users 95 percent of UG, 83 percent of PG, 60 percent of RS and only 4 percent of staff visit the library daily.

41. The Chi-square test revealed that the frequency of library visits depends upon the categories of users.

Duration of library use

42. Duration of time spent in the library by the users as a whole, is not considerable. The study showed that for a larger percentage (52%) of UG, 37 percent of PG and 24 percent of RS, the average time spent in the library is between 1-2 hours. A larger percentage of RS (32%) spend more than 3 hours in the library while 83 percent of staff spend less than one hour in the library.
43. Low percentage of use of the library is attributed to the fact that many of them are having a personal collection of books, more than 2000.
44. The Chi-square test revealed that the duration of library use depends on the categories of users.
45. Out of the fifty CC&S libraries surveyed for the study, only seven CC&S libraries are already computerized, twenty four are in the process of computerization and 19 libraries are planning for the computerization.
46. The major areas of computer applications in the computerized CC&S libraries are acquisition, cataloging, circulation control periodical control and indexing services
47. All the computerized CC&S libraries have given more importance to the catalogue and circulation section.
48. The operating system, which has been used by most of the CC&S libraries, was Windows NT and now they are using LINUX. Some of them used MS DOS, WINDOWS NT and WINDOWS 2000 also.
49. There is one library, Thrissur Major Seminary, that has the LAN facility.
50. Software packages developed locally by the computer centres of the institutions are preferred by majority of the CC&S libraries because of the high cost involved in the purchase of commercial library management packages.

51. Since computers have become the most essential tool in all the CC&S libraries, eighty four percent of CC&S libraries in Kerala have acquired them.
52. Majority of CC&S libraries have the problem of shortage of funds for the introduction of computerization.
53. Eighty four percent of CC&S libraries have either initiated computerization or some of the library operations such as acquisition, cataloguing circulation have been computerized.
54. Majority of the major seminary libraries are functioning just like an academic library with a librarian, and so they do not find any difficulty in giving access to the public. But the GPL are attached to a religious congregation and they have practical difficulties in giving access to the public.
55. The professionally qualified library personnel provided to the CC&S library is inadequate from the point of view of both quantity and quality.
56. The main reason behind the non-computerized CC&S library facilities are:
    - (i) Lack of awareness of management about the importance of computerization.
    - (ii) Lack of technical confidence among the librarians to convince the management or authority about the advantages of computerization.
    - (iii) The high cost of the hardware and software.
    - (iv) Lack of reasonably priced appropriate software packages for library management.

10. SUGGESTIONS

The survey has helped to obtain a total perspective of the impact of IT on the organization and services of libraries attached to Christian congregations and seminaries in Kerala. It has brought to light some of the inadequacies and drawbacks in various aspects of the functioning of CC&S libraries and helped to identify areas, which need improvement. A thorough study of the suggestions put forward by the users and librarians enabled the investigator to evolve possible procedures and programmes for improving the CC&S library setup. The following are the some of the suggestions for the improvement of CC&S libraries in Kerala.

Administrative setup

1. In all CC&S libraries the librarian should have an active participation in decision-making process especially in relating to purchase of books and subscription of periodicals.
2. There should be effective communication between the librarian and the rector.
3. All the CC&S librarians except GPL librarians opined that public should be given access to the library.

Library collection

4. The management should recognize the importance of the library; such interest in the library can improve the overall quality of library collection.
5. The book stock of the CC&S libraries should include the most frequently required reference books.
6. The collection should be updated by adding the latest publications and weeding out the outdated items.
7. The collection of the CC&S libraries are specialized and are of archival nature, they can hardly be found in book shops or other libraries. Therefore, these items are to be preserved for posterity and for this, either microfilming facility should be provided or these items should be digitalized.

Library services

8. In seminary, students have to learn many foreign languages such as Syriac, Greek, Latin, and Hebrew.
9. The major seminary library should be kept open for 12 to 14 hours a day so as to help the users to make use of it effectively.

10. Use of the library by the users should be promoted by displaying new books, accession lists, and important book reviews etc. Further a guide to the library (library manual or handbook) outlining services available such as hours of service, type of materials, location of materials etc. in the library should be made available to the users in order to encourage them to make full use of library resources and services.
11. Library orientation courses should be conducted for all categories of users to make them aware of the services provided by the library.
12. There should be sufficient number of comfortable seats in the library to enable the users to do their reference at ease. The library should provide a reference area where reference books can be consulted.

Library budget

13. Adequate funds must be allotted for the CC&S libraries with a major share for undertaking modernization. Management should take interest to set apart a separate budget for the CC&S libraries.

Library personnel

14. The CC&S libraries in general must have efficient and well qualified staff to deal with various problems of the computerization and to serve various kinds of users. Such persons are equipped with the concepts of technical processing such as classification and cataloguing.
15. The practice of appointing non-professional staff to carryout library works should be discontinued.
16. The library staff should be paid good salary according to the qualification and experience in par with the school or college librarians.
17. In- service training and refresher courses in computer application for the CC&S librarians should be provided at the earliest. This would help the librarians to get a better background in proper reference techniques and

in the principles and methods of storage and retrieval of information.

18. There should be an organization of CC&S librarians and this means pooling of knowledge and ideas that eventually lead to a standardization of practices. Management should realize the value of its librarians maintaining professional membership and attending appropriate conferences. This will help the librarian to keep abreast of new trends and developments in the field and is able to adopt these developments.
19. The psychological aversion towards computerization of CC&S libraries is the main social problem that we have to face at the initial stage. This can be removed by providing computer in library through short term training programmes and visits to computerized CC&S libraries also be arranged.
20. It is better to receive the guidance of other CC&S libraries that are computerized in order to provide better services.
21. The librarian should be familiar with the management and procedures of other CC&S libraries out side Kerala and visiting these libraries is useful as some of their techniques can be adopted.
22. Many of the users expressed the view that professionally qualified librarian should be appointed.

Physical facilities

23. The location of the library should be inside or as near the seminary as possible.
24. The layout of the library should be orderly and free of interruption.
25. The library must be well -lit; well ventilated and must get sufficient natural light.
26. There should be enough space for all the activities of the library.
27. There should be sufficient number of seats for readers and racks to accommodate the book collection and the

back volumes of periodicals and newspapers. Adequate telephone lines to the library are essential.

Impact of IT

28. The selection of computer system should be purely on the basis of its service efficiency and the collection of the library.
29. The choice of the system depends on the extent of the activities computerized in CC&S libraries.
30. The management should be made aware of the need for efficient library and information service, which can be provided through computerization of the library operations, and services.
31. User's need should be taken into consideration while planning for installation of the computer in CC&S libraries.
32. The KCBC (Kerala Catholic Bishop's Conference) CBCI (Catholic Bishops Conference of India) and CRI (Conference of Religious in India) should lay down the policies and guidelines for the application of information and communication technologies in CC&S libraries in Kerala and they should liberally release its grants to CC&S libraries for modernization
33. All the CC&S libraries should understand the advantages of networking and resource sharing; computerization is the first step towards it.

11. SUGGESTIONS FOR FURTHER RESEARCH

The present study as indicated above was conducted to make a survey of the present state of the CC&S libraries with regard to their administrative and organizational set up, computerization status, resources, services, personnel, physical facilities and the utilization of information facilities by the different categories of users. There are certain areas that require further attention for more detailed and focused study. These are enumerated below:

1. The studies can be extended using large sample from each Christian denomination.
2. Automation of CC&S libraries, their problems and prospectus is another possible area of study.
3. The problems faced by the users of CC&S libraries can be studied in depth.
4. A detailed study of the archives and manuscript collection attached to the religious institutions and seminaries may be conducted.
5. The reading habits of the users of the CC&S libraries in Kerala can be dealt with.
6. Attitude of the users and managements towards the organization of CC&S libraries using advanced technologies can be conducted.
7. The study can be further extended to libraries attached to similar religious institutions such as churches, Islamic institutions, Ashrams etc.
8. Comparative study of the administrative and organizational setup, and functioning of CC&S libraries.
9. Comparative study of administrative and organizational setup and functioning of seminary libraries in Kerala with other seminaries in other states of India.
10. Studies can be further conducted in libraries maintained by Catholic hospital libraries. Further studies can be carried out by AIACHE (All India Association of Christian Higher Education) regarding the functioning of libraries among its member institutions.

12. CONCLUSION

The range and nature of impact of IT on the organization and services of CC&S libraries should definitely be varying needs, but what is more important is

(a) Whether within the unavoidable constraints the library system produces optimum service to the user community.

(b) Whether the system is capable of meeting the expressed as well as the latent needs of the user community.

(c) Whether the system is capable of stimulating demands and to satisfy them from organized information systems outside the institution.

(d) Whether the institution helps the user community to have global access of Christian literature.

Libraries who can give positive answers to these questions can effectively think of a network development programme for sharing the resources available, uplifting the facilities for global access of information.

REFERENCES

1. Faris, John D. (1985) *The communion of Catholic Churches. Terminology and Ecclesiology.* New York: Brooklyn.
2. Gergan Elijah. (1999) "Moravian Church Library – Leh, Ladakh." *Dharma Deepika. June:* 59-61
3. Graham, Hedges. (1979) "Christian Library and Information Service: A Survey." *Christian Libraries.* 3: 14-19.
4. Gupta, Sushma. (1986) "The role of library in the life of an African church." *Librarians Christian fellowship new letter.* 37: 38-40.
5. Gupta, Sushma. (1989) "Role of the Library in the Life of a Black African Church." *International Library Movement.* 2(1): 179-182.
6. Halporn Barbara. (1984) "The Carthusian Library at Basil." *The Library Quarterly.* 54(3): 223-243.
7. Hanakovic, S. (1997) "Prerequisites and conditions for the inclusion of libraries attached to church organizations and associations." *Kniznice a informacie.* 29(1): 1-3.
8. Hannaford, Claudia. (1984) "The Christian librarian: an essential volunteer." *Catholic Library World.* 56(5) December: 217-222.

9. Harrington, John H. (1960) "Catholic Theological Seminary and their Libraries." *Library Trends.* 9(2): 162.
10. Harrington, John H. (1960) " Catholic Theological Seminary and their Libraries". *Library Trends.* 9(2): 151.
11. Harvey, John F. (1986) "An Introductory World Survey of Popular Church and Synagogue Libraries." *International Library Review.* 18 : 347-372.
12. Harvey, John F. (1987) "Scholarly and popular Religious Libraries." *International Library Review.* 19: 359-386.
13. Hedges, Graham. (1979) "Christian library and information services: A Survey." *Christian Librarian.* 3: 14-19.
14. Hedges, Graham. (1986) "Church libraries." *Librarians Christian fellowship new letter.* 32: 25-29.
15. Howard, John V. (1985) "Theological School Libraries." *Bulletin of the Association of British Theological and Philosophical Libraries.* 32 (3): 9-14.
16. Jordahl, R. (1994) "Theological Education and Libraries." *Journal of Religious and Theological Information.* 1(2): 1-19.
17. Jordahl, Ron. (1993) "Megatrends, Theological Education and Libraries". *Journal of Religious and Theological Information.* 1(2): 9.
18. Kemper, A. (1995) "Faculty status of theological Librarians in the American Library Association." *Journal of Religious and Theological Information.* 2(1): 1-16.
19. Klicka, K. (1994) "Bibliotheca Apostolica Vaticana in Rome." *Kniznice a informacie.* 25(12): 532 – 534.
20. Koodapuzha, Xavier. (1996) *Oriental Churches an Introduction.* Kottayam: Oriental Institute of Religious Studies in India Publications.
21. Koodapuzha, Xavier. (1996) *Oriental Churches an Introduction.* Kottayam: Oriental Institute of Religious Studies in India Publications.

22. Koodapuzha, Xavier.(1982) *Faith and communion of the Indian Church of the Thomas Christians.* Kottayam: Oriental Institute of Religious Studies.
23. Koodapuzha, Xavier. (1998) *Christianity in India.* Kottayam: Oriental Institute of Religious Studies, India.
24. Kriegar, M.T. (1993) "Providing access to a special theological collection." *Journal of Religious and Theological Information.* 1(1): 59-68.
25. Kriegar, M.T. (1996) "The Seminary Libraries of the Franciscan Province of St. John the Baptists." *Libraries and Culture.* 30(3): 284 – 308.

9
Socio-economic Profiles and Reading Interest of Students

— Dr. G. Devarajan

1. INTRODUCTION

Reading is the art of interpreting printed and written words. It is basic tool of education and one of the powerful and lasting influence in the promotion of one's personal development in particular and social progress in general. Regular and systematic reading sharpens one's intellect, refines his emotions, elevates tastes and provides perspectives and there by prepares him for an effective participation in the social and political life. It gives a unifying and civilizing force tending to unite social groups through the dissemination of common experiences.

Considering the social goal of reading, it is worthwhile to understand the reading habits of students community. The attempts in the field of reading habits of secondary school students are few. Moreover, sufficient study of the socio-economic factors on the reading habits of students especially of adolescent group in Indian setting is lacking. Another important reason habits of students in the secondary schools in Kerala.

2. OBJECTIVES

The primary goal of study is to analyse the impact of socio-economic factors on the reading habits of students in the secondary schools in Kerala. More specifically the study is aimed at the following.

(i) Relation between the socio-economic background and the reading habits of students:

(ii) Variation in the nature of reading habits amongst students hailing from schools situated in urban, semi-urban and rural areas; and

(iii) The degree of variance between socio-economic variables and reading materials.

3. SAMPLE AND METHODOLOGY

For data collection, primarily questionnaire method was used. In order to corroborate the findings arrived at from the questionnaire, interview method was also used on a selective basis.

Data was collected from 32 schools. 1850 questionnaires were distributed among students in VIIIth, IXth and Xth classes in these schools in an equitable distribution. Out of these 1226 questionnaires duly filled up by the students were collected. Hence 1226 questionnaires stand as the baseline data for analysis and interpretation of the study.

4. ANALYSIS

The primary data collected through the questionnaire and interview methods were subjected to a detailed analysis. A correlative study is carried out in order to understand how far the socio-economic factors influence the reading habits of students in the secondary schools in Kottayam, Educational District, Kerala. Different variables such as subject interest, types of reading materials preferred to read etc. were correlated with the socio-economic factors of the students such as sex, place of residence, caste, parents, occupation, income etc. The analysis was carried out under the following heads:

SUBJECT INTEREST VS. SOCIO- ECONOMIC FACTORS

On correlation of variables it is seen that socio-economic factors influence the subject interest among students. The following observations will show how far the socio-economic factors affect the subject interest.

The data show that the region in which students reside has significant impact on their subject interest. Students from the rural areas prefer to read a higher percentage of literature especially novels when compared to students from urban areas. It has also been noted that the percentage is slightly higher than the general pattern of reading interest in science books among students from urban areas. The data show that community varies the subject interest among students. Among SC/ST students the interest for reading literature especially novels is slightly higher when compared to forward community students when compared to backward and SC/ST students. Sex is another factor which influences the subject interest among students. It is seen that male students read a higher percentage of literature books when compared to girl students. Moreover, the interest for reading Science books is more among male students than girls. Girls read biographical studies more than male students. Father's occupation is another factor which generally affects the reading interest in subject among students. Among students whose fathers are farmers a higher percentage (71%) are interested in reading literature especially novels. Among students whose fathers are manual labourers (coolies) the percentage of students reading literature especially novels is students whose fathers are in other occupational groups such as teachers, engineers, doctors etc.

READING STORY BOOKS VS. SOCIO-ECONOMIC FACTORS

It has been seen from the general trend that the detective stories are the type of story books popularly read by the students. But variations are noticed while correlating with socio-economic variables as below.

The data show that there are slight variations in the reading habit of different types of story books and students' palace of residence. The interest for reading of comedy stories, students residing in the rural areas shows more interest that urban students. Community is another factor which influences even in the reading of type story books. The data show that interest in reading detective stories is comparatively high among backward community students when compared to students from other communities. But forward community students show a relatively high interest in reading comedy stories. Sex is another important factor which influence the reading habit of types of books. The data reveal that boys read more detective stories and pictorial stories, more interest has been shows by girls than boys. As per the data, it would become evident that reading detective stories is more among students from high income group. The fancy for reading detective is less among students from low income group. Interest for reading comedy stories is also comparatively high in low income groups.

MAGAZINE READING VS. SOCIO-ECONOMIC FACTORS

It has been seen that irrespective of the socio-economic factors majority of the students read 'Balarama'. Their second and third preferences are 'Malayala Manorama' and 'Mangalam'. But slight variations are noticed while correlating with socio-economic variables. These observations are given below.

The community to which the students belong plays a vital role in influencing the reading habits. The SC/ST have given their first preference to 'Malayala Manorama' while the first preference for the backward community and forward community students is 'Balarama'. Moreover the SC/ST students are not at all interested in reading English magazines. Of course, the backward community and forward community students have shown only a slight interest in reading English magazines. It is a well known fact that the data it will become obvious that the familiar magazine among girls is 'Balarama' whereas 'Malayala Manorama' is the favourite magazine among boys. In respect of reading of English magazines, the boys have shown more interest than girls.

Parent's income have a direct bearing on the reading habits of their children. This is very true in the case of magazine reading. Buying capacity of parents and their interest for reading have a lot of influence on their children's reading habits. Data show that students from high income group show more interest in reading 'Balarama' wheareas the interest for reading 'Malayala Manorama' weekly is more among students of low income groups. The trend in the reading interest of 'Malayala Manorama' is in a decreasing one from low income group to middle income group to high income group. In respect of the reading of English magazines the above trends is just the reverse i.e. from high income group to middle income group and from middle group to low income group.

It is clear from data that the place residence of students has influenced the magazine reading habits. 'Balarama' and 'Malayala Manorama' weeklies are popularly read in the rural areas. Reading of English language magazine is very significant among students residing in the urban areas when compared to students residing in the rural areas.

NEWS PAPER READING VS. SOCIO-ECONOMIC FACTORS

It would be very interesting to note that the students read and how various factors influence their choice of newspapers. The observations are given below

It is clear from the data that sex influences the reading habits of newspapers reading among students. The data show that a high percentage of female students prefer to read ' Malayala Manorama' than male students. But in respect of the reading of 'Deepika' boy students shows more interest than girl students.

The SC/ST students show a higher percentage of interest when compared to the general trends in reading the daily ' Malayala Manorama' The percentage in the reading interest of 'Malayala Manorama' is in a decreasing trend from backward community students to forward community students. In the case of SC/ST students their second choice of news paper is the ' Mangalam'. This is contrary to the general trend in the reading interest of the population under study.

The data show that irrespective of the socio-economic background of the population the daily 'Malayala Manorama' is the most favourite among the urban students. In the use of English dailies, the 'Indian Express' is preferred by the urban as well as rural students without much difference. But in the case 'The Hindu' it is preferred only by students residing in the urban areas.

As the general pattern of interest, the 'Malayala Manorama' is the most favourite news paper among the population under study. This may be due to the fact, that it is a paper published from Kottayam where from the sample is taken from study. However slight variations are noticed among students because of the occupation of their parents. It is observed from the data that 'Malayala Manorama' is the most favourite among students whose fathers are manual labourers. Regarding the second choice of news paper, students whose fathers are farmers prefers to read ' Deepika'. As regards reading of English dailies, an appreciable percentage of students whose fathers are businessmen, government employees etc. read them.

Income is an important variable which influences the news paper reading habit among students. It can be seen from the data that 'Malayala Manorama' is the most favourite news paper among students of low income families. Of course slight variations are observed from the general trend in the news paper reading among middle income and high income groups. Regarding English news paper reading the preferences for ' The Hindu and Indian Express are in an ascending order from low income groups to middle income groups then to higher income groups. In fact it can be inferred that students belonging to different income levels have varying tastes in the reading of news paper.

READING OF NEWS PAPER COLUMNS VS. SOCIO-ECONOMIC FACTORS

The socio-economic factors even influence students in the reading of the newspaper columns. The following would show how far the reading tastes varies from the general pattern due to the socio-economic factors. It can be seen from the data that there are variations in the reading interest due to the differences in the place of residence of the students. The sensation news column attracts more students residing in the urban areas. The urban students have shown relatively a higher percentage of interest than rural students in reading sports columns. It is also noted that interest in reading other news paper columns such as advertisement, editorial, cinema etc. varies with place of residence of students.

Table I would show that caste is another factor which influences the reading of various columns in the news papers. It can be seen from the data that the interest for reading sensational news is so predominant among SC/ST students when compared to students from other communities. As regards interest for reading sports and politics columns as ascending trend is noticed from SC/ST to backward communities and then to forward community students.

Table 1. Reading of News Paper Columns Vs. Caste

Name of News Paper	***SC/ST Community***	***Backward Community***	***Forward Community***	***Total***
Advertisement (13.9%)	12 (8.7%)	25 (7.1%)	60 (8%)	97
Editorial (3.4%)	3 (5.5%)	16 (12.3%)	103 (10.1%)	122
Letter to Editor (1.1%)	1 (2.7%)	8 (0.5%)	5 (1.1%)	14
Sports Column (4.6%)	21 (5.9%)	84 (4.1%)	246 (4.6%)	351
Politics (3.4%)	3 (3.8%)	11 (8.6%)	72 (7.1%)	86
Sensational News (48.8%)	42 (43.7%)	125 (37.6%)	314 (39.8%)	481

The sex is another variable which influence the reading of various columns in the news papers by students. Regarding the sensational news, female students are more attracted (44.2%) than male students (34.3%). In the reading of sports columns boys shows more interest than girls.

LANGUAGE VS. SOCIO-ECONOMIC FACTORS

The general trend in the reading habits of students shows that majority of them prefer to read Malayalam language books. This is due to the fact that Malayalam is the mother tongue of the majority of the population under study. But variations are noticed in the percentage of preferences for reading English books also. These variations from the general trends can be seen from the following observations.

The regions in which students reside is a factor which influences the selection of the language of the books by the students. It is interesting to note that a good number of students in the urban areas prefer to read English language books. This may be because of the existence of English medium schools in the urban areas. But students are not so attracted in reading books in English language.

The language of the books chosen by the students and the community of the students have a direct relationship, It can be seen that SC/ST students prefer to read Malayalam language books (99.8%). But the interest in reading Malayalam books is in a decreasing trend in the backward community students. As regards reading of books in English language, students from forward community have shown more interest. The choice of English language books is in a decreasing trend among backward and SC/ST community students.

The sex is another factor which influence the reading habits among students. The data shows that female students read more Malayalam books (98.3%) than male students. But in the reading of English language books boys show relatively more interest than girls.

LEISURE TIME ACTIVITIES VS. SOCIO-ECONOMIC FACTORS

It is interesting to note how far socio-economic factors influence even the leisure time activities of students. The following observations are made under this head.

It can be seen from the data that there are variations in the leisure time activities from the general trend. Reading is the most preferred leisure time activity by the population under study. But this percentage of preference is high among students from forward community. Playing is the second preferred leisure time activity by the population. But the level of interest for playing as a leisure time activity is high among SC/ST student. The interest for viewing cinema decrease from SC/ST to upper communities.

The sex is another important variable which influences the leisure time activities of students. The data show that boys spend most of their leisure time for playing whereas the girls spend their time for reading.

Moreover, interest for viewing cinema as a leisure time activity is more among boys whereas viewing television is a leisure time activity among girls.

It can be seen from the data that income is another factor which affect the leisure time activities of the students. The students from high income families spend more of their leisure time in reading whereas the time spent for reading is relatively less in low income groups. The students from low income group families spend relatively more time for playing when compared to other income groups. The time spent for viewing TV is comparatively less among students from low income groups. This may be because of the non- availability of TV sets in the low income families.

ANALYSIS OF VARIANCE

A two-way analysis of variance is also undertaken here so as to understand the degree of difference between the variables, socio-economic factors and reading materials. Variables which have show very significant differences alone are discussed here.

The two-way analysis of variables viz. story books vs family income shows that there is a significant difference in the choice of different types of story books by students. It is also found that the difference is significant in the reading of different types of story books by students from various income groups. This will become clear from the following estimation.

Source of Variations	*S.S*	*D.F*	*F-ratio*	*5% of F-limit*
Between rows (between type of story books)	42455.36	6	6.003928	2.66
Between columns (various income groups)	32918.97	3	9.310632	3.16
Residual	21213.79	18		

The two-way analysis of variables viz magazine reading vs community shows that there is a significant difference in the choice of magazines by students. The difference is also significant in the case of students belonging to different communities. This is statistically explained as follows:

Source of Variations	*S.S*	*D.F*	*F-ratio*	*5% of F-limit*
Between rows (magazine reading	97347.52	17	3.332036	2.00
Between columns (between communities)	16910.71	2	4.920004	3.23
Residual	58431.26	34		

The analysis of variables viz magazine reading vs income shows that there is significant variance between magazine reading and family income of students. The degree of variance is estimated as follows:

Source of Variations	*S.S*	*D.F*	*F-ratio*	*5% of F-limit*
Between rows (magazine reading	73010.61	17	4.095529	1.70
Between columns (income levels)	13171.28	3	4.186775	2.68
Residual	53480.72	51		

The aforesaid analysis shows that a number of socio-economic factors influence the reading habits of students in the secondary schools in Kerala. It is also statistically proved that the degree of variance is very significant, especially in variables like income and community, in the choice of reading materials.

5. FINDINGS AND CONCLUSION

The analysis of the data has given very interesting results. It was found that socio-economic factors have significant influence on the reading habits of the students. The following are the major observation that could be made from the study:

(i) A higher percentage of students from the rural areas prefer to read literature especially novels when compared to students from urban areas. Among SC/ST students the interest for reading literature especially novels is slightly higher when compared to forward community students and backward community student. Male students read a higher percentage of literature books when compared to girl students. Among students whose parents are farmers and manual labourers the interest for reading literature especially novel is high when compared to students whose parents belong to other occupational groups.

(ii) The interest for reading detective stories is more among urban students. In the reading of comedy stories student residing in the rural areas shows more interest than urban students. The interest for reading detective stories is comparatively high among backward community students when compared to students from other communities. Boys read more detective stories than girls. More students from high income families read detective stories.

(iii) The SC/ST students prefer to read 'Malayala Manorama' weekly while the students from backward community and forward community students prefer to read 'Balarama'. The SC/ST students are not at all interested in reading English magazines. The most favourite magazine among girl students is 'Balarama' whereas

'Malayala Manoram' is the favourite among boys. The students from high income group show more interest in reading 'Balarama' whereas the interest for reading 'Malayala Manorama' weekly is more among students from low income families.

(iv) Female students prefer to read 'Malayala Manorama' daily that male students. In respect of reading of 'Deepika daily, boys show more interest than girls. The 'Malayala Manorama is the most favourite among the urban students. As regards of English dailies, The Indian Express is preferred by the urban as wellas rural students without much difference whereas 'The Hindu' is preferred only by students residing in the urban areas. The 'Malayala Manorama' is the most favourite newspaper among students of low income groups.

(v) The sensational news columns in newspapers attract more students residing in the urban areas. The urban students have shown relatively a higher percentage of interest than rural students in reading sports columns. Interest for reading sensational news is so predominant among SC/ST students when compared to students from other communities. In the reading of sports columns boys show more interest than girls.

(vi) The students whose fathers are Government employees and businessmen show significant interest in reading English language books. But SC/ST students prefer to read Malayalam language books. Female students prefer to read more Malayalam books than male students.

(vii) Reading is the most preferred leisure time activity by the population under study. But this percentage of preference is high among students from forward community. The most favourite leisure time activity of boys is playing whereas reading is the favourite among girls. The students form high income families spend more of their leisure time in reading whereas the time spent for reading is relatively less among students in low income groups.

A number of socio-economic factors influence the reading habits of students in the secondary schools in Kerala. The degree of variance in very significant especially in variables like income and community in the choice of reading materials.

REFERENCES

1. Anderson, Verna Divkman : (1968) "Reading and Young Children", London, Macmillan.
2. Bound, Goy L, et al; (1979) "Reading Difficulties their Diagnosis and Connection", N.J.Prentice Hall
3. Devarajan G : (1992) "Impact of socio-economic Factors on the Reading Habits of Students in the Secondary Schools Students". (ICSSR Project), Trivandrum, University of Kerala
4. Gopinathan S: (1978) "A Measure of Reading", IE Survey of Reading interest and Habits, Singapore Institution of Education.
5. Singhal R.P.: (1988) "Indian Schools : A study of Teacher Pupil Relation", New Delhi, Vikas.
6. Staiger, Ralph,Ed: (1979) "The Teacher of Reading", Paris, UNISCO
7. Vasistha K.K : (1979) "Teacher Education in India", New Delhi Concept.

Index